Praise for the First Edition

"*The Resilient Practitioner* is a 'must' read for every practitioner. Skovholt gives clear explanations of practitioner stress and provides remedies that can be implemented. I really enjoyed the real-life examples and was impressed by the extensive research that forms the background for the book. Skovholt is a master teacher and practitioner. I recommend that practitioners keep this book close by and reread it throughout their careers."

—**Clara Hill, PhD, University of Maryland**

"This is a wonderful book that merits careful reading by all helping professionals. Well written, engrossing, and amply documented, *The Resilient Practitioner* is recommended with unqualified enthusiasm."

—**Ted Packard, PhD, University of Utah; President, American Board of Professional Psychology**

"In this remarkable book, the author is eloquent in his perceptive description of the demands on the practitioner. At several points, I felt like I was reading from the pages of my own personal journal. This is a wonderfully stimulating book!"

—**William Parham, PhD, University of California–Los Angeles; Associate Director, Counseling Services**

"Over the past ten years, I have been asked by publishers to review hundreds of manuscripts. This is one of the best written! The author has a very engaging writing style and his humanity permeates the content. The book has that scholarly foundation yet is very accessible, very alive, and rich with real-life illustrations. What a wonderful job!"

—**Mark Kiselica, PhD, The College of New Jersey**

"At all career stages, caring professionals will find this book to be a rich resource of encouragement for professional development. It is a bountiful gift to us all."

—Jaquie Resnick, PhD, University of Florida

"This visionary work is essential reading for practitioners and students in the helping fields. With poetic wisdom and academic clarity, Tom Skovholt addresses the issues involved in sustaining professional validity."

—Sally Hage, PhD, State University of New York

"In *The Resilient Practitioner*, Tom Skovholt demonstrates a compassionate appreciation for the complexities of the helping fields. Clearly, he has experienced these development challenges, and has listened and guided well as others have navigated these challenging tasks. Now, in this book, his wisdom can be shared with many other 'high-touch' professionals."

—Kate F. Hays, PhD, Sport Psychologist; Director, The Performing Edge, Toronto, Canada

"Tom Skovholt has identified precisely the difficult career issues for practitioners in the helping professions. He specifies particular steps in balancing care for others and self, sustaining the professional and personal selves, and preventing burnout. Skovholt stimulated me to consider self-care in a whole new way—not as a narcissistic withdrawal from responsibility, but as a means to sustain intellectual excitement and emotional commitment to those with whom I work."

—Susan Neufeldt, PhD, Clinical Supervisor, University of California–Santa Barbara

THE
RESILIENT
PRACTITIONER

COUNSELING AND PSYCHOTHERAPY:
INVESTIGATING PRACTICE FROM SCIENTIFIC, HISTORICAL, AND CULTURAL PERSPECTIVES

A Routledge book series
Editor, Bruce E. Wampold, University of Wisconsin

This innovative new series is devoted to grasping the vast complexities of the practice of counseling and psychotherapy. As a set of healing practices delivered in a context shaped by health delivery systems and the attitudes and values of consumers, practitioners, and researchers, counseling and psychotherapy must be examined critically. By understanding the historical and cultural context of counseling and psychotherapy and by examining the extant research, these critical inquiries seek a deeper, richer understanding of what is a remarkably effective endeavor.

Published

Counseling and Therapy With Clients Who Abuse Alcohol or Other Drugs
Cynthia E. Glidden-Tracy

The Great Psychothearpy Debate
Bruce Wampold

The Psychology of Working: Implications for Career Development, Counseling, and Public Policy
David Blustein

Neuropsychotherapy: How the Neurosciences Inform Effective Psychotherapy
Klaus Grawe

Principles of Multicultural Counseling
Uwe P. Gielen, Juris G. Draguns, Jefferson M. Fish

Beyond Evidence-Based Psychotherapy: Fostering the Eight Sources of Change in Child and Adolescent Treatment
George Rosenfeld

Cognitive Behavioral Therapy for Deaf and Hearing Persons With Language and Learning Challenges
Neil Glickman

Pharmacology and Treatment of Substance Abuse: Evidence and Outcome Based Perspectives
Lee Cohen, Frank Collins, Alice Young, Dennis McChargue, Thad R. Leffingwell, Katrina Cook

IDM Supervision: An Integrated Developmental Model for Supervising Counselors and Therapists, Third Edition
Cal Stoltenberg and Brian McNeill

Culture and the Therapeutic Process: A Guide for Mental Health Professionals
Mark M. Leach and Jamie Aten

The Resilient Practitioner: Burnout Prevention and Self-Care Strategies for Counselors, Therapists, Teachers, and Health Professionals, Second Edition
Thomas M. Skovholt and Michelle Trotter-Mathison

Forthcoming

The Handbook of Therapeutic Assessment
Stephen E. Finn

The Great Psychotherapy Debate, Revised Edition
Bruce Wampold

THE
RESILIENT PRACTITIONER

BURNOUT PREVENTION AND SELF-CARE STRATEGIES FOR COUNSELORS, THERAPISTS, TEACHERS, AND HEALTH PROFESSIONALS

SECOND EDITION

THOMAS M. SKOVHOLT AND MICHELLE TROTTER-MATHISON

Routledge
Taylor & Francis Group
New York   London

Routledge
Taylor & Francis Group
270 Madison Avenue
New York, NY 10016

Routledge
Taylor & Francis Group
27 Church Road
Hove, East Sussex BN3 2FA

International Standard Book Number: 978-0-415-98938-1 (Hardback) 978-0-415-98939-8 (Paperback)

Library of Congress Cataloging-in-Publication Data

Skovholt, Thomas M.
    The resilient practitioner : burnout prevention and self-care strategies for
counselors, therapists, teachers, and health professionals / Thomas Skovholt, Michelle
Trotter-Mathison. -- 2nd ed.
        p. cm. -- (Counseling and psychotherapy: investigating practice from scientific,
        historical, and cultural perspectives)
    Summary: "This informative and inspirational volume creates a map for new
mental health practitioners - one that provides a positive trinity of validity, clarity,
and hope for novices, their teachers, and their supervisors"-- Provided by publisher.
    Includes bibliographical references and index.
    ISBN 978-0-415-98938-1 (hardback)
    1. Medical personnel--Mental health. 2. Psychotherapists--Mental health. 3.
Teachers--Mental health. 4. Counselors--Mental health. 5. Medical personnel--Job
stress. 6. Psychotherapists--Job stress. 7. Teachers--Job stress. 8. Counselors--Job
stress. 9. Burn-out (Psychology)--Prevention. I. Trotter-Mathison, Michelle. II. Title.
III. Series.

RC451.4.M44S57 2010
616.89'14--dc22
        2010026034

Visit the Taylor & Francis Web site at
http://www.taylorandfrancis.com

and the Routledge Web site at
http://www.routledgementalhealth.com

*For my daughter Rachel whose birth was a beautiful
moment and whose continual presence is a pleasure*

—Tom Skovholt

For John

—Michelle Trotter-Mathison

*And to counselors, therapists, teachers, and health professionals
everywhere whose professional caring for others makes this a better world*

Contents

Part Two

Series Editor's Foreword

This series is devoted to understanding the complexities of the practice of counseling and psychotherapy. As a set of healing practices, delivered in a context molded by health delivery systems and the attitudes and values of consumers, practitioners, and researchers, counseling and psychotherapy must be examined critically. Volumes in this series discuss counseling and psychotherapy from empirical, historical, anthropological, and theoretical perspectives. These critical inquiries avoid making assumptions about the nature of counseling and psychotherapy and seek a deeper understanding of the bases of what is a remarkably effective endeavor.

Lest we forget, it is the therapist who makes psychotherapy (and other helping professions) effective. Accumulating research demonstrates that in practice, as well as in clinical trials, much of the variability in outcomes is attributable to the therapist, regardless of the treatment being delivered. However, even the best therapists will fail to produce optimal benefits if the act of helping leads to burnout. Therapy, as well as other helping professions (e.g., teaching, medicine, social work), is demanding because of the nature of the work. Skovholt and Trotter-Mathison have carefully described the manner in which these professionals can, if they are not careful, burn out—basically by giving too much attention to our clients and too little attention to ourselves. *The Resilient Practitioner* is a guide to a caring for ourselves, while caring for our clients. This material is vital for the practitioner—but also for their clients. The effectiveness of helpers depends on their health and well being.

Bruce E. Wampold, PhD, ABPP
Series Editor
University of Wisconsin–Madison

Preface

How does the opera singer take care of the voice?
    The baseball pitcher, the arm?
    The woodcutter, the axe?
    The photographer, the eyes?
    The ballerina, the legs and feet?
    The counselor, therapist, teacher, or health professional, the self?

In this book, we address people in the caring professions—the helping professions, education, health occupations, and the clergy. Some readers may not identify with this broad occupational group (counselors, therapists, teachers, professors, social workers, clergy, nurses, doctors, physical therapists, and other health professionals) because they seem so different. For example, a public school teacher may think that her work is very different from that of a nurse or a counselor. Our own experience in counseling, education, and health services has helped us to see that there are great commonalities among counseling, teaching, and healing. We feel that there are many work concerns that are shared among these professional groups. We view all of these as caring professions because of common work ingredients.

A leading career development inventory, the Campbell Interest and Skill Survey, combines "helping others through teaching, healing and counseling" into one of seven work orientations (Campbell, 1994, p. 2), providing evidence for similarity among these fields. When reading this material, we invite you to consider the commonalities rather than the differences in the careers. If the commonalities can be understood, then this material may be of use to a variety of individuals working in different caring professions.

The questions to be asked by all are: How do those in the caring professions, who use their own self as a method of change, prevent burnout and maintain professional vitality? How does one establish balance between other-care and self-care? What are the keys to practitioner resiliency?

Acknowledgments

As a part of the first edition, Tom acknowledged the following individuals: Lynda Borchers, Dan Detzner, Sally Hage, Len Jennings, Fran LaFave, Susan Lee, Mary Mullenbach, John Romano, Helge Rønnestad, and L. P. Smith. In addition, he noted the sustaining love from his family: his mother and father, Jane and Annie, Glen and Anna, David, Rachel, Hanna, and Cathy. He also appreciated the friendship of Shirley, Rachel, and David. Elisabeth Nealy and Carla Hill were able and patient with word processing through many drafts of the first edition. Thanks to them.

Many people contributed to the second edition. Thank you to Lidan Gu, Ruth Swartwood, and Alexandra Stillman for your work. Tom appreciates the valuable feedback, since the first edition of this book, about professional resiliency from students and participants in workshops. He is thankful for the help, support, and love from his family, friends, and Lisa. Michelle is grateful for the ever-present love and support from friends and family including her parents, Nick and Judy; her husband, John; and wonderful friends Maren, Eli, Julie, Sandy, Andy, Kelly, and Sharmi. We also wish to thank Dana Bliss, Chris Tominich, and Tara Nieuwesteeg at Routledge for their support and guidance as we developed the second edition, as well as Mary Farquhar and Shawn Rutka in the Counseling Program of the Department of Educational Psychology at the University of Minnesota.

About the Authors

Thomas Skovholt, PhD, is a professor of counseling and student personnel psychology at the University of Minnesota and a licensed psychologist. He has been a part-time practitioner for many years. He is board certified by ABPP and a fellow of APA. He was a Fulbright lecturer in Turkey and has also taught in Singapore. Dr. Skovholt's books include *Voices from the Field: Defining Moments in Counselor and Therapist Development*, *Master Therapists*, *Helping Skills and Strategies*, *The Evolving Professional Self*, and *Ethical Practices in Small Communities*. He received the 2010 Award for Lifetime Contributions to Education and Training in Counseling Psychology.

Michelle Trotter-Mathison, PhD, is a therapist at Boynton Health Service at the University of Minnesota. She teaches within the Counseling and Psychological Services Program at Saint Mary's University of Minnesota. Dr. Trotter-Mathison completed her MA and PhD at the University of Minnesota in the Counseling and Student Personnel Psychology program. She is coeditor of *Voices from the Field: Defining Moments in Counselor and Therapist Development*.

Skovholt Practitioner Professional Resiliency and Self-Care Inventory

by Thomas M. Skovholt

The purpose of the inventory is to provide self-reflection for practitioners and students in the caring professions. "Practitioner" here refers to individuals in the caring professions—such as the helping professions, teaching, and health care. Examples include the psychologist, counselor, social worker, academic advisor, K–12 teacher, college professor, clergy, human resources specialist, physician, registered nurse, dentist, and family law attorney.

Questions are addressed to both active practitioners and also students in training programs. There is no total number that is considered best. In fact, some of the questions are not relevant to some professionals or students who fill out this inventory. The inventory is intended to help decrease stress, not increase it.

The checklist consists of four subscales: Professional Vitality, Personal Vitality, Professional Stress, and Personal Stress.

1 = Strongly disagree, 2 = Disagree, 3 = Undecided, 4 = Agree, 5 = Strongly agree

Circle your response.

Professional Vitality

1. I find my work as a practitioner or as a student to be meaningful.	1 2 3 4 5
2. I view self-care as an ongoing part of my professional work/student life.	1 2 3 4 5
3. I am interested in making positive attachments with my clients/students/patients.	1 2 3 4 5
4. I have the energy to make these positive attachments with my clients/students/patients.	1 2 3 4 5
5. The director/chair at my site/school is dedicated to practitioner welfare.	1 2 3 4 5

(Continued)

(*Continued*)

Professional Vitality

6. On the dimension of control of my work/schooling, I am closer to high control　　1 2 3 4 5
than low control.

7. On the dimension of demands at my work/schooling, I have reasonable demands　　1 2 3 4 5
rather than excessive demands from others.

8. My work environment is like a greenhouse—where everything grows—because　　1 2 3 4 5
the conditions are such that I feel supported in my professional work.

Subscale Score for Professional Vitality (Possible score is 8–40) _____

Personal Vitality

---

9. I have plenty of humor and laughter in my life.　　1 2 3 4 5

10. I have a strong code of values/ethics that gives me a sense of direction and integrity.　　1 2 3 4 5

11. I feel loved by intimate others.　　1 2 3 4 5

12. I have positive/close friendships.　　1 2 3 4 5

13. I am physically active and receive the benefits of exercise.　　1 2 3 4 5

14. My financial life (expenses, savings, and spending) is in balance.　　1 2 3 4 5

15. I have lots of fun in my life.　　1 2 3 4 5

16. I have one or more abundant sources of high energy for my life (e.g., other　　1 2 3 4 5
people, pleasurable hobby, enjoyable pet, the natural world, a favorite activity).

17. To balance the ambiguity of work in the caring professions, I have some concrete　　1 2 3 4 5
activities in my life that I enjoy where results are clear cut (e.g., a rock collection,
painting walls, growing tomatoes, washing the car).

18. My eating habits are good for my body.　　1 2 3 4 5

19. My sleep pattern is restorative.　　1 2 3 4 5

Subscale Score for Professional Vitality (Possible score is 11–55) _____

Professional Stress

---

20. There are many contradictory messages about both practicing self-care and　　1 2 3 4 5
meeting expectations of being a highly competent practitioner/student. I am
working to find a way through these contradictory messages.

21. Overall, I have been able to find a satisfactory level of "boundaried generosity"　　1 2 3 4 5
(defined as having both limits and giving of oneself) in my work with clients/
students/patients.

22. Witnessing human suffering is central in the caring professions (e.g., client grief,　　1 2 3 4 5
student failure, patient physical pain). I am able to be very present to this
suffering, but not be overwhelmed by it or experience too much of what is called
"sadness of the soul."

23. I have found a way to have high standards for my work yet avoid unreachable　　1 2 3 4 5
perfectionism.

24. My work is intrinsically pleasurable most of the time.　　1 2 3 4 5

(*Continued*)

(Continued)

Professional Stress

25. Although judging success in the caring professions is often confusing, I have been able to find useful ways to judge my own professional success.   1 2 3 4 5

26. I have at least one very positive relationship with a clinical supervisor/mentor/teacher.   1 2 3 4 5

27. I am excited to learn new ideas, methods, theories, and techniques in my field.   1 2 3 4 5

28. The level of conflict between staff/faculty at my organization is low.   1 2 3 4 5

Subscale Score for Professional Vitality (Possible score is 9–45) _____

Personal Stress

29. There are different ways that I can get away from stress and relax (e.g., TV, meditating, reading for fun, watching sports).   1 2 3 4 5

30. My personal life does not have an excessive number of one-way caring relationships where I am the caring one.   1 2 3 4 5

31. My level of physical pain/disability is tolerable.   1 2 3 4 5

32. My family relations are satisfying.   1 2 3 4 5

33. I derive strength from my religious/spiritual practices and beliefs.   1 2 3 4 5

34. I am not facing major betrayal in my personal life.   1 2 3 4 5

35. I have a supportive community where I feel connected.   1 2 3 4 5

36. I am able to cope with significant losses in my life.   1 2 3 4 5

37. I have time for reflective activities such as journaling, expressive writing, or solitude.   1 2 3 4 5

38. When I feel the need, I am able to get help for myself.   1 2 3 4 5

Subscale Score for Personal Stress (Possible score is 10–50) _____

Total Score for the Four Subscales (Possible score is 38–190) _____

There are a total of 38 questions in the Skovholt Professional Resiliency and Self-Care Inventory. All are scored in a positive direction with 1 low and 5 high. As stated earlier, the scoring system is a method for self-reflection by practitioners and students in the caring professions. There is no total number that is considered best.

As a way to consider professional resiliency and self-care in your career work, consider these questions.

First, scan the questions and focus on your high answers, those with responses of 4 and 5. What do you conclude?

_____

_____

_____

_____
_____
_____
_____
_____

Then focus on your low answers, those with responses of 1 and 2. What do you conclude?

_____
_____
_____
_____
_____
_____
_____
_____

Then look across the four categories of Professional Vitality, Personal Vitality, Professional Stress, and Personal Stress. Are they in balance? If not in balance, what remedies could you consider?

_____
_____
_____
_____
_____
_____
_____
_____

Finally, consider the different topics covered in the inventory, your answers, and the comments you made for future self-reflection, clinical supervision, and discussion with others. Best wishes!

Part One

1

Caring for Others Versus Self-Care
The Great Human Drama

Too often, we therapists neglect our personal relationships. Our work becomes our life. At the end of our workday, having given so much of ourselves, we feel drained of desire for more relationship.

—I. D. Yalom (2002, p. 252)

I tend to give my time away to others before I take it for myself.

—Junior high school teacher, 1996

I have always been better at caring for and looking after others than I have been at caring for myself. But in these later years, I have made progress.

—Carl Rogers at age 75 (Rogers, 1995, p. 80)

There is a continual pull, constant strain, a tautness. It may not be intense. The common form is subtle, felt as body tension. Usually it doesn't knock one over. It is more like a small wave rippling through—maybe a wave going in two directions or waves pulling in three directions. Or is it four? Sometimes it is a skirmish that quickly becomes war.

Exhausted when saying yes, guilty when saying no—it is between giving and taking, between other-care and self-care. This is a universal dilemma in the human drama. It is just more intense for those who are, by nature and inclination, emotionally attuned to the needs of others. It gets highly illuminated when intense human interaction—helping, teaching, guiding, advising, or healing—is the occupational core. Here, giving of oneself is the constant requirement for success. Caring for others is the precious commodity. It is caring for the other, when by nature we are as a species geared to needs of the self, that provides much of the strength of these caring fields.

The best ones who enter these helping fields have this natural lean to the needs of others. They see, feel, smell, touch, and hear human need all around them and want to respond.

The best ones struggle the most and figure it out or leave or burn, from the inside to the outside, while hope dies. It is not natural to put the other before the self. The human senses—smell, sight, taste, touch, hearing—are there to protect the me, to promote the me. To know the world through the senses of the other is like swimming upstream, naturally hard and easy to resist. How much should one work for the other—this moment, this hour, this day, this week, this month, this year, this decade, this career? How much to give this hour to the one I am trying to help when there will be another day of many hours, and another week of many more hours, and another month of even more hours? How much to give of the self for the other this hour?

To be successful in the high-touch professions, we must continually maintain professional vitality and avoid depleted caring. For counselors, therapists, teachers, clergy, and health professionals, this can be a very difficult task. Since Freudenberger (1974) first used the term *burnout*, many authors have discussed the difficulty of professional vitality in the helping and related fields (Baker, 2003; Canfield, 2005; Larson, 1993; Linley & Joseph, 2007; Maslach, 1982; Papastylianou, Kaila, & Polychronopoulos, 2009; Robinson, 1992; Rothschild, 2006; Shirom, Oliver, & Stein, 2009; Sussman, 1995).

A central occupational strength in the caring professions—perspective taking—makes the boundary regulation between the needs of others and the needs of self a difficult task. Occupationally, we are trained to see life from the perspective of the other, and by personality, perhaps we do this naturally. L. King (personal communication, February 1996) suggests that we often have a personal history of active caring for others: "We are often the great friend who listens, the 'fixer' in a relationship, the diplomatic person in a disagreement, and/or the 'helper' within the family of origin." In another place, Skovholt (1988) wrote:

> One of the most distinguished characteristics of our profession is our intense focusing on highly skilled perspective taking: a combination of empathy, perceptual flexibility, tolerance for ambiguity and affective sensitivity. When successful, all of this translates into a profound ability to understand the world as other people understand it. This well-honed ability, one of our occupational strengths, is not possessed by many people in other occupations. (p. 283)

In the theater of life, the other becomes the illuminated part of the stage; our I is often outside the illumination. The lives of others—their hopes, ideas, goals, aspirations, pains, fears, despair, anger—are in focus. Like a leaf under a microscope, we see all of this in highly illuminated detail. As a counselor, therapist, educator, clergy member, or health practitioner, the other gets our attention. Out of the illuminated microscope, we can easily lose sight of our own needs. We even lose sight of the need to not respond to all needs around us.

In addition to perspective taking that focuses on the needs of the other, we often are pulled to see things from multiple perspectives. That way we can naturally engage in activities such as family counseling where we can see the issues from the viewpoint all family members as, for example, the mother, father, daughter, and son. Some people would hear of the Wallace Stevens (1923) poem "Thirteen Ways of Looking at a Blackbird" and say "Wow, there are thirteen ways?" Those in the helping professions use multiple lenses at the same time to understand others.

Being able to see the world of human need through multiple viewpoints can be valuable. Sometimes, though, those in the caring professions lose touch with their own viewpoint, their own needs.

Settings of intense human need can be very unsettling for those in the helping, teaching, and caring professions. This occurs because we are taught to assess, experience, and respond to human need at a much more intense level than the public. That is the goal of training. Nursing homes are an example of a difficult arena. With a honed ability to do perspective taking, one can easily feel the loneliness, fear, and despair of the residents. One practitioner struggled mightily to visit her client in such a place without being overwhelmed by all the other human need. She was caught in the option of exhaustion versus guilt while searching for boundaries of when to reach out and when to pull back. Here, the "shoemaker has no shoes" problem of low self-care can easily occur. Sussman (1995) comments:

> Many therapists, for example, grew up playing the role of caretaker, go-between, parentified child or burden-bearer within their families of origin. Having learned at an early age to attune themselves to others, therapists often have great difficulty attending to their own emotional needs. (p. 4)

Where in the practitioner's life is self-preservation and self-care held and nurtured? Perhaps the answer can be found in the struggle between altruism and self-preservation within the bigger human drama. As a species, we have been remarkably able to increase our numbers. In recent years, it has been at an astonishing rate, from 2.5 billion in 1950 to 6.7 billion in 2009 (U.S. Census Bureau, 2009). We have accomplished this growth and domination of all other living species with an acute sense of species self-preservation.

Biologically, each of us is wired to preserve the self. The senses continually warn us of danger. The physical defense system fights disease and threat with white blood cells, energy pouring from the adrenal glands, and other miraculous processes. The desire to have children is often thought of as a biological self-preservation. The psychological defenses keep us from harm through the use of denial, rationalization, and projection.

Just as self-preservation seems to be such an urgent human drive, we can find evidence for altruism and self-sacrifice as central. How about the altruism and self-sacrifice of winners of the Medal of Honor, the nation's highest award for bravery? One citation reads:

First Lieut. John R. Fox, Cincinnati

An organized attack by uniformed German formations was launched [near Sommocolonia, Italy] around 0400 hours, 26 December 1944.... Although most of the U.S. infantry forces withdrew from the town, Lieutenant Fox reported at 0800 hours that the Germans were in the streets and attacking in strength. He called for artillery fire increasingly close to his own position. ... His commander protested that ... the bombardment would be too close. ... The Germans continued to press forward in large numbers, surrounding the position. Lieutenant Fox again called for artillery fire with the commander protesting again ... "Fox, that will be on you!" The last communication from Lieutenant Fox was: "Fire it! There's more of them than there are of us. Give them hell!" The bodies of Lieutenant Fox and his party were found in the vicinity of his position when his position was taken. ... [His action] inflicted heavy casualties, causing the deaths of approximately 100 German soldiers, thereby delaying the advance of the enemy. (As cited in Bennet, 1997, p. E7)

Books such as *Man's Search for Meaning* (Frankl, 1946/1959) and *Do Unto Others: Extraordinary Acts of Ordinary People* (Oliner, 2003) tell of ordinary people who made extraordinary sacrifices of the self. Kohlberg (1979), a leading scholar in moral development, measures morality with the famous case of Heinz, a boy caught in the dilemma of either stealing medications to keep his mother alive or not stealing—caring for others versus self-preservation.

The dilemma of Heinz is a sample of the larger human drama of altruism versus self-care. Within this larger human pull of altruism versus self-care, counselors, therapists, teachers, clergy, and health professionals do their work, attempting to live on the balance beam between too much other-care and too much self-care. For example, how much sleep deprivation should the practitioner endure to adequately prepare to help the client, student, parishioner, or patient the next day? This is just one example of many dilemmas continually faced by practitioners in the high-touch fields.

Exploration of the practitioner's world begins in the next chapter. There, we explore the deep satisfaction of the work. We are speaking of the deep, and often subtle, pleasure that comes when enveloped by work that aims to make life better for others.

Self-Reflection Exercises

In this chapter we attempted to describe a major human theme: Should one's energies go toward the well-being of others or the self? Or a combination? Of what? When?

1. What kind of reaction did you have to the ideas of Chapter 1?

_____
_____
_____
_____
_____
_____
_____
_____

2. How accurate is the description in the first pages of the chapter for you?

_____
_____
_____
_____
_____
_____
_____
_____

2

Joys, Rewards, and Gifts of Practice

In teaching others, we teach ourselves.

—**Proverb**

There is no greater pleasure than knowing that you made a real, lasting difference in the life of another human being—a common experience for the effective psychotherapist, one that never loses its special meaning.

—**J. C. Norcross and J. D. Guy (2007, p. 21)**

This is the true joy in life, the being used for a purpose recognized by yourself as a mighty one; the being thoroughly worn out before you are thrown on the scrap heap; the being a force of Nature instead of a feverish selfish little clod of ailments and grievances complaining that the world will not devote itself to making you happy.

—**George Bernard Shaw (Larson, 1993, p. 2)**

A teacher affects eternity; he can never tell where his influence stops.

—**H. Adams (1918, p. 300)**

A person who saves one life, is as if he saved a whole world.

—**The Talmud (danby, 1933, p. 388)**

The reward of teaching is knowing that your life made a difference.

—**W. Ayers (1993, p. 24)**

Most readers of this book are nurturers of human development. This can be very rewarding. Making a positive difference in human life—in the growth

9

and health of the other is a central career interest for counselors, therapists, teachers, clergy, health professionals, and other practitioners, too. The close connection to others and the opportunity to help, teach, guide, advise, and heal people brings the joys, rewards, and gifts of practice. Being successful in high-touch work can produce a profound sense of satisfaction.

People have asked why we did not choose a research career in a lab or a technical field such as software design. We have a variety of answers such as experiencing an innate sense of satisfaction in working with people struggling with life's difficulties. One consistent answer is why work with things when you can work with people. Interacting closely with the most complex of all species is a great deal. The opportunity to try to make human life better is an even better deal. And to get some money for the effort is even a better deal.

What are some of the specific joys, rewards, and gifts of practice?

Joys of Practice

The focus of the work is on positively affecting human need. This goal can be elusive and difficult to achieve, a reality quite familiar to veteran practitioners. Consequently, when the practitioner hits a bull's-eye of success, there is a joy-of-practice reaction. Witness these joy-of-practice reactions.

Larson (1993) asked nurses to describe "the most positive moment he or she ever had as a helper." Three of them said:

> When a wife of a patient whose case I just opened called the office after I left their home and told my supervisor, "Thank you for sending us such a wonderful nurse."
> When a patient said to me, "I'm so glad you're my nurse today— because I wanted you to be the one to be with me on the day I die." She died at the end of my shift that day.
> A mother of a child with leukemia once said, "We come to this clinic every week and know that you care for many, many children, but when you come to see us, I feel like we are the only people you have seen that day." (pp. 6–7)

A senior psychologist at a Southern university described to Tom a joy in his practice:

> I had a very nice phone message when I checked in yesterday (on my birthday); a client who I worked with about four years ago had called to tell me that she is doing very well, is about to be married, and feels that

the only reason she is alive and living so happily now is because of the work we did together. She had been clinically depressed and suicidal for months, and I had worked my butt off with her; such a nice result!

For a member of the clergy, the pleasure of helping came in this way:

One day he went to visit a woman who was very ill. As he started to leave the room, the woman spoke to him: "You have been such an important person in my life. I want you to know that I have great love for you." These kind words sailed straight into the minister's heart. (Rupp, 1994, p. 17)

An elementary school teacher experienced a similar "practitioner joy":

This past fall I received in the mail two letters from two former students, then beginning fifth grade. They were asked by their teacher to write a letter to their favorite elementary teacher. These two girls each wrote to me, telling me that I had been their favorite, and they each had their reasons why. ... The letters brought tears to my eyes, and I know I will save them forever. I kept them at my desk this whole past year, as a reminder that I'm a good teacher and that I am positively influencing children's lives. Receiving those letters was one of the happiest moments during my teaching career. (S. McNeill, personal communication, 1996)

Michelle recalls a practitioner joy that drew her into the professional helping field:

As a lay helper right out of college, I worked at a summer residential camp for adolescents who were struggling with emotional and behavioral issues. I worked with one young woman who I will call Mary. Slowly, through my work with Mary, I was seeing small indications that Mary liked setting goals and making changes in her life. After a special outing celebrating Mary's birthday, she came to me and said: "I had a really fun day today. All my other birthdays I was gone—drunk or high, but today I had a lot of fun. Thank you, thank you for today." Hearing this from this young woman at camp helped me to know that the caring professions were for me. I wanted to be there to help others, like Mary, connect to themselves and their capacity growth.

Can you think of anything better than to have a ringside seat in the human drama and, at times, assist in making the drama turn out well? We are fortunate to be in the helping professions. We acknowledge this with happy memories of past practitioner experiences, enjoyable present work, and positive anticipation of the future in this field.

Rewards of Practice

I do not try to help the other grow in order to actualize myself, but by helping the other grow I do actualize myself.

—**M. Mayeroff (1990, p. 40)**

There is richness to the experience of relating on an intimate level with many people.

—**P. P. Heppner (1989, p. 74)**

As described in the Mayeroff and Heppner quotations, the high-touch fields can provide many "psychic income" rewards. Radeke and Mahoney (2000) describe some of the rewards in the high-touch field of psychotherapy (see Table 2.1). In comparing the experience of research psychologists and psychotherapists, the therapists were significantly higher on important dimensions. In their book, *Leaving It at the Office,* Norcross and Guy (2007) cite the following as some of the rewards of practice: satisfaction of helping, freedom and independence, variety of experiences, intellectual stimulation, emotional growth, reinforcement for personality qualities, and life meaning.

Some rewards are related to the "helper therapy principle," an idea first described by Reissman in an important 1965 article. Essentially, the idea is that

TABLE 2.1
Rewards of Psychotherapy

	Percentage Agreement	
Dimensions	Psychological Researchers	Psychotherapists
Made me a better person	78	94**
Made me a wiser person	81	92**
Increased my self-awareness	69	92**
Appreciation for human relationships	56	90**
Accelerated psychological development	69	89**
Increased tolerance for ambiguity	58	81**
Increased capacity to enjoy life	51	75**
Felt like a form of spiritual service	25	74**
Resulted in changes in my value system	68	61**

Source: Items taken from "Comparing the Personal Lives of Psychotherapists and Research Psychologists," by J. T. Radeke and M. J. Mahoney, 2000, *Professional Psychology: Research and Practice, 31,* pp. 82–84.
** $p < .001$.

the giver in a human exchange gets a lot from giving. An example is the sponsor role in Alcoholics Anonymous (AA). In an article, Skovholt (1974) elaborated on Reissman's idea by suggesting four ways that giving is rewarding:

1. *Identity development*—The idea here is that the giving role gives the practitioner a sense of identity. Also, the need for effectance motivation (the joy of being a cause) and competence motivation (the innate desire to be competent) is met through the practitioner's work. Last, a close connection with others reduces a sense of loneliness. In recent years, much professional literature in psychology has documented the importance of social connections for wellness. For example, Rupert, Stevanovic, and Hunley (2009) found that when surveying psychologists, family support was an important ingredient for well-being, whereas conflict between work and family were associated with burnout.

2. *Social exchange theory*—Theories of social exchange attempt to explain the human rules used in resource exchange. Foa (1971) developed a six-resource model: love, status, information, money, goods, and services. In essence, by giving one or more professional resources—information and services—the practitioner receives versions of love, status, and money. People, including practitioners, treasure receiving these resources.

3. *Modeling*—The modeling literature is rich with examples of how we learn by observation. Examples are learning to teach by watching one's teacher and learning to parent by watching one's parent. This is a powerful human development method. Practitioners closely observe those they work with when attempting to make positive changes in an emotional, intellectual, spiritual, or physical area.

   Much of the interaction and observation occurs in private space, although some is public (i.e., the classroom). Like a cultural anthropologist in these encounters, the high-touch practitioner is able to closely observe human behavior and learn from it. Of course, this must be done in an ethical way in which the needs of the other are primary. Yet, these encounters do provide rich opportunities to learn via modeling. Often the learning is about deeper human themes, such as the impact of motivation on change, the ingredients of success, ways to encounter pain, and how friends and family affect goals. If done in an ethical way, this modeling can be instructive for the practitioner.

   Here is an example. A few years ago, Tom attended a ceremony for winners of teaching awards. Eight awards were given out. All eight of the award winners spoke passionately about how much they learned from their students. Ironic, in a way. These were distinguished professors. Aren't they supposed to be the givers of knowledge to the unenlightened? No, they spoke of how their students were their teachers and how grateful they were for what they had learned.

4. *Direct reinforcement*—The practitioner's work can lead to direct social reinforcement, such as forms described by Skinner (1953) of attention, approval, and affection. Certainly, getting reactions like these can help make the practitioner's work satisfying.

Gifts of Practice

One great gift of practice is species immortality. This is a term that we use to describe the connection that we, as practitioners, have to the ongoing evolution of our species, *Homo sapiens*. Through helping, teaching, religious and spiritual ministry, and health care, practitioners are connected to the great human life chain that stretches from the far past into the far future. Like sharing one's DNA with others in a biological chain, practitioners, through their acts of empowering human growth, are connected in a positive way to the ongoing human story.

Connecting oneself to the growth and development of the species can provide enormous meaning, sometimes clearly felt and sometimes unconscious, for the practitioner. When the search for meaning is elusive for so many in contemporary society, finding a source of meaning is a great gift to the high-touch practitioner. Conversely, meaning burnout, a concept explored in Chapter 7, can be very distressing for the practitioner because the gift of meaning seems to be gone.

A master therapist quoted in Norcross and Guy (2007) expresses this sentiment about the value of meaningful work:

> I have learned so much about life through the experiences of my clients. They have changed me, and I'm a better person for having been a part of their struggles and pain. I've lived several lifetimes and viewed life through the eyes of literally hundreds of people. This can't help but improve my own chances for a happy life. (p. 30)

In summary, there can be great joys, rewards, and gifts for the practitioner. They can combine in unique forms at different times during a practitioner's life. They can vary in form and intensity across different practitioners and different caring career fields. Yet, although differences exist, the positive quality of the work—the joys, rewards, and gifts—can be very real and sustaining.

Self-Reflection Exercises

In this chapter, we described moments of intense satisfaction for practitioners. Nurses, teachers, and counselors were quoted about special times when their work seemed very helpful to others. This significant helping of others has been called the "psychic income" of the work. It can make it all worthwhile.

1. While preserving the privacy of clients, students, and patients, describe one to three specific joy-of-practice experiences (moments of intense work satisfaction) for you in your life as a practitioner. What was the specific positive impact on the other person? What did you find most meaningful about this work?

_____

_____

_____

_____

_____

_____

_____

2. Perhaps one or more joy-of-practice experiences were powerful critical incidents or defining moments, which are events that often serve as turning points in our professional lives. We suddenly see ourselves in a new way because the event leads us to view ourselves differently. Sometimes, critical incidents/defining moments lead us to understand theory or practice with sudden insight. Here, describe a joy-of-practice critical incident/defining moment. What happened? How did it impact your life?

_____

_____

_____

_____

_____

_____

_____

3. If you are a seasoned practitioner, address these questions. Do you judge situations as joy-of-practice experiences in a different way than you did in the past? If so, what has changed? Are you pleased or disappointed with the impact of time and experience on your satisfaction with the work?

_____

_____

_____

_____

_____

_____

_____

_____

4. It is important for those of us in the caring professions to have meaningful, positive work experiences. Some practitioners do not have them on a daily basis. However, on a random and intermittent basis, they can be very reinforcing for us. Write below in response to these questions: Are you having a high ratio of positive work experiences in your work life? If not, what is missing? What can you do to increase the ratio of positive experiences in your life as a practitioner?

_____

_____

_____

_____

_____

_____

_____

_____

3

The Cycle of Caring as the Practice Essential

Winter is necessary for the bursting of spring, which leads to the radiance of summer that unfolds into the gorgeous colors of fall that bring on the quiet beauty of the snows of winter. This cycle of the seasons, and its beauty and its energy and its excitement, is reflected in the life of the practitioner in the cycle of caring (Figure 3.1). Here, in this chapter, we will introduce this concept to you.

Caring as Central in Counseling, Therapy, Teaching, and Health Careers

> People who have had a great teacher almost always say, "That teacher saw something in me that I was unable to see in myself."
>
> **—P. J. Palmer (2004, p. 82)**

> Care is a state composed of the recognition of another, a fellow human being like one's self: identification of one's self with the pain or joy of the other; of guilt, pity and the awareness that we all stand on the base of a common humanity from which we all stem.
>
> **—R. May (1969, p. 284)**

The essential ingredient that makes psychotherapy effective and successful … is human involvement and struggle. It is the willingness of
the therapist to extend himself or herself.

—M. S. Peck (1978, p. 173)

It is better to know the patient who has the disease than it is to know
the disease which the patient has.

—Hippocrates (460 BC–377 BC)

In a world where technological innovation is illuminated in splendor and
applause, it seems much too simple to say that something more basic is more
important. Yet, in the counseling, therapy, teaching, health, and religious
fields, the research evidence overwhelmingly points to the power of human
caring as the essential among essentials.

Skovholt and D'Rozario (2000) asked people to describe in two words the
teacher they *most liked* in their experience as students. Others were asked to
describe their *best* teacher. Each person in this sample of 171 individuals gave
two words for a total of 342 words. The favorite word chosen did not describe
how brilliant or well-educated the teacher was, the prestige of the teacher's
university training, the methods of teacher education that the teacher learned
or practiced, or the teacher's physical attractiveness. The most popular word
described whether the person as a student felt cherished by the teacher in a
personal way. The overwhelmingly popular word used to describe the most
liked or best teacher was *caring.* Themes were created from the words in
this study, with the strongest theme being *caring and understanding.* For this
theme, the following words—*caring, understanding, kind, patient, concerned,
helpful,* and *loving*—were stitched together to highlight the importance of
the connection that the teacher makes with a student.

Since this study in 2000, we have asked others in resiliency workshops and
classes about their favorite teacher and have come up with similar results. For
example, in September 2008, 14 doctoral students in a Midwest program
in professional psychology were asked to use three words to describe their
favorite teacher. Their answers were consistent with other results, and again
caring was the most popular word. Related words were *patient, supportive,
kind, invested, engaged,* and *positive.* Another dimension was humorous. They
also mentioned ideas like knowledgeable, recognized my abilities, and high
expectations.

Right now, we ask that you think about your favorite teacher. What were
her or his most amazing traits? Your results may not be consistent with the

results presented earlier. Your answer is your answer. In a fundamental way, your favorite teacher probably altered you. It may have been in your own view of your ability. Maybe your favorite teacher opened up a new field of study or way of understanding the world. Most people have some feeling of connection with their favorite teacher. Most describe the person as knowing about them personally and being concerned about them as a student. When there is a combination of your teacher being very knowledgeable in the content area, highly skilled in teaching the content, deeply committed to your welfare, and passionately caring for you as a person—there is a favorite teacher! Without the personal caring, the other factors usually lose their powerful effect.

Reflecting on your favorite teacher: What were his or her most amazing traits? (Use the following oval to list your responses.)

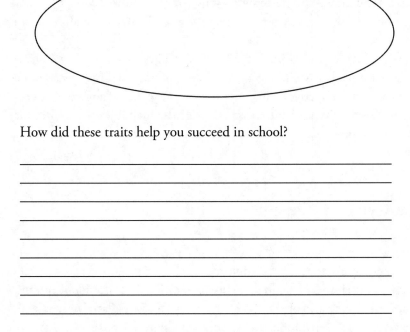

How did these traits help you succeed in school?

_____

_____

_____

_____

_____

_____

_____

Examining factors in student achievement, Klem and Connell (2004) found that teachers' support and caring were central to student success and participation: "Teacher support is important to student engagement in school as reported by students and teachers. Students who perceive teachers as creating a caring, well-structured learning environment in which expectations are high, clear, and fair are more likely to report engagement in school" (p. 270).

Mayeroff (1990) describes the benefits of caring this way: "Perhaps few things are more encouraging to another than to realize that his growth evokes admiration, a spontaneous delight or joy, in the one who cares for him" (p. 56).

The process seems to work as described by psychiatrist Scott Peck (1978) when illuminating the crucial importance of parental love for the child. He wrote: "For when children know that they are valued, when they truly feel valued in the deepest parts of themselves, then they feel valuable. The feeling of being valuable—'I am a valuable person'—is essential to mental health and is a cornerstone of self-discipline" (p. 24). Here, this idea of the capacity for self-discipline, an essential skill for student success, may help us understand why teacher caring is valued so highly by students. As additional evidence, let us mention how caring, defined as love, is the bedrock, central element in the parent–child bond. And think of popular songs on the radio. No matter what song, singer, country, year, or decade, they often speak of one kind of caring—romantic love—usually found or broken.

Our premise is that caring is the essential quality that must be *maintained* in the career fields where there are high levels of need and high levels of personal connection. Here, the inability to care is the most dangerous signal of burnout, ineffectiveness, and incompetence. The inability to care, therefore, must be strongly guarded against during one's career in these high-touch career fields.

The Cycle of Caring

Over and over again—with client, student, patient, advisee, parishioner—the practitioner must engage in a minicycle of closeness and then some level of grief with the ending of an often intense, professional connection. Let us now turn to the four parts of the Cycle of Caring: empathic attachment, active involvement, felt separation, and re-creation (Figure 3.1). In many ways, in counseling, therapy, teaching, spiritual guidance, advising, and healing, we constantly must first care for the other, be involved, then separate—being able to feel for, be involved with, and then separate from person after person in a highly effective, competent, useful way.

FIGURE 3.1
Cycle of Caring

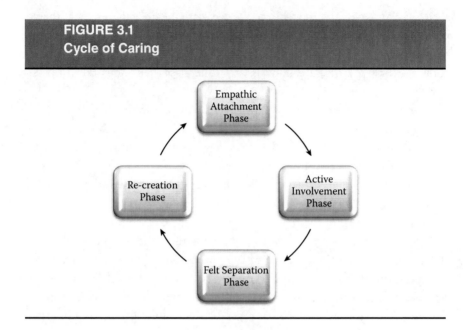

One essence of practice in the helping, teaching, and healing fields is to be a highly skilled relationship maker who constantly attaches, is involved, separates well, then steps away from the professional intensity, then does it again with a new person. We could, in fact, say this is the essence of the work; it is a very concise summary of a 40-year career.

In a major contribution in understanding human development, Bowlby described these processes in the classic books *Attachment* (1969), *Separation* (1973), and *Loss* (1980). This practitioner's work mirrors the larger human drama of connection and disconnection between people.

This process continues over and over in interaction with those we try to counsel, teach, guide, or heal: empathic attachment phase → active involvement phase → felt separation phase → re-creation phase → empathic attachment phase, then repeat. Making positive attachments, being engaged, and making positive separations with others in need of counseling, therapy, learning, or healing is the core professional skill for practitioners in the caring professions.

How many children does the preschool teacher greet as another week starts Monday morning? How many student–teacher–parent consults does the school counselor have each day? How many therapy clients do the marriage and family therapist see each week? How many helping contacts does the social worker have each month? How many patients does the physical therapist work with every 6 months? How many students does the schoolteacher instruct per year? How many suddenly fired clients does the outplacement counselor have per decade? How many funeral services does the minister have during a career?

How does one do this over and over again? How is this done well? Person after person—attach, be involved, then separate, re-create, attach, be involved, separate, re-create—day after day, week after week, month after month, year after year. Long-term social workers, counselors, therapists, teachers, clergy and health professionals work 30 to 40 years. They make attachments, involvements, and separations over and over again. Hundreds of them. Thousands of them.

It is the endless cycle of caring, with distinct phases, that makes up the life of the practitioner. Each of the phases—attachment, involvement, separation, re-creation—is important in itself, and each will be discussed separately. However, it is also important to focus on the cycle of caring as a whole and the need for competent practitioners to be skilled at all phases of the cycle. It is not easy to be skilled at each phase because they are distinct and call for different practitioner attributes. Attachment demands an emotional connection and openness to the experience of the other. Involvement demands the content skills of the practitioner and the energy to do the work. Separation paradoxically demands the opposite of attachment. To remove one's self is the opposite of connecting one's self. It reminds us of the saying about the tasks of parenting—"roots and wings." Parents who make roots often find it hard to give wings because of the emotional connection to their sons and daughters. Giving wings is easy for the parent who never develops deep roots, although the child usually suffers in such a situation. The same dilemma confronts the practitioner, yet, as with good parenting, the challenge is to be good at both attachment (roots) and separation (wings). The last stage of re-creation can be hard for a variety of reasons. We want extremely responsible and conscientious individuals to enter the caring professions because of the ethics of caring for vulnerable people. Yet, being highly meticulous and diligent as a person does not easily translate to the re-creation phase. This is the letting go, resting, having fun part of the cycle, in order to attach again.

Some individuals are extremely good at involvement but less skilled at attachment or separation. Teachers who focus on specialized content (e.g., high school physics) may have this orientation. The specialized content or skills may be the focus for the individual's work (e.g., teaching high school physics, critical care nursing, psychological assessment), and the emotional connection–disconnection may be less a focus. The emotional dimension at the active involvement phase, however, is also important for ideal results in the counseling, therapy, teaching, and health professions. Now, for a discussion of each phase.

Empathetic Attachment Phase

> The therapeutic value of empathy continues to receive strong support.
>
> **—A. Bachelor and A. Horvath (1999, p. 142)**

Attaching, connecting, bonding—these are key terms that describe the emotional oxygen-giving link between the counselor, social worker, therapist, teacher, clergy, or health professional and the other. Attachment theory, described by Bowlby (1988), is considered the most important conceptual work in understanding how a child becomes emotionally secure and able to be close to others. Pistole (2003) and Pistole and Fitch (2008) have provided rich applications of attachment theory to the caring professions.

The literature in the counseling and psychotherapy field supports the power of the human relationship dimensions in this work. In a 72-page literature review on the counseling relationship, Sexton and Whiston (1994) state in the *first* line of their abstract: "The quality of the counseling relationship has consistently been found to have the most significant impact on successful client outcome" (p. 6). They go on to say:

> The success of any therapeutic endeavor depends on the participants establishing an open, trusting, collaborative relationship or alliance. ... Research has shown that failure to form such an alliance is strongly associated with client noncompliance with treatment plans ... premature termination ... as well as poor outcome. (p. 7)

Further the importance of the therapeutic alliance is emphasized by Strauss et al. (2006). They assert:

> The strength of the alliance early in therapy is one factor that influences treatment engagement, retention, and outcomes. Ruptures in the alliance also occur and can be therapeutic or can be associated with early dropouts and worse outcomes, if not handled properly. (p. 337)

In a review of the literature on the working alliance, Castonguay, Constantino, and Grosse Holtforth (2006) report that one of the most notable findings that emerged from their review of the research was that the "alliance correlates positively with therapeutic change across a variety of treatment modalities and clinical issues" (p. 272). Lambert, Garfield, & Bergin (2009) speak to what is now called "common factors," in which basic therapeutic factors have been identified as promoting positive change regardless of the theoretical underpinnings of a particular therapist's counseling style:

> The humanistic, phenomenological perspective, suggests that the common factor is a caring relationship characterized by warmth, support, attention, understanding, and acceptance. These ingredients are said to have direct healing properties somewhat like the effects of good nutrition or solar radiation, which strengthen the organism and stimulate growth. (p. 809)

Attaching With Our "Underside of the Turtle" Side   What is the nature of this attachment process? How is this important but difficult task done well? To do this well, we often need to attach with our caring side; we call it the underside of the turtle versus the hard shell. With the hard shell, we cannot get hurt, but we cannot attach very well either. So we must continually present our soft side and attach with it. And we must do this with individuals who are often struggling with emotional, intellectual, spiritual, or physical needs. Learning an optimal level of attachment—in which the practitioner experiences the world of the other, but is not overwhelmed—is an essential professional skill and a complex one. Learning how to regulate and modulate the level of emotional attachment in the curative relational process takes time. It is a paradoxical skill—learning how to be emotionally involved yet emotionally distant, united but separate. Baker (2003) described this as self-other differentiation and discussed how this is an important part of practitioner self-care.

Often, the job of the counselor, social worker, therapist, teacher, clergy, or health professional is to establish a good relationship with individuals who cannot relate well or are highly distressed. Children who are socially rejected often believe that others with good intentions actually want to harm them (Dodge & Feldman, 1990). The helper must often relate to people who have psychological or physical complaints and want things to be figured out for them, or want answers to their questions, or are confused or lacking in confidence, or are hostile or depressed. Often the person is highly distressed, in pain, or feels unsuccessful. There may be a loss or struggle of some kind. For example, Harmon, Hawkins, Lambert, Slade, and Whipple (2005) presume that "some clients, because of their interpersonal histories, find it difficult to establish a trusting relationship with a therapist (or any person), and that these clients are especially sensitive to therapist characteristics and actions that spark memories of past painful experiences" (p. 177).

Mallinckrodt and Wei (2005) suggest that "continuing struggle [by the practitioner] to build a more secure therapeutic attachment and productive working alliance results in a corrective emotional experience that the client, equipped with new social competencies, can generalize to other relationships" (p. 358). To be effective, other-care givers are expected to be able to attach successfully with these highly distressed individuals. Being highly skilled at creating positive human relationships is, as shown by Mallinckrodt's research, an essential occupational trait for counselors, therapists, teachers, and health professionals.

The responsibility for competent, ethical, professional relationship making is with the practitioner, not the client, student, parishioner, or patient. The client may be very depressed or angry; the student may feel very stupid and ashamed about academic challenges; the church member may be struggling with the sacred; the patient may have a serious physical illness. The practitioner must step forward and create a positive human connection so that counseling, advocacy, therapy, teaching, or healing can occur. To do the job well, the practitioner must absorb so much from the other, especially in the more emotionally demanding fields within the caring professions, such as psychotherapy.

Learning how to attach with the caring side—the underside of the turtle versus the hard shell—is a part of all degree-training programs in the caring professions. For example, school counselors, social workers, elementary teachers, nurses, physicians, priests, and physical therapists are all taught professional relationship skills and how to be empathetic with their clients, students, parish members, and patients. Practitioners spend hours trying to learn the attachment skills of attending, intense listening, emotional sensitivity, and nonverbal understanding. Accurately absorbing the reality of the other, caring about the other, and feeling the feelings of the other are essential in this skill of empathic attachment. They learn metaphors for helping, such as "the ocean," a visual way of thinking about immersing oneself in the world of the other, an empathic immersion. For some individuals in the caring professions, learning to be empathic is difficult. These individuals often leave this work while in training, voluntarily or upon request, because of an inadequate ability to connect and just as likely because of a lack of interest in committing such a huge amount of one's emotional energy to the work.

Optimal Attachment

What do clients and patients recall when they look back, years later, on their experience in therapy? More often than not, they remember the positive support. The focus in training in the caring professions is on teaching the student practitioner to care enough by use of verbal and nonverbal attending behavior. Often, in reality, the problem for many in the helping fields is caring too much—excessively feeling the distress emotions of the other, such as sadness, fear, shame, anxiety, and despair, and replaying the "movie" of the other's life repeatedly in one's own mind. The practitioner can be engulfed by the other's pain and even experience vicarious traumatization, a process described in Chapter 6. Learning an optimal level of attachment, in which the practitioner experiences the world of the other but is not overwhelmed, takes years of training, practice, and supervision. It is an essential professional skill and a complex one. Learning how to regulate and modulate the level of emotional attachment takes time. It is a paradoxical skill—learning how to be emotionally involved yet emotionally distant, united but separate. The demand to be attuned, to be interested, to be energetic for the other— the other who is often in misery, anger, defiance, or hopelessness—and to continue to do it over and over again with client after client is taxing, as well as deeply rewarding, work.

Novices in the caring professions are especially vulnerable to being overwhelmed by the realities of others. We describe this problem under the term *emotional boundaries* in Chapter 5 about stress experienced by novices. Learning physical boundaries, such as with touching between practitioner and client/student/patient is important. Learning the skills involving emotional boundaries can be even more difficult. For example, a school social worker asked, "When a student or family is really upset and there are no easy answers, I keep trying, and then I take it home with me. How can I leave it at the office?" (I. Smith, personal communication, February 21, 1996). Is this optimal attachment? Being able to know an optimal level and artfully perform the sequence of attach–involve–separate–break is a characteristic of a skilled practitioner.

Larson (1993), writing about emotional demands in the helping fields, describes "the helper's pit" where the practitioner becomes overinvolved emotionally and then experiences the pain in a way that puts him or her in

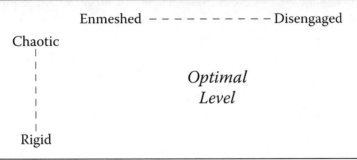

FIGURE 3.2
Levels of Family Functioning

Enmeshed – – – – – – – – – – Disengaged

Chaotic

Optimal
Level

Rigid

Source: From Olson, D. H., *Journal of Family Therapy, 22*(2), 2000.

a pit of distress feelings. Reflecting an earlier idea by Lief and Fox (1963) about detached concern as ideal for physicians, Larson suggests "detached concern" as an optimal style of involvement and writes that it is "the state of being emotionally involved while simultaneously maintaining a certain emotional distance" (p. 38). Writing about family functioning, Olson (2000) describes the optimal level of family functioning as a midpoint between enmeshed and disengaged on one dimension and chaotic and rigid on another dimension (Figure 3.2). Perhaps this can also be a guide to practitioner attachment.

Difficulty in Attaching   The task of attaching to the other is especially hard when the client, for example, does not have the skills for positive attachment. Repeatedly forming optimal, positive professional attachments is often especially difficult for practitioners or those in training who have had serious attachment distress in their personal lives. If the practitioner had intense stress in his or her primary attachments in childhood or adolescence, such as a very distressed relationship with a parent, then forming consistent, optimal professional attachments in later life can be difficult. To paraphrase Freud, sometimes the child is the parent of the adult, which means that childhood events can profoundly affect adult life. Other attachment distress examples include losses such as a major geographic move and its effects such as culture shock.

In *Fear of Intimacy*, Firestone and Catlett (1999) make a compelling case for the impact of early life experiences on later life capacity for intimacy. For example, the authors argue that the child can be strongly affected by the same-sex parent's modeling of intimacy and nonintimacy behavior. Unless the child, when an adult, consciously addresses the fear of closeness, the internalized early life messages can overwhelm any other reality and produce an extreme reaction of fear and avoidance.

As an extension, personal life attachment behavior can have a direct bearing on the practitioner's professional attachment style. The effect on professional attachment may mean that the practitioner either attaches too deeply; is unable to attach sufficiently to understand clients, students, or patients or make them feel cared about; or expresses an inconsistent attachment style with one person or across a number of clients, students, or patients. The inconsistency can seriously affect the quality of the professional relationship and, therefore, the possible benefits for the other. As mentioned earlier, Pistole and Fitch (2008) provide a valuable perspective in their application of attachment theory to counseling work.

The skill of professional attachment is complex. It is more than just trying to help. For optimal effectiveness, there must be a profound understanding of the other. The helper-healer in the following short story was aiming for skilled professional attachment but missed a key element.

Some Other Day

Preserve me from the occupational therapist, God.
She means well, but I'm too busy to make baskets.
I want to relive a day in July when Sam and I went berrying.
I was eighteen,
  My hair was long and thick
  And I braided it and wound it round my head so it wouldn't get
  caught on the briars.
But when we sat in the shade to rest I unpinned it and it came
  tumbling down.
And Sam proposed.
I suppose it wasn't fair to use my hair to make him fall in love
  with me,
But it turned out to be a good marriage.
Oh, here she comes, the therapist with scissors and paste.
Would I like to try decoupage?
"No," I say, "I haven't got time."
"Nonsense," she says, "you're going to live a long, long time."

That's not what I mean,
  I mean that all my life I've been doing things
  For people, with people. I have to catch up
  On my thinking and feeling.
About Sam's death, for one thing.
Close to the end, I asked if there was anything I could do. ...
He said, "Yes, unpin your hair."
I said, "Oh, Sam, it's so thin now and gray."
"Please," he said, "unpin it anyway."
I did and he reached out his hand—the skin transparent, I could
  see the blue veins—
  And stroked my hair.
If I close my eyes, I can feel it. Sam
"Please open your eyes," the therapist says;
"You don't want to sleep the day away."
She wants to know what I used to do.
Knit? Crochet?
Yes, I did those things,
  And cooked and cleaned
  And raised five children
  And had things happen to me.
Beautiful things, terrible things.
I need to think about them,
  Arrange them on the shelves of my mind.
The therapist is showing me glittery beads.
She asks if I like to make jewelry.
She's a dear child and means well.
So I tell her I might
Some other day.

—E. Maclay (1977, pp. 46–48)

Active Involvement Phase

> By far the most common and important way in which we can exer-
> cise our attention is by listening. ... How difficult it is to listen well.
> Listening well is an exercise of attention and by necessity hard work....
> There are times when I shudder at the enormity of what I am doing
> when I accept another patient.

—M. S. Peck (1978, pp. 121, 141)

Trust in the other to grow and in my own ability to care gives me courage to go into the unknown. ... And clearly, the greater the sense of going into the unknown, the more courage is called for in caring.

—M. Mayeroff (1990, pp. 34–35)

This is the work phase for the practitioner. One's content area expertise—counseling with adolescents, teaching adults to read, explaining the Bible by being able to read old Greek, repairing teeth, helping patients maintain adequate blood sugar levels—rises as a dominant part of this phase. A central question becomes: Does the practitioner know how to assess the problem and make things better? However, the focus of this book is not about the content areas of the caring professions. These fields vary greatly (e.g., from psychotherapy to physical therapy), and covering all the specific content skills here would remove us from the focus of this book—the wear and tear of emotional giving in one's professional work.

The active involvement phase demands the continuous attachment of the practitioner to the client, student, person, or patient. The consistent, sustained work for the other makes the active involvement phase of the cycle. An analogy is with the work of parenting, in which the long phase of active involvement follows the early days of birthing and attachment. The consistent caring for one's child over the days, weeks, months, and decades is one indicator of positive parenting.

The practitioner's consistent emotional caring is part of the active involvement phase. This time period may be the mental health counselor's contract for 10 sessions, the teacher's rhythm of an academic year, or the physician's following of an elderly patient's long, slow decline. The active involvement phase can also be the majority minutes of a one-session meeting, the time between attachment and separation. This could be, for example, a one-time advising appointment, tutoring session, or home nurse visit.

Separating Well Phase

With every hello there is a goodbye.

—S. Larson, junior high school teacher

Parting is such sweet sorrow.

—William Shakespeare (Romeo and Juliet, Act 2, Scene 2)

All counseling relationships must eventually end.

—R. Goodyear (1981, p. 347)

From terminations that are highly satisfying to those that are down-right disturbing, the provider's emotional experience receives scant, if any, attention.

—D. D. Davis (2008, p. 173)

We know much less about the practitioner's experience with professional separations than with the empathetic attachment phase. In personal life, attachments and separations are connected, as in the accepted thesis that the quality of previous attachments and separations predicts future attachments and separations. If so, do professional separations take on as much impor-tance as professional attachments? Perhaps the ability to separate well, to be energized paradoxically by the professional loss process, may be a key attri-bute for the relationship-building elements of long-term professional vitality in the helping and related professions.

How then do highly competent practitioners separate? Teachers of chil-dren give hints of their attachment when they speak of their students as "my kids." Are there, in fact, elements of loss and grief in this professional separa-tion process? Are there elements of a grief process that operate positively and enable the practitioner to attach again to another client, student, parishioner, or patient? Some examples of the dynamics of professional attachment and separation follow.

When Tom taught undergraduate courses more than he does now, each course was one academic quarter of 10 weeks. He would often have a group of 30 students—living, feeling, thinking, acting human beings with names, faces, hopes, fears, and dreams. He would struggle to learn their names, and they may have thought that he was indifferent to them for one reason or another. He realized in time that, each quarter, he was still struggling with the loss of the classes that he had the quarter before and that he was still pos-sessed by those classes. It was a kind of emotional, retroactive inhibition. A class can, after all, be a living group, a living organism, that, all of a sudden with the final test, disappears and dies forever. It would usually take until the sixth or seventh week of the new quarter for his grief (Is that the right word for this loss? Do we even have language to describe the loss of profes-sional attachments?) to wane and his embarrassment at not knowing names to grow. Then he would learn the names, only to have the whole process repeat itself the following quarter. He did not understand this attachment, involvement, and separation process for a number of years. He is sure most of the undergraduates knew nothing of it. They just hoped to be treated well, learn something, get a good grade, and move on.

A colleague working as a residence hall director in the past spoke of a similar loss reaction. For years, he experienced a three-week depression in June when the resident assistants and students left the dorm. The dormitory, teeming with people to whom he was professionally attached, suddenly was empty. He expected to be relieved and elated. Instead, he felt lost. For years, he did not really understand his reaction.

An internship training director described her struggles, when she was a student in training, with professional separation (S. Renninger, personal communication, February 1995):

> The more clients that I see, and the more clients that I terminate with, the more I am aware that this is a process of loss. I believe it is currently affecting my professional work as I am increasingly having difficulty getting close to my clients. I find myself hardening and retreating behind my "expertise." ... I believe that this year I feel the losses more than ever before, and I think it is connected to the brief therapy I am providing. I saw most of my clients at my past therapy site for the entire year. We had time to connect and time to terminate over a period of several sessions.

Do highly experienced, highly competent practitioners—experts in attachment, involvement, separation and re-creation—experience the separation process in a way that permits them to attach again? Is there a way to do this that distinguishes positive professional separations from negative professional separations in terms of the ability to attach again? Is there a pattern of attachment, involvement, and separation that continues, cycle after cycle, and produces good, ongoing professional attachments, involvements, and separations for proficient practitioners? Our suggestion is that an optimal level of other-care versus self-care highly correlates with proficient professional attachments for counselors, therapists, teachers, clergy, and health professionals.

The concepts of "anticipating grief" and "honoring the loss" can facilitate the separation. Anticipating grief means the internal preparation a person does, often without much conscious awareness, in preparing psychologically for change in one's life. Examples include the death of a loved one after a long, slow illness; the end of school and graduation; or a long-planned geographic move. Practitioners know that the cycle of empathic attachment → active involvement → felt separation → re-creation with clients, students, parishioners, and patients is contained within very specific limits and internally prepare for the change.

Davis (2008) discusses five kinds of termination in mental health work with clients: prospective, flexible, complex, oblique, and unprofessional. She also says "termination may be likened to a pilot's task of landing an aircraft" (p. 1).

Using her metaphor of landing a plane, we will provide some examples. Prospective termination consists of a long planning process by practitioner and client, talking about the trip during the descent, and a real smooth landing. The plane stops and they both get out and go their own ways. This is a positive process for the practitioner and tends to energize the practitioner to enter the cycle of caring again. Flexible termination lacks the long planning process. Suddenly, it is time to land the plane as, for example, the client announces in midsession, "I think this will be my last visit."

The practitioner as pilot then shifts the focus to termination and together they do the separating well phase work together. Again, an ending that gives energy to the practitioner.

Complex termination does not have a smooth landing. The plane gets to the runway and stops but it is often a harrowing event for both practitioner as pilot and client as passenger. External events may force termination such as a college internship training site where both graduate-student clinician and student client stop when the school year ends. Other examples involve a conflicted therapy relationship that slowly gets worse or a stalled therapy process with either practitioner or client not satisfied with the work. Then it ends perhaps by the client not returning for the next appointment. Complex termination can deplete the practitioner for the next cycle of caring.

Oblique termination can be likened to the client as passenger jumping from the rear of the plane via a parachute while the pilot is guiding the plane unaware that the passenger left. This happens when the client cancels an appointment and disappears while the practitioner had been thinking that the work was going well and that they were in midstream. This can be depleting for the practitioner.

This lack of closure for the practitioner is a stressful experience we call ambiguous professional loss. Ambiguous loss (Boss, 1999) is often stressful for a person because the factors of loss are unclear—is a MIA soldier returning or not? For us in the caring fields, ambiguous professional loss occurs during all those times when things end without an ending in our work with clients, students, parishioners, and patients. We will discuss the stress of ambiguous professional loss and remedies for it in later chapters of this book.

Back to the pilot metaphor and the last kind of termination in the group of five by Davis (2008). Unprofessional termination occurs when the practitioner acts in an unprofessional manner and the helping relationship ends. The metaphor is that the plane crashes because of pilot error. There are many reasons for pilot error but none are acceptable for the passenger, just as unprofessional conduct by the practitioner, for whatever reason, is never acceptable.

The varieties of termination offered by Davis are all part of the ending process in helping relationships; all human relationships have a beginning and an end. A good termination is positive for both parties. Honoring the loss means building in a time and energy commitment for the separation. This is not idle practitioner work. Practitioners need to do professional attachments again and soon. Doing separations well permits new attachments to emerge.

Grief work is not about dying. Grief work is for living; it makes intensity in living possible. That is why it is so important. Do not misunderstand. We are not suggesting that every practitioner, after only a short contact with a client, for example, engage in a long mourning ceremony. Professional grieving of the loss reflects the depth of the attachment and involvement, just as in one's personal life; therefore, more contact with the other leads to more time and energy for honoring the loss. For example, a nursing home nurse may go to the funeral of a resident that she cared for over a long period. An elementary teacher may devote the last days of the school year to honoring the loss of her students and of the class as a living, breathing group that will never reappear in the same way. She may engage in a series of goodbye and transition activities to help the children and herself. A counselor or therapist may spend all of a last session with a client reviewing progress made, talking about goals for the client, and saying goodbye.

Some practitioners develop separation rituals for themselves. These may involve internal thought processes (i.e., thinking about the work with the individual in a certain way) or external events (e.g., a ritualistic walk within one's office area). Using one's own creativity and imagination can be fruitful for doing this. One academic advisor, writing about her ritual, said:

> It is helpful to think of ways I can say goodbye and separate in ways that leave me feeling renewed and ready for new connections with clients. My own ritual is to picture each client as a great novel, one that I have the pleasure of reading as I become engrossed in the character's life. But always I know that I am merely a page-turner, a facilitator, an active reader who both affects and is affected by the humanness of the words on the page. Upon termination, I envision closing "the book," my access to the client's life, and place it on an important shelf in my mind. (J. Langer, personal communication, July 1998)

Re-Creation Phase

Re-creation is the fourth phase of the cycle of caring. It is the getting away from the work phase. It is the "off button" phase as opposed to the three previous "on button" phases. It is as important as the three on-button phases (empathetic attachment, active involvement, and felt separation) because, without an off button, eventually there will not be any on-button phases.

The light switch in a room symbolizes this. Let us imagine that the light switch is attached to a solar panel that collects energy from the sun only when the light is off. When the light is off, energy is generated. Then when the light switch is turned on, there is illumination. And not just dim illumination. A rather, strong, intense illumination. It is the illumination of the highly caring practitioner deeply devoted to the other, the one in need of help, assistance, guidance, teaching, or healing.

The re-creation phase can be understood using many different words that start with the letter *r*. These include renewal, rest, refurbishment, repair, restoration, renovation, restitution, and return. Other terms include having a break, time-out, and goof off. We like to use the word re-creation because it communicates the paradox of the seriousness of the fun; recreation is about the re-creation of the self. And that is important.

Practitioners vary in the quality and quantity of their time off, their restoration. Some are good at this activity, a kind of self-care. Others never seem to get to it. And that eventually is dangerous, for restoration is necessary for growth.

The Cycle in Summary

> I have learned one important thing in my life—how to begin again.
>
> **—Sam Keen (As cited in Goodyear, 1981, p. 347)**

All phases are important just as the great seasonal differences in northern climates depend on one another. Winter is necessary for the bursting of spring, which leads to the radiance of summer, which unfolds into the gorgeous colors of fall, which bring on the quiet beauty of the snows of winter.

Sustaining one's self, being vital, and being active in the caring professions means being fully present for the other. But how does the practitioner maintain such a presence for person after person? How does the practitioner empathically attach with the "underside of the turtle" side, get involved in working with the client, student, parish member, or patient, then end the work in a felt and positive way, then take a break only to start again with another and then another? Being able to do this well is a central focus of this book. The exact nature of the cycle differs across occupations and the nature of the contact within occupations. Yet, whatever the differences, the principle of proficiency with the endless caring cycle remains a measure of a successful practitioner.

The cycle of caring is one definition of the essence of the helping professions. It is what practitioners do over and over again thousands of times over a 40-year career. This is noble and courageous work and so valuable too when it is done well. May you learn to be highly talented and skilled at the art form of the cycle of caring.

Self-Reflection Exercises

We have described the four engagement phases within the cycle of caring as empathic attachment, active involvement, felt separation, and re-creation. We have also said that the most successful work in the high-touch fields involves a connection with the practitioner's "underside of the turtle." Considering the cycle, let us ask you some questions.

1. Describe how you feel about your skill level at each of these engagement phases.

   Empathic attachment: _____

   _____

   _____

   _____

   Active involvement: _____

   _____

   _____

   _____

   Felt separation: _____

   _____

   Re-creation: _____

   _____

   _____

2. Which of the four engagement phases is most satisfying for you? Most exhausting for you? Why?

_____

_____

_____

_____

_____

_____

_____

_____

_____

_____

3. What is your rhythm like in connecting and then disconnecting with your clients, students, or patients?

_____

_____

_____

_____

_____

_____

_____

_____

_____

_____

_____

4

The Long, Textured Path From Novice to Senior Practitioner

Thomas M. Skovholt and Michael H. Rønnestad

Ellis Island is an important place in American history. Situated near the Statue of Liberty, Ellis Island is where the immigrant entered the new land. The immigrant had to first leave the homeland, often a painful decision. After finding and entering Ellis Island, the new immigrant would explore the land to find a place to live. For some, this meant a long road across the American landscape to a place later called home.

Entering a career in helping, teaching, or healing is like the immigrant experience. Who am I? Where do I fit? What do I want? What can I do well? What provides opportunity? These immigrant questions are also the questions for someone considering a caring profession. And like the new immigrant, the person seeking to enter a field cannot envision or understand the whole picture. Walking along a path, in life or in a career, is like a long hike on a challenging trail. It is step by step.

As research colleagues, we have tried to describe the steps along the bigger occupational hike. In writing we have tried to describe the long path of professional development traveled by practitioners (Rønnestad & Skovholt, 2003; Skovholt & Rønnestad, 1995). In this research and writing, we have focused on the career of the counselor and psychotherapist and have used an extensive 6-year research process including 160 practitioner interviews. In the present chapter, however, we use our work in this one career field and broadly apply it to a wide rainbow of helping, teaching, and healing careers.

This chapter is divided into two sections: a section describing themes of professional growth and one describing phases of practitioner development. It is a revision of the chapter from the first edition (Skovholt, 2001) with modifications from Rønnestad and Skovholt (2003).

Themes in Professional Development

Organizing content according to phases, which we describe later, has advantages and disadvantages. One disadvantage is that the phase concept, although not as much as the stage concept, seems to communicate breaks between time periods; however, in real life, change is more gradual, like with seasons. To combat the disadvantages of phases, we have also organized the content according to themes, which comprise this section of the chapter.

Theme 1: Professional Development Involves an Increasing Higher Order Integration of the Professional Self and the Personal Self

How do I improve and get better at the work, you may ask? First, we can ask how competence develops. There are many ways: watching practitioners develop, reading the research literature, working as a practitioner, teaching novices and supervising them—all of these activities, and more, are part of the slow evolutionary growth that leads to practitioner competence.

If we were to hike together on the long, textured career path, we would come across experienced hikers, each with his or her own style of hiking. The stride, pace, body slope, and use of a walking stick could vary greatly among hikers. With time and experience, a hiker develops an individual style. So do practitioners. It is, in fact, the process of developing an individual style that is so important to practitioner identity. The embracing of a unique, individual style can, we believe, be an important factor in career vitality. Let us mention the long career of the great painter Georgia O'Keeffe. Her work changed as she changed, and with it, her originality emerged (Lisle, 1987). In its optimal expression, integration involves a process akin to Rogers's (1957) concept of congruence, where experiences are consistent with the (professional) self-concept.

Although it may seem simple and painless, the winnowing of the professional self can be difficult. It involves the merging of one's values, theoretical beliefs, and skills. It involves shedding values, beliefs, and skills that no longer fit and adding others. Like hiking, this individuation process requires constant effort. This individuation process is done through a two-sided process of aloneness and connection and is similar to the work of Grotevant and Cooper's (1986) individuation process. Their definition includes both the "qualities of individuality and connectedness" (p. 89). Recent work on individuation is from Blatt (2008), who described the two polarities of experience as relatedness and self-definition.

In our research interviews, we have observed numerous expressions of movements toward better integration. Examples include therapists and counselors who have changed their theoretical orientations. The older method, perhaps very well known, is discarded or radically modified to fit with the practitioner's emerging identity. There may have been significant and transforming events in their personal lives. As a result, professional and personal identity is altered with a necessary integration between them.

Theme 2: The Focus of Functioning Shifts Dramatically Over Time, From Internal to External to Internal

There are three parts of this theme that describe changes over time in the practitioner's development:

1. *Pretraining*—The conventional mode. Just as hikers hike without instruction, so do untrained helpers, teachers, and healers who operate according to conventional and nonprofessional ways of helping, teaching, and healing. Natural rules and personal experience govern role, working style, and methods used.

   During this period the individual operates from a commonsense base. Behaviors and conceptions of helping, teaching, and healing reflect each individual's interpretation of effective ways; ways that are fueled by both personal dispositions and popular ways of doing it. For example, for the lay helper, some characteristics of conventional helping in our culture are to define the problem quickly, to provide strong emotional support, to provide sympathy as contrasted to empathy, and to give advice based on one's own experience. There is a personal base of helping that contributes to helping being experienced as authentic and natural.

2. *Training*—The external, rigid mode. Suddenly, the path meets a bridge between the lay world of high-touch work and the high-touch professions. On the other side of the bridge, there are experts in professional hiking who strongly believe in only using certain methods, skills, attitudes, and approaches. These experts teach people to be

qualified for practitioner fields (such as counseling, advising, social work, psychotherapy, human resource development, elementary and secondary teaching, college teaching, nursing, physical therapy, and medicine). All of these fields attempt to help people, although the focus may vary greatly.

After basic training Marine recruits are suddenly enveloped by the right way to do things. So too are recruits to the high-touch professions after they cross the bridge. The recruit's reaction to criticism of lay methods is to try to do everything correctly according to professional standards. We call this the external, rigid mode. The novice helper, teacher, or healer is often trying desperately to do things the correct way to pass through gates and jump over hurdles on the training part of the path. This is an exhausting process that takes much of the person's energy.

Behavior becomes less natural, loose and more rigid. The use of humor may be seen as an index of this movement from natural and loose/flexible in pretraining to nonnatural and rigid during training and back to natural and flexible with more professional experience. Use of humor typically disappears for the student practitioner to reappear with the professional self-confidence of the experienced practitioner.

3. *Posttraining*—The loosening, internal mode. *Commencement* celebrates the end of school, but the term really means the beginning. Now, the practitioner begins the self-directed professional development process. During this long period after training, which lasts decades, there is a moving away from prescribed ways taught during the externalizing period. There is shedding and adding as part of the sculpting of the professional self.

Theme 3: Continuous Reflection Is a Prerequisite for Optimal Learning and Professional Development at All Levels of Experience

Learning from experience, a powerful possibility, is not always a reality. Professional experience does not always increase expertise. Why, you may ask. There seem to be two routes on the path. The practitioner can have years of experience—rich, textured, illuminating, practice-changing professional experience in a helping, teaching, or health occupation. Or a person can have one year of experience repeated over and over. This happens because feedback from the work with clients, students, or patients is not used to transform practice.

As will be described in more detail later, the ability and willingness to reflect upon one's professional experiences in general and on challenges and hardships in particular is a prerequisite to avoid the stagnant process that ensures a mismatch between competence and task. A stimulating and supportive work environment, including informal dialogues among colleagues and in formal supervision, impact the reflective capacity and adaptive handling of the challenges encountered. The concepts of scaffolding (Wood, Bruner, & Ross, 1976) and proximal zone of development (Vygotsky, 1962) may inform us of the supportive and relational conditions that stimulate reflection, learning, and development at all levels.

In our view, valuable learning from experience, a wonderful part of the practitioner years, only occurs when three conditions are present:

1. *Professional and personal experience*—Researchers of expertise development (Chi, Glaser, & Farr, 1988) studied chess players, taxi drivers, and physicians and concluded that experience is essential to develop expertise in a domain. So one ingredient of increased competence is experience in the domain. Some teachers in a domain (e.g., counseling, teaching, health care) also practice. Others do not and risk teaching in a way that is not effectively honed by practice.

2. *Open, supportive work environment*—A dogmatic work environment, one where certain truth is already known, does not permit the essential searching process. The novice in such an environment quickly learns that certain answers are better than others. Whereas some certainty and structure are helpful in sorting out the complex, ambiguous data of the work, too much leads to a process that we call pseudodevelopment. Administrative and supervisor support for an open work climate is an important feature. In such a setting, the practitioner can bring in the data from the work and dwell with it.

3. *Reflective stance*—"Dwelling with it" is called reflectivity in the literature on professional development (Neufeldt, Karno, & Nelson, 1996). This dwelling means thinking about, pondering, considering, and processing the reality of the profound experience of meeting with a client, student, or patient. The reflective stance is well described by Benner and Wrubel (1982):

   Experience is necessary for moving from one level of expertise to another, but experience is not the equivalent of longevity, seniority, or the simple passage of time. Experience means living through actual situations in such a way that it informs the practitioner's perception and understanding of all subsequent situations. (p. 28)

One challenge to the dwelling is the frantic work pace for many practitioners. If one is so busy *doing,* there is no chance to *be.* Yet, it is the *being* that produces the chance to learn. The clinical supervision process, if done right, also provides an environment for reflection.

Theme 4: An Intense Commitment to Learn Propels the Developmental Process

The practitioner's own motivation to grow professionally is an important fuel that propels professional development. Hiking along the professional path depends on the hiker actually doing the hiking. Most of our research informants, whether students or practitioners, impressed us with an attitude of reflective awareness and an eagerness to learn and develop. Trying new ways of hiking, going down side routes to explore and try to improve—these are important for professional growth. Commitment to learn and willingness within ethical boundaries to take risks and to be open to new learning are building blocks of increased professional functioning.

Our informants told us of periods of moratorium, times when they needed to stop and rest, to not keep going forward. We came to see these rest periods—these times of moratorium—as positive. Although the achievement culture of training programs and the professions focus on excellence and lots of it, there is also an important place for dwelling in a place for a time before going on. The sequence of hiking–rest–hiking–rest–hiking is well known to those who make long-term progress on the trail. We also learned of periods of stagnation and decline, but most reports conveyed a message of an urgency, commitment, and intensity in motivation to develop professionally.

Research on master therapists (Skovholt & Jennings, 2004) has shown a continual motivation to grow professionally for these colleague-nominated experts. This is also the case with an international sample of practitioners. Research within the Collaborative Research Network (Orlinsky et al., 1999) has shown that therapists' sense of currently experienced professional growth did not decline as a function of years in practice. Survey responses of therapists with two or more decades of professional experience also reported a sense of growth characterized by experiences of improving, becoming skillful, and feeling a growing sense of enthusiasm about doing therapy. The researcher interpretation of the results was that "therapists' sense of currently experienced growth reflects a renewal of the morale and motivation needed to practice therapy, a replenishment of the energy and refreshing of the acumen demanded by therapeutic work" (Orlinsky et al., 1999, p. 212).

*Theme 5: The Cognitive Map Changes; Beginning Practitioners Rely on
External Expertise, Seasoned Practitioners Rely on Internal Expertise*

A wonderful reality gradually emerges for the practitioner as he or she hikes
down the path over the years. Instruction books on hiking are gradually discarded as the practitioner discovers a self-developed method that works. Over
a long period of time and great effort, lessons from the instruction books have
been combined with the rich knowledge gained from one's own hiking.

You may ask what has happened. We contend that external expertise has
been replaced by internal expertise. It is a positive change in a practitioner's
professional life. Experience-based generalizations and accumulated wisdom
have replaced global theory developed by others. There is a rich literature in
the study of expertise, which helps us understand the path from novice to
master (Ericsson, 2007; Ericsson, Charness, Feltovich, & Hoffman, 2006).
Expertise entails a "rich structure of domain specific knowledge" (Glaser &
Chi, 1988, p. xxi). The practitioner now has this expertise after hundreds
of hours of practice in a domain and the active use of reflection about that
practice. Using Winston Churchill's words from a more extreme situation, it
has come from "blood, sweat and toil."

Dreyfus and Dreyfus (1986) describe this progression from external to
internal expertise as

> the progression from the analytic behavior of a detached subject,
> consciously decomposing his environment into recognizable ele-
> ments, and following abstract rules, to involved skilled behavior
> based on an accumulation of concrete experiences and the uncon-
> scious recognition of new situations as similar to whole remembered
> ones. (p. 35)

From looking for external guidance to looking for internal guidance, this
is one of the most profound ways that the hiking of the practitioner is altered
during the long time on the path. Another way of saying this is that there is
movement from received knowledge toward constructed knowledge. Belenky
et al. (1986) have formulated a model for understanding the evolution in
knowledge development that we have observed. Anchoring their model in
Perry's (1981) model of cognitive meaning and development, they described
seven levels of ways of knowing. Received knowledge is the entry level, and
constructed knowledge is the highest of seven levels of knowing. Beginning
practitioners, as new students, seem to fit the entry level: "While received
knowers can be very open to take in what others have to offer, they have very

little confidence in their own ability to speak. Believing that truth comes from others, they still their own voices to hear the voices of others" (Belenky et al., 1986, p. 37). Senior practitioners seem to fit the highest level.

> All knowledge is constructed, and the knower is an intimate part of the known. ... To see that all knowledge is a construction and that truth is a matter of the context in which it is embedded is to greatly expand the possibilities of how to think about anything ... theories become not truth but models for approximate experience. (Belenky et al., 1986, pp. 137–139)

This movement from external expertise to internal expertise profoundly affects the practitioner's functioning.

Theme 6: Optimal Professional Development Is a Long, Slow, and Erratic Process

Lewis and Clark had quite an adventure in their journey across the American frontier. Ambrose (1996) describes this adventure of making a path through the wilderness. Sometimes things went well for these explorers; other times there was great uncertainty and danger. Hardship could always be around the next corner. A route would appear and then disappear, and it took so much time for them to progress. In the end, however, they traversed the American continent.

Each practitioner, like Lewis or Clark, encounters a similar long, slow, and erratic trek on the professional development path. It takes a long time to make real progress. The development of expertise in the complexity of difficult human work takes hours. Understanding the reality of the long journey can help pale the coupled novice feelings of frantic insecurity and lusting for quick competence. The practitioner generally experiences professional development as a continual increase in competence and mastery. Our data suggest that this process may at any point in time be barely noticeable but appear as substantial in the retrospective view.

The practitioner's pace through his or her own developmental wilderness is also erratic. Sometimes the change process is slow, other times rapid. For example, there are recycling loops of anxiety, self-doubt, and feelings of dejection that come and go. Critical incidence (Skovholt & McCarthy, 1988) or defining moments (Trotter-Mathison, Koch, Sanger, & Skovholt, 2010) often produce rapid development. Piaget (1972) calls the overall change in cognitive complexity assimilation followed by accommodation.

Theme 7: Professional Development Is a Life-Long Process

This theme follows closely on the previous one. Commencement is thought to be an end. Actually, the word means the beginning. And this is true for professional development. When formal school is over, the practitioner is now in charge of one's own development. The postgraduate years are crucial for optimal development. The importance of the postgraduate years was a notable result of our research—so much literature concentrates on student growth. It reminds us of human development models that emphasize the early years without much attention to the events of adult life. For example, Freud's last stage covered all events from adolescence to the senior years.

Many models of development within the counseling and therapy professions are in fact models of student development. "Little is known about the postgraduate counselor. … Such studies are necessary for a complete understanding of counselor development across the professional life span" (Borders, 1989, p. 21).

Major changes in many aspects of work and the professional self happened after graduation. Practitioners improve their competence, handle difficulties and challenges more adequately, and become more skillful in regulating responsibilities. In addition, senior activities such as being a mentor, supervisor, or teacher fuel professional growth.

This concentration on student growth makes it appear that most of the path is walked during those days; however, the reality is more like Lewis and Clark. In the first weeks of their trek across the American continent, they got started, but that was about it. The cold winter of 1805 was ahead, as was dysentery and a grizzly attack. So was seeing, for the first time in the same week, the grandeur of the great falls of the Missouri River and the beauty of the Rocky Mountains (Ambrose, 1996). If the practitioner trek is more a marathon than a sprint, it is important for those who want to achieve higher levels of competence to understand it this way, as a life-long process.

Theme 8: Many Beginning Practitioners Experience Much Anxiety in Their Professional Work; Over Time, Anxiety Is Mastered by Most

Like tiny seeds prudently sown and nurtured, professional experience in helping, teaching, and healing can lead to a rich harvest. The harvest brings a competent practitioner who can skillfully perform multiple professional tasks. One result of the harvest is a major decline in performance anxiety from novice to senior practitioner.

Many elements combine to increase performance anxiety in the beginner. Examples are a lack of professional knowledge, the high achievement expectations of the academic culture, and the fear of being unsuited for the work ("imposter syndrome"). One practitioner, looking back, told us he was so scared he barely heard what the client was saying. The anxiety of the beginner has been discussed by many authors since Robinson's description of social work trainees in 1936 (as cited in Gysbers & Rønnestad, 1974). With increasing experience and an accompanying sense of mastery and expertise, anxiety levels diminish markedly. One greatly respected senior informant told us in the research interview: "In time you are no longer afraid of your clients." (Skovholt & Rønnestad, 1995, p. 96). Describing the underpinnings for the decline in anxiety and increase in confidence, Martin, Slemon, Hiebert, Halberg, and Cummings (1989) say that the work "equips seasoned practitioners with efficient sets of schema that they consistently draw on. ... These schemata probably have tremendous practical advantages in both economy of time and energy and felt confidence" (p. 399).

Theme 9: Clients, Students, or Patients Serve As a Major Source of Influence and Serve As Primary Teachers

It may sound strange to talk of the client as teacher. The practitioner is the teacher, not the other way around. So, you may ask: "What does this mean?" Here we are talking about the professional relationship between the practitioner and the other. In their interactions, the client, student, or patient constantly gives feedback. This is the source of "teaching by the client" for the practitioner. As one experienced practitioner told Tom, "If you really listen, you can really learn a lot from those you are trying to help about what helps." In fact, our sample group emphatically told us that their clients served as primary teachers. This is also supported by other research such as a study of therapists from 20 countries (Orlinsky, Botermans, & Rønnestad, 2001). In this study, experience in therapy with clients was rated as the most important source of influence for professional development.

By extension, students and patients serve the same primary role. People-oriented practitioners usually do not talk about learning so directly from the other in the high-touch professional interaction. Of course, the learning has to be in an ethical context. The reaction of the client, student, or patient, however, continually gives data for reflection.

Openness to the feedback, especially when the data is part of the "series of humiliations" experienced by all practitioners, is critical. Otherwise, the other is a mute teacher, and nothing is heard.

A common major crisis, often in the beginning years, involves the use of a major, highly valued approach in the field. The novice works hard to learn the approach and then energetically applies it. The result is often disappointment not success. The practitioner senses the poor result because the client, student, or patient does not change. As part of growing, the practitioner must struggle with this stressful information. This is an example, often painful but valuable, of how the client, student, or patient serves as a primary teacher.

The counseling/therapy room, the classroom, the doctor's office—these are all laboratories for learning. Client, student, or patient reactions continually influence the practitioner. Through the close interpersonal contact, the feedback provided adds intensity to the learning process. Negative feedback can impact how practitioners understand what is working and what is not.

Although often difficult, learning to listen to negative client, student, or patient feedback is especially important in order to fully use the client as teacher for professional development. Of course, positive feedback from the client, student, or patient is valuable, too. And how nice and empowering it is to get this kind of feedback.

Theme 10: Personal Life Is a Central Component of Professional Functioning

How do we know? Where does the knowledge come from? In professional fields like psychotherapy and counseling, teaching, and health care, knowledge is said to come from empirical research studies. And it does. However, there are other powerful areas too including as we said clients, students, and patients as teachers. Now with the present theme, we are discussing another source of knowledge, another epistemology. In these high-touch human fields, the practitioner also learns from her or his own life.

In the people-oriented fields, the practitioner's own personal life is highly influential. Motivation for entering the work, for example, often has a personal part. Many novices are inspired by someone close to them such as a relative. Some are also given assistance by a caring and competent practitioner in therapy, education, or physical health at a critical point. Examples here are the college student, at a point of emotional anguish, greatly helped by a skilled therapist; the junior high student awash in an unstable home empowered by a towering teacher; and the child elevated from illness by a dedicated nurse. Motivation to enter professional training may come from personal pain, like a child who witnessed the devastation of parental alcoholism or saw acute physical illness steal life away from a loved one.

These examples concern just one personal element—motivation for high-touch work. Throughout one's high-touch career, personal life keeps swirling around the practitioner. Bountiful lessons come from the practitioner's normative life events, such as one's personal aging march through life. Each decade provides so many lessons about emotional, intellectual, or physical development. Equally instructive are the unusual realities, such as acute loss (e.g., job loss) or glorious success (e.g., an award for competence). For optimal professional development, the practitioner illuminates, reflects on, and uses these ongoing personal realities in a highly instructive, nonbiased way to improve his or her work.

The impacts of personal life on professional functioning was clearly demonstrated as we interviewed the most experienced therapists for the second time, when they averaged 74 years old. Two of the learning arenas that we identified and described were in personal life domains. They were profound impact of early life experience and profound personal experiences in adult life (Rønnestad & Skovholt, 2001). Adversities and crises in adult personal life were seen to exert an immediate negative influence on professional functioning. Sometimes personal suffering increases professional sensitivity. In our work, we found this to be particularly so for suffering in the adult years. Examples of intense personal experiences that in the long run were instructive include death of spouse and children, physical disability, or severe psychological impairment of members of family. Examples of positive consequences were increased ability to understand and relate to clients, increased tolerance and patience, heightened credibility as model, and greater awareness of what is effective helping. Marriage was often described as highly sustaining with supportive and caring spouses convincingly portrayed as impactful. Measures of life and marital satisfaction were significantly associated with the way therapists related to clients.

Theme 11: Interpersonal Encounters Are More
Influential Than Impersonal Data

In the people-oriented professions, where intense people contact and caring about the other are central, it is not surprising that the drama of human contact is a great teacher. In fact, we were told by our sample group, in 160 interviews, that interpersonal encounters were more instructive than the theory and research of the profession. Meaningful contact with people was the catalyst for growth. People most often mentioned were clients, professional elders (i.e., supervisors, personal therapists, professors, mentors), professional peers, friends, family members, and, later in one's career, younger colleagues.

When interviewing our informants and examining the impact of different sources of influence at different levels of professional functioning, strong human relationships emerged as more important than impersonal data. When asking in the interviews about the impact of theories and research, we thought that theory and research would be perceived as of central importance for subjects' development. However, in the interviews, the subjects kept telling us most about person impact and least about empirical research results.

For our informants as a group, person impact in the work context occurred in this order: clients as most impactful, then professional elders, then peers, then being a professional elder for others. Of course, there is a great variety across individuals in their ranking of person impact. In time, being a professional elder can also be very impactful for the individual. Theory and research is often mediated through these individuals, and in this way, both people and theory/research are of importance.

Theme 12: Newer Members of the Field View Professional Elders and Graduate Training With Strong Affective Reactions

Professional elders are of extreme importance to new members in any helping, teaching, or healing career field. Beginners are often dependent on more established members (i.e., clinical supervisors, professors, mentors, more experienced peers) of the field for career advancement and feel vulnerable to their judgment. Students are continually scrutinizing and evaluating professors, teachers, and supervisors. Students want to learn from and model seniors they see as competent. By possessing the key for entry into the profession, professors and supervisors are seen as having the power to control the students' entry into the profession.

This sense of power difference and vulnerability contributes to tendencies by the novice to either idealize or devalue the more senior member. Students admire practitioners who are more advanced and have characteristics such as intellectual brilliance, strong therapeutic skills, outstanding supervision ability, unusual emotional support for beginners, and the modeling of professional values in personal life.

Our research showed that negative reactions to professional elders were just as common and intense. Students tend to devalue some seniors with the same intensity that they idealize others. Being in a dependent and relatively low power position is the fuel that propels the sometimes strong reaction. Professional elders are devalued if they possess behaviors perceived as highly negative. These include individuals such as a supervisor who is perceived as unfairly critical or a professor who teaches content but seems unable to practice it.

In time, and with more experience and less dependency by the novice, seniors are viewed with less affective intensity. In time, the younger practitioner, usually years later, may go through normative transitions in the way most regard parents: from idealizing the parent as a child, through devaluating/criticizing parents as an adolescent, to seeing the parent as a person with all the ordinary humanness of people in general. Beyond graduate school, professional elders are idealized and devalued less, and their humanness (ordinariness, strengths/weaknesses, uniqueness) is more clearly seen.

Training programs also receive intense scrutiny by new members of the people-oriented fields. The student's roller coaster of feelings often starts with a peak of excitement and idealization, leading to a valley of strong disappointment later in training. This disappointment often occurs when the beginner feels unprepared for the rigors of performing (i.e., a first clinical practicum, practice teaching, interviews by the student with patients in health care).

Most practitioners experience some disillusionment regarding their graduate education and training. Participants report a strong expectation to be taught specifically and concretely how to do the work, an expectation that is often not met. A common question from students, often seasoned by frustration, across training programs is: Why didn't they train us better for this?

Here we are addressing the classic gap between theory and practice that is a fundamental part of all professions where there is intense human interaction and helping of the other as a core activity. This is a major topic for investigation by researchers and teachers of professional education. If the work was simply doing something to the other, like using a can of spray paint to change the color of an object, precise instructions could be carried out. However, in the people-oriented professions, there is interaction with the other that is like a complex multiple-person art form. Theory cannot translate directly to practice. It takes time, lots of time, to learn how to do the work. Professors know this painful gap is one that all students go through, just as they did as students. Disappointment and disillusionment come to the student when the theory–practice gap is experienced. Good supervision seems to buffer against the student confusion caused by the theory–practice gap. Long after graduation, the roller coaster hills and valleys diminish and are replaced with a more objective—some good parts, some not so good—evaluation of graduate training.

In a more general way, how can we describe the commonalities where students struggle with the theory–practice gap? Here we are talking of fields that are very different yet very similar such as counseling, medicine, teaching, physical therapy, and the ministry. One analysis of the characteristics of these people-oriented professions suggests some common aspects. These aspects are (1) the process of change takes place in a *relationship* between the professional, student, or patient; (2) the process of change can be conceptualized as *communicative practice*; (3) the process of change can be conceptualized as *emotional practice*; and (4) the professional practice requires the professional to exercise an *ethical responsibility*. There is reason to believe that these commonalities make it particularly demanding to acquire, maintain, and develop a high level of professional competence within these professions (Rønnestad, 2008). These four characteristics help explain why students cannot simply and directly apply theory in their work and why there can be so much frustration for students as they struggle to become competent.

Theme 13: Extensive Experience With Suffering Contributes to Heightened Recognition, Acceptance, and Appreciation of Human Variability

With the passing of professional and personal time and all the experiences life brings, the practitioner usually becomes less judgmental of others. The practitioner has been a witness to so many intense lived moments with clients, students, or patients. The practitioner has seen many attempts by the other and many resolutions to make improvements in the domain (emotional, intellectual, or physical) needing change. The practitioner's own life has also been a school in which the lessons have produced a more understanding stance toward self and others.

Contributing to wisdom is an awareness of the unpredictability of life, uncertainties as to the best way to handle difficult life situations (Baltes & Smith, 1990), and increased tolerance for human variability. Research on the development of wisdom suggests that the self-evaluation and self-acceptance that follow the inner-directed life review process contribute to wisdom (Hartmann, 2001). Interviews with our informants suggest that insight, introspection, and reflection contribute to the development of wisdom and its elements of social judgment and integrity as conceptualized by Erickson (1950). Our informants told us of the varieties of personal and professional experiences that have combined to influence them in unique and diverse ways (Rønnestad & Skovholt, 2001).

Theme 14: For the Practitioner, There Is a Realignment From Self As Hero to Client As Hero

Practitioners in the high-touch caring professions enter the fields of helping, education, and health to positively impact the other. It is a central motivation for being drawn to these occupations. Entering the work world, the new student is unsure of the amount of emotional, intellectual, or physical improvement there will be for the client, student, or patient. Drawn to the field, some new students make an error in believing that the work can bring change more quickly and more completely than is realistic. It takes a long time for the practitioner to sort out the realistic from the ideal. This error is often coupled with a belief that one may possess a strong helping impulse— one that can really make a difference, meaning a belief by the practitioner that he or she can be an instrument for wondrous change. In time, there is a more textured understanding of the change process, with the practitioner being only one part of success.

With experience of both failures and successes with a large variety of clients, students, and patients, there is a gradual shift in understanding the change process. This change can be formulated as a movement from practitioner power to client power. This shift in attitude parallels the recent emphasis in the contemporary psychotherapy literature of the heroic client by Duncan and Miller (2000). Although practitioners feel more confident and assured as professionals with the passing of time, they also experience a "series of humiliations" that contribute to increased realism as to what can be accomplished in professional work. If these "blows to the ego" are processed and integrated into the practitioner's self-experience, they may contribute to the paradox of increased sense of confidence and competence while also feeling more humble and less powerful as a practitioner. This general movement is also similar to how Skovholt and Jennings (2004) describe master therapists.

Phases of Practitioner Development

One way to understand human development is to think in stages, such as the classic stages described by Freud, Piaget, and Erikson. Usually, the stage perspective describes changes that occur suddenly and sequentially. Many stage models are not suited to capturing changes that occur gradually, continually, or chaotically; however, for many human realities, there are no sudden shifts as suggested by stage models. Stage models have strengths and limitations. In our first formulation we did use the stage concept. Now, in our reformulation (Rønnestad & Skovholt, 2003) we are using the term *phase* to indicate less abrupt changes. We hope that the following descriptions of the phases in our model will be of use for you in understanding your own development as a practitioner.

Phase 1: The Lay Helper Phase

In roles as parents, friends, sisters, brothers, grandparents, children, colleagues, and volunteers, people help other people. Looking at this picture through a historic and cross-cultural lens, we see patterns of counseling, therapy, teaching, and healing where kin, rather than professionals, fill these roles. For generation after generation, people have cared for each other emotionally and given guidance and advice, usually through relationships of blood, marriage, or friendship. In these worlds, parents, older siblings, and other relatives are the primary teachers of children. Health care, as in first aid, is also given by those close to a person.

In recent years, in a variety of countries, as kin relationships have loosened, professional helping, teaching, and healing occupations have grown. Also, volunteer and paraprofessional relationships of giving through helping, teaching, and healing have increased. These are not primarily blood related. In the United States, for example, most adults volunteer in the community in one capacity or another. Across cultures and across time, there have been different patterns of caring that are not driven by the professional socialization of careers such as social worker, secondary teacher, or registered nurse. Here, we attempt to describe this pattern of helping, teaching, and healing in the lay helper phase.

The central task in the lay helper phase is to use one's abilities and skills to be helpful to the other. The lay helper often identifies the problem quickly, which contrasts with the expert in the helping fields who often takes considerable time to identify the problem. It may be that the expert is processing so much data about the problem that it takes longer to really understand it. Quick problem identification for the lay helper is often accompanied by strong emotional support and advice.

Although individuals without professional training in helping populate this phase, the goal is still quite close to that of the caring professions—giving to the other emotional, educational, or health help. Perhaps this is because of kinship obligations, close relationship connections, or a sense of wanting to be a successful volunteer.

Usually there is sympathy toward the other and an interest in assisting the other. The sympathy of the lay helper, a feeling sorry for the other, may have a component of overidentification with the other and a getting lost in the sympathy. Sympathy can feel enveloping for the lay helper.

This is in contrast to the empathy of the professional helper. Empathy consists of a temporary identification with the other. One definition of empathy is from Bohart, Elliot, Greenberg, and Watson (2002): "The therapist's sensitive ability and willingness to understand the client's thoughts, feelings and struggles from the client's point of view" (p. 85). One is not the other; there is more of an as-if quality rather than being lost in the sympathy. This as-if formulation is from Rogers (1957) and suggests the separation of the self from the other. Regulating emotional engagement is a characteristic of professional empathy.

Sometimes the lay helper does not have an emotional investment in the helping of the other. There is more of a distance than an overwhelming connection to the other's problems.

The advice will come from the lay helper's own personal life. Knowledge, perspective, and approach come from what life, in one way or another, has taught a person. For example, a young woman who is having trouble with her boyfriend turns to a female friend for help. Most often, the friend will give advice based on her own life experience. It is a kind of "based on my life, here is what to do" approach. As much as the friend's life offers useful help, then the lay helper phase approach is useful. It also has limits, however, because the friend's helping method and solution, based on her own life, may not be a "glove that fits." The same principle of competence to assist another coming from one's life experience governs other high-touch assisting efforts, such as teaching a child to read, helping an adult to be happy, or offering spiritual guidance.

There is a projection of one's own experiences and one's own solutions on to the life of the other. The lay helper often gives answers and these can have a base in the notion of common sense. There will usually not be a self-consciousness or reflectivity about the helping process. Rather, there will be a naturalness in the whole process. For example, when unsure whether to take one path or another the lay helper may say, "This is what I did. Try that," or give romantic advice like "You are better off without him" or "Keep trying."

At the lay helper phase, there is usually less self-awareness of the concerns that students in professional training programs have, like "Am I doing this right?" or "Am I any good at this work?" At the beginning student phase there is often an acute self-consciousness about performing in a helping role in a professional way. Here, there is a more relaxed, commonsense approach to both the work method and evaluation of success.

Phase 2: Beginning Student Phase

The people-oriented professions are marked by an unusual paradox. The core work of these careers is reserved for only a few yet open to all. For example, the psychotherapist consoles a person enveloped in intense grief. So does the sister, father, or friend. An essential reason for the large overlap between exclusive and inclusive is the core work of caring for the other. The career essential of caring for the other is the occupational glue in the people-oriented professions. Of course, caring for the other is also the glue that marks the human bond in families, friendships, and volunteer activities, therefore, the overlap.

The beginning student phase is the bridge from a land of the known lay helper phase to the land of the complex professional world of intense training and exacting standards. By entering the beginning student phase, the student is crossing the bridge to the professional field. By doing so, the person is volunteering to give up old ways of thinking, acting, and feeling in order to learn the professionally correct methods, whatever they are. In this phase there is a movement from open to all to reserved for just some (from inclusive to exclusive). These movements are exemplified by teaching a child to count (open to all) to teaching linguistic theory to university students (reserved for some). This phase is marked first by the transition from the known to the unknown. The known is the conventional way that the lay helper functions as a helper, teacher, or healer, and the unknown is the prescribed ways of a profession, such as mental health counseling, secondary teaching, or nursing.

While crossing the bridge, the professional novice-to-be is often filled with excitement and enthusiasm. The person has chosen this field for advanced training, perhaps in part because of positive volunteer experiences and looks forward to learning new skills. There is also worry about an unpredictable and unknown future.

The approach to this phase and the movement through it and other phases are influenced by age and life experience. An older person with experience in a people-oriented profession will move through the training stages faster than a younger person with less life experience. A 40-year-old explained how she was different than a 23-year-old when beginning a graduate training program:

> Perhaps part of this is a function of being older and already having two careers which have been rewarding and engrossing for me: teacher and mother. From these I have brought the knowledge that I could work effectively with people. … I also have the notion that in any field there are many theories and that I can comfortably pick and choose and combine elements. (Skovholt & Rønnestad, 1995, p. 25)*

When school begins, the new student is exposed to theories, ideas, perspectives, facts, approaches, and visions. This formal schooling brings new information cascading onto the student. Two elements, self-assessment of skill level and theoretical approaches, absorb the novice's time and attention. What is first welcomed quickly becomes overwhelming. Suddenly, there is so much to learn and know. One student said, "There was too much data, too many conflicting ideas, and the techniques learned in class seemed kind of wooden and sometimes made things worse" (p. 27).

Having a first client is a sign of moving from the known of the lay helper role to the unknown of the professional role. The student often feels the chasm between theory and practice. Questions such as "How do you keep talking for a whole hour?" are very important at this point. The beginning student can be preoccupied with trying to apply classroom methods to actual practice and finds it difficult to do so.

Two influential groups in training are one's teachers and one's peers. Both of these groups begin to exert a strong influence on the beginning student. In addition, both the new ideas and the new people serve as catalysts for the novice's life review. The past begins to be examined through a new lens. This is especially true for some occupations such as family therapy, where one's family of origin is examined in new ways, and teaching, where one's own teachers are examined as models of teaching.

In trying on the professional role, a person is often eager but unsure. One student said, "I was very motivated to be in the right saddle but didn't know what that saddle felt like" (p. 26). Another said, "If I don't have success I get disillusioned with myself" (p. 29). In time, the transition to professional immersion is not as raw and new.

---

* All quotations throughout the rest of this chapter are from this source unless otherwise cited.

The counselor, therapist, teacher, or health professional is now into professional schooling, which provides so much new information—research, theory, technique, skill, and approach—that the student is swimming in it, swimming in a swirling pool that is rising and growing in strength. The possibility of drowning in the professional newness can be a suddenly felt threat. In reaction, the high-touch professional-in-training often searches for a life vest to use in the swirling water, turmoil, and confusion. Two popular life vests are (1) modeling oneself after an expert and (2) searching for an understandable theoretical model that explains the confusion about human beings. Questions can be: How do people develop problems? What approaches are the best in improving human life in areas like counseling, teaching, or health care?

One of the central tasks at this phase is to grab onto a life vest and use it to keep from drowning, while realizing that authentic practitioner development means that eventually one must swim without a life vest. Translating the metaphor, this means that the challenge for the student is to remain open at the metalevel while making tentative choices at the microlevel. These choices are about what to embrace in terms of theory and practice. Making tentative choices provides a temporary relief from the anxiety that can threaten the student. The anxiety arises from not knowing. There has been an increase in understanding the complexity of the professional world like recognizing the difference between what emerges when one is looking at a leaf from a distance and under a microscope. If the anxiety of not knowing is too strong, the student may retreat. Leaving the field or rigidly clinging to one way of understanding reality (one theoretical approach) are two retreat styles that reduce anxiety but, unfortunately, also reduce the capacity for cognitive complexity, a long-term key to senior expertise.

If a life vest is used, the anxiety of bewilderment gives way to temporary relief and calm; therefore, searching for a life vest has the built-in motivation of a teachable moment. The student is ready and often frustrated when a life vest is not available.

Life vest #1 is to use a senior practitioner as a model. One counseling student stated this simply: "I wanted to absorb from the counselors I observed" (p. 31). Students of teaching watch their teachers teach, students of medicine watch their teachers interact with patients, and teachers of counseling are intensely observed while demonstrating a client interview. The style, mannerisms, thinking method, and approach of positive models—national or local experts and even admired peers—are readily adopted. It is a quick way to feeling more competent. Video or live demonstrations are popular.

As a profession, marriage and family therapy has led the way in the use of modeling to learn the profession.

Negative models are also used to cut down the complexity of choice. If something can be eliminated, then confusion can be lessened. Negative models, usually more advanced practitioners judged harshly by the student, provide a movie of "things I do not want to do." A classic example is the teacher of teaching methods judged to be a poor teacher by the student of teaching. A more general negative model in the caring professions is the senior practitioner who no longer seems to care about the client, student, or patient. Such a practitioner, perceived to be burned out, is sternly judged and avoided. There is a strong factor in the negative view; the student fears, "I may end up like that."

For *life vest #2,* the search is on for a theoretical approach to lessen the confusion. It is another teachable moment. First, a reminder that the larger task is for the beginning student to be open to the confusion and to create gradually one's own professional identity. It is a painfully slow process. Here is one student's description of this process:

> I'm putting together a jigsaw puzzle. First I pick up a piece to see how it fits with another. I turn it around and try to get it to fit. I try lots of different combinations. If a piece fits, I keep it and it becomes a natural part of the puzzle. If it doesn't fit, I keep trying to find a place for it. Eventually with no place, it gets dropped. (p. 33)

The life vest is an easily learned method that suggests "pay attention to this" and "do this." How, for example, should the nursing student provide care to an elderly patient during a routine health visit? The theoretical model, read in a text or heard about in class, suggests a few key variables. In the mental health professions, students quickly grab a simple theoretical model such as versions of basic helping skills or cognitive therapy. A simple cognitive approach, for example, suggests that, in the great complexity of the human being, one can be an effective helper by just paying attention to faulty thinking patterns with a goal of correcting "stinking thinking."

If neither of the two life vests is available to students in ways that meet their needs, they usually begin criticizing their training. The initial excitement of being in school turns to disappointment and frustration, feelings most often voiced to one's peers. Without a life vest, rather than being more prepared for the work, the student feels more vulnerable. One person expressed it this way: "The intensity of the anger comes from the next set of challenges. The person must perform at a consistent level and often feels unprepared" (p. 35).

A central task here—being open to professional complexity while finding safety in temporary solutions—continues as the student enters the next phase.

Openness to new learning is important for the student at this point. Yet, the openness presents a problem that has been described as "trying to drink from a fire hose." There is so much to think about and decide about. So, as we stated, one or more life vests can be valuable. Openness to new learning means a willingness to recognize that professional work is complex. It can be disconcerting to become aware that the circle of not knowing grows about as fast as the circle of knowing. This realization runs counter to the reason to go to school: to feel more competent, not to feel that confusion and clarity are neck to neck in a professional development race.

In spite of the struggles between confusion and clarity, too much of a closed attitude fosters professional stagnation. Conversely, accepting the slow process of professional development and an acceptance toward oneself as a learner in a learning community helps the professional development process.

The complexities of professional work need to be addressed. But, how to do it? We think that the developmental approach has an accepting quality and that it is a process that takes times. It has an exploring, active, searching, trying-out quality and is understood, at least somewhat, by the novice as a long-term project.

The nondevelopmental (eventually stagnant) approach attempts to limit the confusion by focusing not on exploration but rather on fitting all the data into one way of understanding the client and one way of proceeding. It has an experience-limiting, defensive, anxiety-reducing quality with impression management (Goffman, 1967) being the focus. Here, looking good is more important than being open about the struggles that accompany long-term professional development.

The impression management route is attractive because of the accumulative impact of a variety of forces. First, the training program is usually part of the intense achievement culture of a university. Perfection is the goal and doing well at everything is expected. The normative struggles of the novice period do not get support in such a culture. There is also the power differential between the supervisor or instructor and the student in practicum, internship, or field placement. This power differential is exaggerated by the evaluative function of the educational system. Last, during those times when the novice hits the tidal wave of confusion and low self-efficacy, the student is likely to engage more actively in impression management.

Students vary in how confident and competent they feel while in training. Some, because of previous work experience in the helping professions or related fields such as teaching, have more confidence. Life experience and personal maturity fuel a sense of professional confidence. Others trace the learning curve in their practitioner work with the learning curve of another area where they started with no skill and then gradually got much better. Students in class have made analogies to skills such as learning to be a debater, learning to be proficient at the piano, learning to play baseball, learning how to integrate complex and diverse knowledge arenas, learning how to live in a foreign culture. Each of these involved early attempts that were helped greatly by a positive teacher or mentor. These first attempts led to increased practice with feedback that improved performance. Some in the beginning student phase seem to be a natural fit with the role. They may be wired by biological inclination or early family role as mediator or helper to the practitioner role. These are all situations where there may be less student anxiety in the early practice days.

It is more common for students to feel threatened and anxious in the early student days (Rønnestad & Skovholt, 2003). Student anxiety during the early practice days seems to be present across countries and cultures. These results are from the most extensive international survey ever done of practitioners from students to the senior level. It is the International Study of the Development of Psychotherapists (Orlinsky & Rønnestad, 2005). From this research, we know that inexperienced therapists in many countries frequently feel overwhelmed and highly challenged in client sessions. Compared to functioning at later phases of development, Norwegian therapists (Rønnestad & von der Lippe, 2002) reported more frequently to experience the following difficulties: (a) lacking in confidence that you can have a beneficial effect on a client, (b) unsure how best to deal with a client, (c) in danger of losing control of the therapeutic situation to a client, (d) distressed by the powerlessness to effect a client's tragic life situation, (e) troubled by moral or ethical issues that have arisen in your work with a client, (f) irritated with a client who is actively blocking your efforts, and (g) guilty about having mishandled a critical situation with a client.

Also, research on supervision within counseling/therapy confirms how threatening training experiences may be for students. The works by Gray, Ladany, Walker, and Ancis (2001), Moskowitz and Rupert (1983), and Ladany, Hill, Corbett, and Nutt (1996) in particular have demonstrated the counterproductivity that may result from a nonoptimal supervision relationship.

Phase 3: The Advanced Student Phase

The people-oriented professions (e.g., university counseling, elementary teaching, physical therapy) differ in many important ways. As an occupational core, however, all focus is on caring for the other, which occurs within the practitioner role. The most intense practitioner training usually occurs in this stage. Here, the practitioner-in-training needs supportive guides for the long, challenging, difficult career path. The supervisor as guide does not do the work of the novice or carry the novice along the path; however, the supervisor does watch as the novice struggles while hiking and may point out hazards and pitfalls on the path, suggesting alternative methods of hiking during arduous parts. When a person hikes with a guide for the first time, it goes by different names, such as field placement, internship, externship, practicum, student teaching, clerkship, and residency.

The central task here is to look, act, think, feel, and perform at a basic established professional level. Many students, however, have higher aspirations for their functioning and want not only to avoid making mistakes but to excel in their work. This takes enormous amounts of student energy, time, and effort. Many feel pressure to do things more perfectly than ever before. The advanced student usually has a seriousness and cautious approach to role and function. They are typically not relaxed, risk taking, or spontaneous. Years later when down the practitioner path, the task is to shed aspects of this narrow professional role. Now, however, the task is to show professional gatekeepers that one has what it takes to pass through the gate.

The internalized high standards for professional functioning for many students contribute to the tendency toward excessive and misunderstood responsibility. A female student at this phase said: "I do a good job of letting myself feel responsible for everything." Another said: "I thought I could and should help everybody," and a third expressed it this way: "Every single request for consultation I wanted to do. I wanted to learn things and to prove to the director of training that I could do the job."

Supervisors are both guide and evaluator. This dual role of guide and evaluator can contribute to student ambivalence toward gatekeepers at the advanced student phase. Most loved are the wise and expert gatekeepers who adroitly teach the trade with large doses of emotional support and small doses of evaluation fear. Most despised and feared are the opposite—incompetent practitioners who unfairly evaluate the student as inadequate. The student dream is for the former. Most supervisors/gatekeepers fall in between these extremes.

When novice practitioners have critical supervisors and clients who do not seem to improve, the situation is ripe for what Orlinsky and Rønnestad (2005) call "double traumatization." This, like other events early in one's career when the experience base is fragile such as a client suicide, can be very harmful to the naturally slow evolutionary growth of practitioner competence.

If the reference point for evaluating one's own competence changes to that of the seasoned professional, the advanced student realizes there it is still much to learn. The advanced student as practitioner may still feel vulnerable and insecure, and actively seek confirmation and feedback from seniors and peers. There is still considerable external dependency.

The reaction of the client, student, or patient lies at the center of the drama at this point. The person at the advanced student phase uses the indirect and direct feedback from the client, student, or patient to judge one's own practitioner self. Am I any good at this work? is a common self-assessment question and a very important one. Other questions are: Can I do it? Will the person I am trying to help think that I am good at this? How about the view of my peers and my supervisor? Do they think I can be a very skilled practitioner? The variable confidence at this phase is expressed by these individuals. One said, "There weren't many times I felt highly competent. I questioned, am I in the right place, is this what I should do?" Said another, "I've gone from being petrified to being comfortable." Another stated, "I'm less afraid of losing patients than in the past."

At this phase, the practitioner-in-training is most interested in pragmatic information that can immediately help the novice with the current client, student, or patient. The social work student with the teenage client suffering from a psychotic break wonders, "What can I read to help me interview her?" The secondary teacher-in-training eagerly seeks out a method to keep order in a class of 35 highly distractible students. Before stitching a wound for the first time, the medical student, like a dry sponge, eagerly soaks up lessons given by the supervisor. Practical, useful information is valued; confusing, impractical theory is read only when there is the external, anxiety-based motivation of a class assignment.

Supervision of beginning practicum students can be a powerful source of influence for the advanced student. One female, reflecting on her internship, said: "It was a concrete realization of what I had learned. It was really valuable. The contrast between them and me helped me see my own style and how far I had come in my development" (p. 44).

Practicing like a professional makes the person eager to move beyond the student role to the world of professional practice. It is, in fact, the act of graduating and leaving school that ushers in the next phase of the long practitioner road.

Phase 4: The Novice Professional Phase

At commencement, the ritual of graduation celebrates the end of school, and students are happy because they are escaping from the demands of formal training. The novice professional phase is a time of freedom for many. It is the dawn of a new time, a time for discovery of a new part of the novice to senior practitioner path. The central task of this phase is searching onward beyond what the individual has already successfully explored.

The novice professional phase encompasses the first years after graduation, although individual paths vary. For most practitioners these years are experienced as intense and engaging. There are many challenges to master and many choices to be made.

In the novice professional phase, there is a sense of being on one's own. In addition, there is a continual process of reformulating, a process of "shedding and adding" at the conceptual and behavioral level. There seems to be a sequentially ordered change that occurs during the first years following graduation. First, there is a period where the practitioner seeks to confirm the validity of training. Second, when confronted with professional challenges inadequately mastered, there follows a period of disillusionment with professional training and self. Third, there is a period with a more intense exploration into self and the professional environment.

The new practitioner is excited to finally leave the student role and be a professional in the world of helping, teaching, and healing. The person is eager to use all the new skills that were gleaned through hard work during the stress and grind of student life. We call this the confirmation subphase because the new professional is eager to confirm the usefulness of one's formal training and the status of the school or university.

In the preceding phase, the practitioner had supervisors and teachers as guides. The supervisor and the built-in structure of the practicum, internship, or clerkship are there to help ensure a positive learning experience. Helpful and instructive developmental supervision is part of this equation. The ideal does not always happen. Sometimes the guides and the structure of the training experience are not ideal. Now, with the freedom of the novice professional phase comes the path without the guide, which is often confusing and dangerous. The long dreamed about freedom may also produce a surprise reaction of anxiety, loss, and confusion. Three individuals at this phase commented: One said, "Having less guidance from professors and supervisors was scary." Another said: "People weren't protecting you from taking on too much anymore." A third had the following reaction:

> I didn't anticipate all of this. I was concerned all the time that things wouldn't work if I didn't finish [my degree]. I used to think that my doubts about me and my despair would go away with the degree. ... It is a disorienting process because I don't know anymore now except that there are more expectations. ... I didn't expect the formal training would lead to feeling adequate until I felt inadequate and then realized how much I expected to know by now. My professional training was over and I lacked so much. (pp. 51–52)

Many will look for workplace mentors who will offer guidance and support, thereby easing the transition to autonomous professional functioning.

The realization that one's schooling was not enough usually comes to the practitioner while performing work tasks. The person starts getting hit with challenges that he or she is not prepared to meet. This most often happens when the feedback from those served—clients, students, and patients—clearly tells the practitioner that his or her work is not totally successful. This may come through what we call "a series of humiliations" that are painfully experienced by the practitioner. The painfully experienced element comes because there is a demand to succeed at helping, teaching, and healing and because the vast majority of people-oriented professionals are highly motivated to provide service to the other. Failure is distressing.

Here is an example of disillusionment: An individual with a math and science undergraduate degree entered a graduate program with a strong research-based empirical approach. As he applied what he had learned, an approach with an emphasis on precision and rationality, to patients with spinal cord injuries, he was overwhelmed by the emotional anguish and pain of these patients. He said: "Sometimes you feel like you were trying to fight a forest fire with a glass of water."

The realization that one's training was insufficient brings on the disillusionment subphase. This realization of inadequacy often accompanies anger at not being better prepared. One female looked back and said: "I realized that graduate training had real gaps. There was much I had to cover that was not offered in graduate school. I remember writing letters to the director of the program, pointing out things that should have been addressed." Others point the finger inward and go through painful self-examination of the inadequacy.

The novice professional is typically experiencing an increased sense of the complexity of practitioner work and is recognizing more profoundly how important the therapeutic relationship is for client progress. As the novice professional is focusing more attention on understanding and mastering relationship issues, the practitioner is also becoming more skillful in defining work roles and regulating boundaries.

The developmental challenge is to continue down the path with self as the primary guide. The key is to be open and searching, to use the reflection process to learn, and to continue to rely on peers for support and professional elders for guidance. Practitioner development is a long process. The novice professional phase practitioner who embraces this reality continues the step-by-step process of growth.

Phase 5: The Experienced Professional Phase

By this phase, the practitioner is highly experienced. Formal schooling occurred years ago, and the hiking boots have now racked up many miles on the career path. The central task on this part of the path is the development of a more authentic, genuine professional self. This means creating a role that is highly congruent with the individual's self-perceptions (including values, interests, attitudes), which makes it possible for the practitioner to apply his or her professional competence in an authentic way. Expressing this authentic self, one research participant at this phase used a music analogy when saying:

> If I know my pieces really well I can then play them individually with ease. Played well together there is a unifying and coherent quality that is difficult to achieve but is beautiful when it occurs. (p. 68)

Major sources that we have found to influence professional development (theories and research, clients, professional elders [professor, supervisors, mentors, therapists], peers and colleagues, one's own personal life, and the social and cultural environment) continue to play an important role in professional functioning. Increasingly, the experienced practitioner reports understanding human behavior through professional literature in related fields such as anthropology or religion; or through reading prose, poetry, and biographies; or through movies, the theater, and other artistic expressions.

A shedding and adding process is the key to forming and shaping an authentic professional self. Consolidation is a major part of the shedding and adding. Examining the professional life of the painter Georgia O'Keeffe shows strong evidence of this shedding and adding process as part of developing the authentic professional self (Lisle, 1987). One practitioner at this stage called it "throwing out the clutter" (p. 62). Other research participants said it in the following ways:

> There was a time I had an investment in one approach in part due to training but exposure to clients, other approaches, and my own therapy led me to change. (p. 64)

One person expressed it this way:

> I learned all the rules [practice guidelines] and so I came to a point—after lots of effort—where I knew the rules very well. Gradually I modified the rules. Then I began to use the rules to let me go where I wanted to go. Lately I haven't been talking so much in terms of rules. (pp. 66–67)

Another said:

> I'm more loose than I used to be in my approach to the work. Sure, everything must be done ethically and professionally. That's a given. I'm just not so frantic about answers or even questions. Now I really feel there isn't a right way to do it, although there is a right process for me. (p. 67)

This personalization of the professional self lets the practitioner express the helping, teaching, and healing self at a higher level of creativity. In sharp contrast with earlier functioning, techniques and methods are not applied in a conforming, rigid, external or mechanical fashion, but can be used in a personalized and flexible way. Expressions of this are seen in the active formulating of a conceptual system and the active developing of a working style that fits the individual. Increasingly, there is little tolerance for lack of close fit and a strong tendency to search for a work environment experienced as compatible with self, a movement consistent with the underlying premise in Holland's (1997) theory of vocational choice. Data to shape the professional self has been coming to the practitioner from a variety of sources for a number of years. The early disillusionment of the previous phase has been replaced by active building of the professional self. The adding and shedding process occurs through trying out a wide variety of methods, approaches, and techniques; insights from direct and indirect feedback from clients, students, and patients; learning from a variety of supervisors and other professional elders; and learning from admired peers.

The practitioner must continue moving forward toward more professional maturity while dodging hazardous elements on the path (dangerous branches, rocks, and roots), translated as becoming stale, exhausted, and apathetic. One element that makes self-awareness of stagnation versus development difficult is the recycling of older concepts, methods, and techniques under new terms. In the people-oriented professions, attention is paid to that which is new, revolutionary, successful, and highly impactful. Researchers get credit for publishing something new, not replicating something old. Practitioners, especially new practitioners, are not drawn to "old ideas that sometimes work." However, the experienced practitioner can sense the "old fish in new wrappers," and a cynicism can emerge. One person said: "I've recently stopped going to workshops. They seemed to be geared to 'Freshman English' and to be old stuff" (p. 78). Is this burnout or the wisdom of experience? It can be difficult for the practitioner to assess this accurately.

The great challenge at this phase is to both settle into a consistent style of walking along the path while also pushing oneself to explore more and develop further. Together, these two forces combine to form the central task of deeper authenticity and individuation.

The practitioner, years after continual interaction with professors, mentors, and clinical supervisors, is no longer guided on the path by these professional gatekeepers. As a source of influence for the practitioner, these professional elders have receded from the illuminated part of the developmental path and are now in the background. The experienced professional phase requires the practitioner to continue to develop professionally with self as director. Life is different, and the experienced professional phase practitioner is now in the front of the professional parade. This does not mean, however, that one's own professional elders are absent. No, they have just been internalized and live on in that manner. Concerning the influence of John, a supervisor 20 years ago, one practitioner said, "I have running around in my mind words, phrases, quotes that I periodically pull back to ... and sometimes I say to myself, how would John handle this situation?" (p. 79). These "internalized mentors" were often recalled with great fondness and appreciation by our research participants.

This professional development process is analogous to a similar process in personal human development. Here is one description:

> [I was] talking with an elderly man who was explaining to me that his wife, whom he cared for deeply, wasn't really dead because the pleasure of their time together lived on inside him. While he spoke these words, ... I began to feel that all the people I'd ever known who had

> died or left me had not in fact gone away, but continued to live on inside me just as the man's wife lived on inside him. (Golden, 1997, p. 427)

The learning process at the experienced professional phase is highly self-directed. The pace, the direction, the focus, and the content are all self-directed. Continuing education requirements must be met, but they usually are structured in a very conventional method of "seat time" with a formal, one-way distribution of information. In contrast, highly impactful continuing education such as critical incidents and defining moments in the practitioner's life are broader in method and focus. Serious learning may also come through watching movies, an intense cross-cultural experience, having personal therapy, teaching a class, or making pottery. As described in the following quote, the key part for development versus stagnation is an ongoing, self-directed effort.

> With a new client I think about cases I've had. I think about how they have gone. Themes come in a case and this stimulates a memory in me. The memory is in the form of a collection of vignettes, stories and scripts. It isn't fully conscious but new cases do kick off the memory—the memory of how things went before provide a foundation to begin the current case. (p. 77)

A strong source of influence is the practitioner's personal maturation and life experience. This is a high-impact arena because the high-touch occupations are, by their nature, focused on human themes of emotional, intellectual, and physical development and health. In addition, the practitioner at the experienced professional phase has now lived more years and has more personal history data on which to draw. For example, becoming a parent—a powerful personal experience—can potentially affect any helper, teacher, or healer in how he or she does their work. Another example is the death of a close relative or friend and the resulting profound mourning. These are examples from the two ends of a central arena of human development: the attachment–loss process.

As we interviewed therapists and counselors with more experience, we increasingly heard stories of the interrelationship between adult personal and professional life. Although some talked about how the fatigue from overburdening work could negatively influence family life, or how professional knowledge and competence could be transferred into one's personal life, there were more tales of "traffic" in the other direction, that is, of how personal life was seen to influence professional functioning. One said: "You learn a lot from your kids just like you learn a lot from your clients" (p. 65).

Another talked of her divorce being the most difficult experience of her life. She found it forced her to see herself as a separate person and not a daughter or wife in relation to others. She said: "It really shocked me to my core. I had to tap into some dark places and look at things about me" (p. 65). The whole experience, she said, increased her connections with human pain, made her more intellectually curious, and ultimately helped her be a better therapist. We heard many similar stories of the long-term positive influence of adverse experiences in therapists and counselors adult personal life.

The immediate influence of adverse personal experiences is often negative. One senior therapist told us her story that moved us deeply. She told us that after losing her husband and her only daughter within a 2-year period, it took another 2 years "before she could breathe again." It was not until after a long period of intense grieving that she could use the traumatic experience constructively in her work.

As previously described, there were several stories of negative experiences in early childhood and family life exerting an adverse and not positive influence on professional functioning (Rønnestad & Skovholt, 2001). This was surprising as it runs counter to a common perception of "the wounded healer" (Henry, 1966), where healed early wounds are understood to contribute to the forma-tion of a more effective helper. Early wounds are not necessarily healed, and may find their expression in adult professional functioning. However, from our interviews, there were several stories indicating that wounds acquired late (i.e., in adult life) can, if they are reflected upon, understood, and assimilated (see Stiles, 1997), contribute to more effective helping. We may add that research within the International Study of the Development on Psychotherapists (ISDP) has shown that the relationship between early family experiences and later therapeutic functioning is positively moderated by therapists' personal therapy (Orlinsky et al., 2005).

Yes, it is true that the personal human development of a practitioner of human development—emotional, intellectual, or physical—is quite natu-rally a source of influence. Yet, paradoxically, some practitioners are not very self-aware or reflective about the impact of personal life on work. Georgia O'Keeffe seemed to be in this camp regarding her flower paintings. She denied that the lush flower paintings had a sexual component although they were painted during the most intensely romantic part of her life (Lisle, 1987). Others are quite aware of the power of personal life. One practitioner stated:

> Certainly my experience has been an important factor. … My experi-ence in the Peace Corps for a few years has taught me … a sense of

> relativity of this culture. Raising children I think is so important. I got
> a chance to go back through development with my own children, and
> to be able to see what it felt like to be them. (p. 79)

An expression of authenticity is more use of one's own professional experience as the epistemological base for one's work. The truth about how to do effective helping, teaching, and healing now comes predominantly from one's own experience-based generalizations and accumulated wisdom. Practitioners at this point voiced this.

> I think that the more you [work] ... you find out more ways of what
> works. So I think with experience, what you end up doing ... you do,
> with all your experience, what you know works, what has worked in the
> past. ... It leaves you with a model that you developed, that fits your
> personality, and also from your experience, you know that it works. You
> start out with a theory and you eventually modify it. (p. 75)

A significant finding in our qualitative study is reflected in this quote above. Practitioners seem to most deeply cognitively embed early experiences in practice. And these early experiences form a cognitive schema for doing practice in the high-touch fields. The power of early practice experiences is evident in a collection of defining moments in counselor and therapist development edited by Trotter-Mathison et al. (2010). Defining moments, like critical incidents, are powerful events that shape one's professional identity and style. Of 87 defining moments, most describe events in early practice such as a client experiences or an experience in clinical supervision.

Later in practice, it is not every client, student, or patient that dramatically affects the practitioner. It tends to be those who are on the extremes—those who do really well or do really poorly. Then the highly experienced practitioner at the experienced professional phase is typically deeply moved if one of their clients, students, or patients experiences a profound event, either positive or negative, when they are working together.

To get to an often deeply satisfying professional level, the practitioner must have moved far down the path. First, there is the absorption from professional elders, and theory and research in the field; then there is the agony of early practice when the novice is lost and confused; then comes the shedding and adding and, most of all, listening to the lessons from experience. With the lessons from practice and the active use of reflection, deeper professional personalization occurs, as described in the previous quotations.

Satisfaction is a common practitioner emotion at this phase. It seems to result from all the effort over the years that has now formed a practitioner who feels competent at many complex professional tasks and is paid, at a modest level or above, for the work. Yet some are not doing so well. From the international survey research, a conclusion is that a minority of therapists report rather substantial difficulties in their practice in combination with a sense of professional decline (Orlinsky & Rønnestad, 2005). Thirteen percent of therapists, including many who had practiced for decades, experienced "distressing practice." In line with what we found in our qualitative interview study, the majority at the experienced professional phase, however, seem well able to regulate their emotions and handle the professional challenges they encounter. The majority also feel they are growing professionally.

Now, practitioner joy relates in part to realistic expectations. Those who have entered the career field to "change the world" either have left the work out of frustration or have modified their expectations. Wanting to have a big impact may be a good way to begin a heroic occupation, that is, one that aims to reduce human suffering. Yet, in time, veteran practitioners see these strivings as dangerous, foolish versions of perfectionism and grandiosity. Thus, in a paradoxical way, the reduction of expectations makes satisfaction and sprinkles of joy more possible.

With experience, as goal setting has become more realistic, with increased awareness of strengths and limitations, and with a clearer definition of and differentiation of responsibility, it is more likely that the involvement level has been fine-tuned in a professional way. The practitioner is typically good at regulating involvement and identification with clients. A male therapist said: "I have a better sense of personal boundaries and blame myself less if things don't work out well" (p. 85). Another said: "When the session is over I can leave it there" (p. 93). This process of letting go of "overresponsibility" is likely a prerequisite for the regulation of emotions and attitude expressed when the practitioner is able to be totally absorbed in client work and then, when the session is over, is able within minutes to refocus attention and subsequently engage in work with another client. When this is successfully and ideally mastered, the practitioner can end many workdays more refreshed and stimulated than exhausted and depleted.

Paralleling realistic outcome replacing ideal outcome and improved regulation of professional boundaries, the experienced professional has learned how to separate the professional role from roles such as that of a friend, parent, or spouse. One female reflected back to her graduate school years when this was more of a problem. Laughing, she said that her daughter gave her useful feedback when she said: "Mother, will you quit being a damn social worker and just be my mother" (p. 69).

Phase 6: The Senior Professional Phase

Practitioners, at this phase, have practiced about 25 years, some more, some less. Many are approaching retirement. This group, the most experienced in our sample, averaged 64 years of age when we interviewed them the first time, and 74 when we interviewed them again. This second set of interviews especially gave us the opportunity to learn about experiences and reflections of practitioners in the very mature professional years. Some at this senior level welcome this change in status, whereas others are not so positive about it. One talked about supervising younger interns and said: "They get brighter all the time: I feel that I learn as much from the interns as I teach them. They have become my teacher" (p. 92). Conversely, another said: "Suddenly I was seen by others as a leader, but I didn't see it that way. I didn't feel I belonged" (p. 80).

From our research, we have concluded that the central career task at this phase is integrity defined as maintaining the fullness of one's individuality. We have framed this central task within the terms of the famous psychologist Erik Erikson (1968), who said that the psychological focus at this point is integrity versus despair. Integrity is often expressed by an alignment of values, much professional experience, high competence, and an integration of the professional and personal selves. A quiet joy seeps out into the work. The idea here at this phase, within the metaphor of the long, textured path, is for the senior practitioner to keep on trekking using the individual style that the senior practitioner has developed during decades of practice. Yet, as much as there can be a positive flow to the work when a person is at the senior professional phase, we also heard objections to the glamorization of being older. For example, one male therapist said: "I think the golden age is not best by any means. As far as I can tell, being old and wise is not better than being young and innocent and energetic" (Rønnestad & Skovholt, 2001, p. 183).

While practicing within the ethical standards of the profession, this phase represents a profound acceptance and full expression of the self. As one senior practitioner said, "I think I am more myself than I have ever been" (p. 87). This full expression by the practitioner requires a chiseling of the professional self over the years of the all the postgraduate phases; the novice professional phase, the experienced professional phase, and now the senior professional phase. With self as director, there has been shedding of unwanted exterior influences while other influences have been added.

Acceptance, a predominant senior practitioner emotion, comes from the fruit of one's labor. Related emotions are serenity, security, humility, and confidence. One senior practitioner described it this way: "The longer I've been at it the more I've become accepting of my limitations. That is just the way it is. Some things I do well, other things not so well" (p. 88). Secondary emotions are excitement about the work and regret, which is related to time gone and the missed opportunities.

Performance anxiety is greatly reduced from the early years. The practitioner does not have the dreaded feeling of not knowing what to do or the strong dependence on professional elders as guides. A major contribution to reduced anxiety is the internalization of expertise. After thousands of hours of experience, knowing what to do no longer comes from others such as textbook and guidebook authors, clinical supervisors, professors, and mentors. The big problem for the novice in using the ideas of others is that they are often generalizations that the novice must customize to the individual client. The senior practitioner does not have that problem because the knowledge base is mostly internal and more easily sculpted to the individual client than with the external expertise of the novice. For the senior, it is experience-based generalizations and accumulated wisdom that now form the autopilot that guides the work. A senior professional phase practitioner expressed this feeling when saying, "Almost never do I feel anxious about my work. I've done everything before and it has turned out all right" (p. 88).

The cascade of influences for the novice practitioner—theory and research; clients, students, or patients; professional elders; and peers and colleagues—is different now. These sources of influence are not absorbed during the senior phase with the same straw-gulping urgency of a thirsty novice who is drinking in the professional knowledge base. Drinking a cold milkshake too fast can lead to an intense feeling in a person's head; this is often the experience of the novice practitioner when being overwhelmed by so much data from so many places.

Now, at the senior phase, things are different. Why is this? Many of these influences have been internalized. They now reside internally and are forceful in role and working style in that way. The senior practitioner tends to get less excited about new ideas in the field. For year after year over decades, he or she has already been exposed to an avalanche of new ideas. For the senior phase practitioner, the similarity of new ideas and old ideas is seen more than the discontinuity. New, revolutionary professional ideas and practices are less often perceived as absolutely better than the old. This does not mean the veteran practitioner is stuck in the old, but rather that there is more adding to what is already there. As one practitioner, at this point, said:

> By the time a person reaches the end of one's work life, he/she has seen the wheel reinvented so many times. ... Old ideas emerge under new names and it can be frustrating ... to see people make a big fuss about something he/she has known for years. This contributes to cynicism for the person. (p. 95)

One source of influence has expanded, which is from the classes of the school of hard knocks. Perhaps of most significance is the depth and wisdom gained from losses. After all, one of the most profound realities of human life is that with every hello, there is a goodbye. For example, almost all mentors and models have gone away in one way or another and peers are often no longer a strong influence. There is also a loss of innocence about the work whether it be teaching, physical healing, counseling, or a related field. There has been a fading of illusions and increased sense of reality in terms of what can be accomplished professionally.

These losses can be instructive for a practitioner in a people-oriented profession. The practitioner must, however, do his or her own grief work and get to a point of resolution (Rønnestad & Skovholt, 2001). Then he or she can speak from this depth and wisdom, as described by the leading character in *Memoirs of a Geisha* who said, "I don't think any of us can speak frankly about pain until we are no longer enduring it" (Golden, 1997, p. 419). So this source of influence, using the depth and wisdom gained from enduring profound human loss, can be of great value to the senior practitioner in helping, teaching, and healing. Many *forces* converge to make the work satisfying for numerous senior practitioners. Performance anxiety is greatly diminished; there is often a strong feeling of competence in the work and control in the work setting. New energy is not needed for miles of hiking on the path, yet the work brings success with clients, students, and patients.

The seductions for practitioners at the senior professional phase are the intellectual apathy and boredom that can come from routine tasks completed over and over again, experiences that can reduce engagement in high-touch work. This is very dangerous because much of the power of the work comes from the human engagement with the other, the powerful I–Thou relationship while avoiding the I–It relationship to use the Martin Buber (Kramer, 2004) language. Researching psychotherapists,

(Orlinsky & Rønnestad (2005) and their colleagues found that most of their sample avoided this disengagement and continued to be committed to grow professionally.

Many forces converge to make the work satisfying for numerous senior practitioners. Performance anxiety is greatly diminished; there is often a strong feeling of competence in the work and control in the work setting. New energy is not needed for miles of hiking on the path, yet the work brings success with clients, students, and patients. One senior professional phase practitioner stated it this way:

> With diminished anxiety, I became less and less afraid of my clients and with that came an ease for me in using my own wide repertoire of skills and procedures. They became more available to me when I needed them. And during those moments it became remarkable to me that someone would have the willingness to share their private world with me and that my work with them would bring very positive results for them. This brought a sense of immense pleasure to me. (p. 96)

We see in this quotation the joy of practice described in Chapter 2 of this book. Now, at the senior professional phase, the most dangerous hiking elements—tree branches, steep incline, dangerous overlooks, and sharp-edged rocks—have been managed. The end is near, and the professional hiker can enjoy the final miles of the long, textured path.

5

The Elevated Stressors of the Novice Practitioner

The formation of a professional self can be and often is quite frightening.

—M. J. Adolson (1995, p. 35)

There is no gathering the rose, without being pricked by the thorns.

—Pilpay (1872, p. 67)

Praemonitus, praemunitas—forewarned, forearmed.

—Latin proverb

Articles connected to students' [and novices'] experiences serve an important function. If only for a moment, they provide validation, clarity, and hope in the midst of great anxiety, discomfort and uncertainty.

—M. Pica (1998, p. 362)

The Ambiguity of Human Interaction

Over and over, graduate student Pica (1998) expresses surprise at his lack of preparation for all the ambiguity of practice: "Struggling with ambiguity is one of those unspoken aspects of clinical training that students do not comprehend until they begin their graduate programs" (p. 361).

Yes, we are all surprised and unprepared while on our own Lewis and Clark exploration through the wilderness of professional preparation for the helping professions. Perhaps Emily Dickinson said it best: "To live is so startling, it leaves but little room" (as cited in Johnson & Ward, 1958, p. 380). The new practitioner, when first grappling with the confusing uncertainty of the work, deserves one chapter in the life journey of surprises.

Students are usually accepted into graduate training in the helping professions because they have excelled in school. They are hard working, conscientious, excel in learning class material, and develop mastery of assigned tasks. They are good at taking on an assignment and completing it at a high level. In fact, they are often nearly perfect in doing what is required. They feel a sense of control as students. This is expressed by getting high grades in classes. Then they decide to be trained in a high-touch human field such as counseling, teaching, therapy, nursing, the ministry, medicine, or other related fields in part because people are interesting. If only each of us knew when entering this work how interesting the most evolved of all species really is; if only each of us knew how hard it is to control ambiguity. For each of us, when taking our turn as a novice, this is when innocence hits reality.

Our work involves close contact with this highly evolved species. The good and bad news, mostly bad for the novice, is that human beings—*Homo sapiens*—are very complicated. After many centuries of effort, the world's playwrights, head doctors, and spiritual leaders are still trying to figure us out. The kind of problems we attempt to solve are full of complexity and ambiguity (e.g., What is human competence, and how do we get there? What is effective counseling? What is the genesis or cure for either depression or anxiety?). To understand this complexity and ambiguity, as practitioners we often use thinking patterns that are not logical, linear, or sequential. Expertise within these webs takes years to develop because complexity and ambiguity are difficult to master. The innocence of the novice hitting the fog of early practice helps produce an assortment of elevated stressors. Here is one description of these stressors.

Trekking With a Crude Map

I didn't teach long enough to know what I was doing.

—**J. Smiley (1991, p. 384)**

Experience is a good teacher, but she sends in terrific bills.

—**Antrim (quoted in Anonymous, 1982, p. 317)**

The requirements for the novice to access, integrate, synthesize and adapt information are exhausting.

—M. Mullenbach (personal communication, March 1999)

The novice enters practice as a new canoeist enters white water—with anxiety, some instruction, a crude map, and some previous life experience. All of a sudden, for example, there is the client in front of the counselor, telling a very personal, real story. The story often comes in an incomplete form. The experience is like the sudden rush of water, rocks, and rapids demanding instant understanding and reaction. The novice often has the urge to both call 911 and appear calm, collected, and professional—whatever that is. In a study of novices in the related practitioner field of medicine, the most stressful situation was the white water experience—having to make clinical decisions while very confused (Zeigler, Kanas, Strull, & Bennet, 1984).

The map is, most of all, a cognitive plan in one's head. It is based on a combination of databases used by the novice (Skovholt & Starkey, in press) including theories learned in class or procedures and techniques acquired in a practice lab. There is also the intense psychologizing and introspection of the new helping professional, such as medical or nursing students wondering about any relationships between diseases they study and their own bodies. There is modeling, too, of advanced practitioners, which is an age-old method, like how the apprentice bricklayer learns by watching the senior craftsman. One's personal life enters the cognitive map regarding how to react to human situations. With more age, one may also have had a parallel career or two that provides part of the map. Most of the map is not part of an internal cognitive schema or map but rather is external to the novice and comes in the form of theories and techniques from others. These are outside of the novice's professional experience. For the novice in the white water, this is not good enough. The status of novice equals an inadequate cognitive map.

Lack of professional experience makes everything more difficult. Inexperience creates a host of problems, and "I didn't know what I was doing" summarizes them. But what does not knowing really mean? It means many things. The novice teacher, for example, does not have a professional, internal cognitive map to navigate the task at hand, such as managing a classroom of bored students. Like much of the work in counseling, therapy, teaching, and health care, confronting this ambiguity requires multiple well-timed reactions in the right dose. It is a difficult dance that all beginners struggle to perform.

The theory and research map used by the inexperienced practitioner comes from others, be they writers of theories, supervisors, teachers, or mentors.

This is the classic gap between theory and practice that hits all novices in fields such as counseling, therapy, teaching, and health. All of this happens after the practitioner in training has worked hard while attending numerous classes, reading countless books and articles, writing many papers, and taking scores of tests. All of a sudden, what one has learned seems irrelevant in practice. Why?

This happens because the cognitive map was developed by someone else as a *broad* guide to cover a *variety* of situations, not the particular situation the novice has now encountered. Also, the roadmap gleaned from one's personal life is often not adequate for the specific challenge. It is like comparing virtual reality to actual reality or learning a foreign language and then going where they speak that language. All of a sudden, the book learning hits the practical world; language is used differently than in the text in terms of usage, style, and syntax. Another problem is that one must continually try to access the expert's cognitive map, the theory of another, and *spontaneously* use it. So the combination of the theory of experts as a broad guide, the fact that it is the theory of others or personal self-theory and not professional self-theory, and that it must be applied spontaneously in novel situations means that the novice will often have limited success. It is a cumbersome process. For example, the new therapist sits with a new client who is highly self-critical. The therapist decides that this data fits with a cognitive therapy approach and then tries to apply the theory to the problem; however, the unique elements of the client's presentation puzzle the novice who struggles to find a useful approach.

After realizing that the practice world of unique situations is different from the academic models that often seemed adequate while a student, the novice searches for an explanation for this distressing reality. This searching often coincides with a sense of frustration or disillusionment with one's training. In fact, there is often an intense disappointment with one's educational program, whether an undergraduate or graduate program. We suggest that, in the posttraining exploration in professional development, a phase of disillusionment follows a phase of confirmation and confidence regarding the adequacy and worth of one's training (Rønnestad & Skovholt, 2003). Most often, the novice, whether in training or soon after, while searching for an explanation for this often overwhelming sense of inadequacy, focuses on the inadequacy of the training program. There is almost universal criticism by individuals at this point, with either specific or general criticism directed to the courses, the professors, or the entire program. It is as if the novice is saying, "If I were better trained, I wouldn't feel so lost and so incompetent just when I need to perform well."

The novice often points a finger of blame also toward the self. When directed toward the self, the novice is saying, "It is me. I am no good at this and just an imposter in this field. Nothing I try seems to work." Pointing the finger at these two fault lines—the inadequacy of one's education and the inadequacy of the self—is captured in a description from life as a novice:

> Even after having graduated from an accredited master's program, I didn't learn nearly enough to actually be a school counselor. I sometimes wonder if I really paid enough attention in class or if I read my textbooks too casually. Maybe I just forgot the important concepts that I need to be a helper of children. Yet if I'm asked, I can glibly explain the core conditions necessary for change. I can give a mini-lecture on irrational beliefs and how they impair daily functioning. I can even describe outcome research studies that begin to pinpoint the actual reasons clients do change. Perhaps I studied the theories with the assumption I would be helping insightful clients who know what changes they want. Does the source of this problem lie in my personal shortcomings or in my training? (Bandhauer, 1997, p. 7)

With extensive experience, one shifts from external expertise to internal expertise, from the theories of others to one's own complex, experience-based rules, procedures, and guidelines for situations. Benner (1982), studying nurses, describes the expert nurse who examines a patient and knows that he is in danger, not because theory says so but because extensive experience says so. Since Benner described this concept over 25 years ago, much of the nursing literature has explored the role of intuition in nursing practice. Through hundreds of hours of experience, internalized theory has developed. The nurse uses these experience-based generalizations to quickly assess the needed approach.

The problem is that there is just too much to know, and one does not really know what will be needed at what point. An analogy is that of a traveler to a foreign country. One packs the suitcases before traveling, hoping to bring the right clothes and articles. Inevitably, necessary items are omitted. The traveler gets anxious and has to compensate in some way. The novice often feels the same. One novice therapist in a study of turning points in therapist development reflected: "I feel like I am on a roller coaster in terms of confidence. ... One day I think, I can do this well, and the next day I am scared to death that I will mess up somebody's life" (Howard, Inman, & Altman, 2006, p. 96). Orlinsky and Rønnestad (2005) also found elevated anxiety for the novice. How does one learn how to handle these very specific situations? Bandhauer (1997) responds to this question when describing his development as a counselor:

> I remember someone once telling me that good judgment comes from those experiences brought on by bad judgment. I'm seeking to become a part of the fraternity of wise people who consistently make confident, appropriate decisions. Since wisdom comes from experience, perhaps the confidence I seek must slowly develop over time. To find my way, I must promise to examine my feelings and reactions to my experiences. When I feel overwhelmed, I must attempt to figure out why. I must try to figure out who owns the problem I'm being asked to solve. I must delve into my experiences to identify what or whom I'm reminded of from the past. Maybe in 10 years wisdom will have arrived. (p. 9)

The professional journey for all means studying long and hard and also attending the "school of hard knocks." This school is necessary but difficult. Sanger (2010) gives an example:

> When my group supervisor at the community mental health center where I was completing my master's practicum presented Grace's (pseudonym) case for disposition, she prefaced it by saying that none of the staff were available to work with this client. What she didn't say outright, but was clear about in her description, was that none of the staff wanted to work with this client. Grace had a long history of bipolar disorder and substance abuse. Her drug of choice was heroin. She had seen the revolving door of inpatient drug treatment more than once and was holding tenuously onto a few weeks of sobriety. In this sense, she didn't necessarily stand out from many of the clients we served at the clinic. But, as I would learn over time, Grace also had a history of burning bridges, with family members and therapists alike. She was quick to lash out in anger and just as quick to apologize beseechingly. She seemed to feel like the world owed her something, and she was determined to exact whatever that was from those around her.
>
> Looking around the room at my peers, it was evident that no one was jumping to work with Grace. It sounded like a lot of work. With only a little reluctance, I allowed my desire to please my supervisor and my novice "I'm gonna save the world one client at a time" attitude to prevail. I agreed to work with Grace. I didn't know at the time that I was bound for failure. ... When we met for the first time, after a volley of back and forth phone calls and multiple initial appointment no-shows, I already knew that I was in over my head. Grace presented

her life as one ongoing crisis; she recounted failed relationships, urges to use heroin, and recurrent thoughts of suicide in a voice that pitched up into a startling crescendo while tears streamed down her face. She spoke so quickly that I was amazed she wasn't constantly tripping over her words. "Breathe," I told her gently. "Breathe!" I told myself, a little more urgently, as I tried to sort out in my head where to begin. I had next to no experience working with dually diagnosed clients and felt nervous about figuring out how to best support Grace's recent sobriety while also attending to her mood disorder and relationship instabilities. The fact that she had uttered the "s" word (suicide) so many times only elevated my pulse further into the aerobic activity zone.

After our first session ended and I had time to regroup and consult, I decided on what seemed like reasonable therapy goals: safety planning, relapse prevention, mood and affect management, bolstering interpersonal skills. As it turned out, it didn't really matter what treatment goals I had chosen, since I don't recall ever having had the chance to really discuss them with Grace. Each time we met there was a new crisis that needed attending to. Not knowing much better at the time, I faithfully followed Grace down the path of each crisis, helping her to put out fires but failing to help her prevent new ones. ...

Despite all of this, we eventually managed to forge what felt like a workable therapeutic relationship. She seemed to trust me. I admired her repeated efforts to engage in a life that had kicked her down so many times in the past. I imagine that, from Grace's perspective, my dogged and naïve persistence to be there for her in whatever way she needed was comforting and relationship enhancing. But it also contributed to growing resentment and emotional exhaustion on my part. It took me awhile to learn that when I feel like I'm doing more work than my client, it's time to co-examine the therapy process. At the time, I couldn't disentangle myself enough to see that my work with Grace had "over-involvement" written all over it.

Grace taught me as a beginner that progress in therapy can be slow, sporadic, and difficult to define. At times, it's imperceptible. It's like one of those flip books that, when paged through rapidly, shows a horse fluidly galloping across the landscape. But, sometimes, the pages catch on your thumb, and the horse stops and starts with a jerk. If you stop on each individual page, the change from one page to the next is almost impossible to discern. Doing therapy with Grace was like flipping through the pages one at a time. Even when I strained, I could barely see any forward movement, even though there was some evidence of change. Over time, she started opening up more in therapy to discuss the big picture—her relationship with her mother, her view of herself, her disappointments and regrets—even while her crises continued. These disclosures, together with our developing therapeutic bond, were progress, but I didn't realize it until much later because it wasn't what I was looking for initially.

When Grace relapsed during the final week of my practicum, my thumb slipped entirely off the edge of the pages of the book. She landed in the hospital, manic, and it seemed as if we hadn't made any forward movement at all. Our last meeting took place on the haphazardly arranged, threadbare couches on the inpatient unit. Grace thanked me for our work together and then asked if I had brought her new underwear like she had asked. I had not. She hugged me. That was it. I walked out feeling devastated. I felt like I had failed.

At times in my work with Grace it felt as if I were trying to balance on a narrow precipice between two deep chasms. On one side was a well of boundless and naïve optimism that, given enough time and effort, I could help anyone. On the other side was a pit of cynicism and hopelessness, into which I sometimes tumbled after losing my footing. When I was in the pit, I felt powerless to do anything. In the middle was that elusive middle ground called reality, in which both extremes had a hint of truth to them.

This sort of non-dualism was a new concept for me. Erich Fromm (1968) described a version of it in The Revolution of Hope when he said, "To hope means to be ready at every moment for that which is not yet born, and yet not become desperate if there is no birth in our lifetime" (p. 9). I had a lot of hopes for Grace—too many, in fact—and this left me vulnerable to feelings of desperation when those hopes weren't realized. (pp. 72–74)

Here is a painful example in which the novice can learn. Sanger is gradually building her experience base. It is a long, slow, erratic process (Rønnestad & Skovholt, 2003) that the novice often wants to speed up to reach the safety of competence. Is it the same wish we ask for in our personal lives? Wouldn't it be wonderful to know the lessons of the last decade without going through the 10 years? Tom is reminded of the Norwegian saying, "Too soon old, too late smart," which describes this very human dilemma. Another example is that of the youngest child in the family who wants desperately to be as old and mature as his or her siblings but can do nothing to speed up the process.

Experience and lots of it is necessary to make the shift to an internal base (Skovholt, Rønnestad, & Jennings, 1997). In Outliers: The Story of Success, Gladwell (2008) discusses the often-used maxim that 10,000 hours in a domain is necessary to excel. The experience must also be of a certain quality, as described by Benner and Wrubel (1982):

Experience is necessary for moving from one level of expertise to another, but experience is not the equivalent of longevity, seniority, or the simple passage of time. Experience means living through actual situations in such a way that it informs the practitioner's perception and understanding of all subsequent situations. (p. 28)

Until experience gives one the internal cognitive map, the novice experiences the elevated stress of inexperience. Being lost and confused in the fog of early practice is part of a painful rite of passage for all new practitioners who attempt to counsel, teach, or heal. The ambiguity of so many practitioner interactions makes the life of the novice, like the teen years in one's personal life, a folder for memories in later years. Some accept their own rookie mistakes. Others, like the now-experienced college teacher from Tennessee, suffer from guilt and regret:

I vividly remember thinking of the song title, "If it wasn't for my bad luck, I'd have no luck at all," when I was told that I'd be teaching 47 under-graduates. ... The hundreds of unsuspecting college freshmen who endured my initial teaching ... should receive a coupon redeemable for three hours of instruction. (Eison, 1985, p. 3)

Acute Need for Positive Mentoring

Mentors and apprentices are partners in an ancient human dance. ... It is the dance of the spiraling generations, in which the old empower the young with their experience and the young empower the old with new life, reweaving the fabric of the human community as they touch and turn.

—**P. J. Palmer (1998, p. 25)**

Thrown into the tumultuous sea of professional practice, the novice eagerly seeks safety from the unpredictable, powerful, and frightening forces that seem to quickly envelop the self. Seeking safety while on the high rolling seas, the novice hopes desperately for a mentor who will quell the danger and let the novice practice steering the ship. Practice here translates to conducting a 50-minute counseling session, teaching a class of lively children, or doing an important health procedure—and then doing it again and again. Ward and House (1998) describe the rough seas for the novice as "increased levels of emotional and cognitive dissonance" (p. 23), which can be translated as the novice not knowing what he or she is doing— the inexperience factor. Help is sought from a wise elder—a supervisor, teacher/professor, or even a more experienced peer who knows the ropes and has developed expertise.

At this point, the novice badly needs and wants this supportive relationship with a mentor, just as in life, a person at times really needs a parent. Yet, we do not choose our parents, and we do not have the power to have them be what we want when we want it. The saying "the teacher will appear when the student is ready" is a truism that, unfortunately, is only sometimes true. The novice wants and needs the mentor to be a certain way—supportive, positive, helpful in specific ways of managing the voyage, and available (Rønnestad & Skovholt, 1993). The absence of a mentor leaves the novice with orphan distress, searching for his or her way on the high seas without experience. Equally distressing is the novice's disillusionment with a mentor who has failed to provide what is desperately needed. Examples include the absent mentor, the critical mentor, and the confusing and convoluted (while giving instructions) mentor. The terms *orphan stress, critical mentor,* and *novice neglect* summarize the fear.

The most effective mentors seem to operate by a structure similar to what we have called the uncertainty/certainty principle of practitioner development (Rønnestad & Skovholt, 1997). Here, the mentor, perhaps as teacher or supervisor, introduces the novice to the process of searching through the uncertainty. Searching through uncertainty via reflection has been described as the best method of novice professional growth (Neufeldt, 1999). The novice is taught to proceed on the voyage within a framework of there being more than one right way to counsel, teach, or heal the other. Yet, within uncertainty, the mentor also introduces certainty, as in specific techniques, methods, and procedures that can be very helpful to the confused novice. This mentor blend of giving answers and providing questions is sometimes hard to find. This increases the difficulty that the novice has in finding the best growth-producing mentoring at the time of great need.

A key to development is the "holding environment" created by the mentor. A strong holding environment comforts the novice against negative forces within and outside the self and acts to promote originality and creativity. Torrence (1996), a leading scholar of creativity, said, "The mentor protects the mentee from the reactions of their peers long enough for the mentee to try out some of their ideas and modify them. The mentor can keep the structure open enough so that originality can occur" (p. ii).

The importance of the mentor, at this point of high vulnerability, can be assessed by asking veteran practitioners of counseling and therapy, teaching, and health services to describe the quality of the mentoring that they received during the critical period of their lives as novices. Through the emotional intensity, either positive or negative, and the acute memory recall of events decades earlier, one can ascertain the importance of mentoring for the novice. Specific situations are described, and strong emotions of affection, appreciation, and adoration, or anger, criticism, and disappointment are expressed. Here are three retrospective stories. First, Brinson (1997) writes:

> When I catapulted out of the womb of graduate school … it seemed as if I spent much of my time babbling, drooling, crawling and falling on my rear end.
>
> Still wet behind the ears and suffering the after-effects of that traumatic birth experience, I longed for the support and nurturing of a trusted confidant to help me adjust to this new and exciting profession. This guidance became increasingly necessary for me the more I realized that my graduate experience had not prepared me for the "political" dimensions of the profession. …
>
> Obviously, anyone who is just starting out in a profession would value the support of individuals who lend their knowledge and expertise toward helping him or her achieve success. While this was certainly true in my situation, I did, however, approach this relationship with a degree of skepticism. Although there was nothing about the behavior or attitude of the individual that gave me reason for pause, the fact that he was a member of a different ethnic group presented a dilemma for me. Since the historical relationship between our ethnic groups has been strained, I was inclined to ask myself, "Why is this person interested in seeing me succeed?" Yet, through spending time and getting to know him as a person, I eventually rid myself of the stereotypes that otherwise would have made it impossible to foster a productive mentoring relationship.
>
> Having a mentor made a world of difference in my growth. … Not only did I find someone who could provide me with the wisdom, knowledge and experience of many years in the profession, but I found someone who was willing to serve as an advocate on my behalf when I faced certain crossroads in my career.
>
> I also found someone to confide in about my fears and concerns of being a novice in the profession, without feeling as if I would be judged as incompetent. … I am grateful for several other ways in which my mentor helped me, especially during times of professional and personal crises when I felt discouraged and dispirited. It made all the difference to have someone in my corner. …
>
> Years later, I now share my experiences with you in hopes of reaching other beginning professionals who are trying to find their way and don't know where to turn. (pp. 165–166)

In this next retrospective account, Osachuk (2010) describes the emotional intensity of a positive mentoring experience years earlier, in the context of being a beginning student therapist and the impact of David, his professor and clinical supervisor:

> It came time to begin my second practicum, and I again requested and hoped to have David as my supervisor. My request was granted. David remembered me from his psychotherapy course. Early in my practicum, during videotape review of my therapy with clients, he was pleased to see the improvement of my skills since the course. Being a new therapist, I was still learning and feeling clumsy and awkward, and I hung on every word of his feedback in supervision, as I was in awe of the depth of his skills and continually wanting to improve. Developmentally I also really needed external affirmation and confirmation of my potential to become a skilled therapist and was hoping at some point to receive this from David in supervision. It was as if David saw the potential in me, believed in me, that I would be all right.
>
> The affirmation and confirmation I was hoping to receive came during a subsequent clinical supervision session. It seems like such a small thing, but it was so important to me at the time. David had shared with me that he had spoken about my growth in a telephone conversation with one of his adult daughters. In essence he shared that initially he was uncertain about how I would do based on his memory of me from the time I was in his psychotherapy course, and he was pleased, actually pleasantly surprised, about the development of my skills since that time. He further shared with me what he anticipated he might experience with me in supervision. He was initially dreading my being his supervisee. He shared his memory of my forced intensity and anxiety while in his psychotherapy course and that it was difficult to be in my presence. He said he was not looking forward to having to work through this with me in supervision. While he did not elaborate, I had the sense that he anticipated that supervising me would personally be very taxing.
>
> The reason he was now pleased was that these qualities were largely absent and that my interactions were no longer forced. He said I had made great strides in being present, hearing my clients, and making empathetic reflections. I was thrilled to hear that. Of course I was still very much a beginner, and that's why I was being supervised. This conversation was a defining moment for me. I was finally able to relax and accept that I was going to be a therapist, that I had made the right choice. This experience would be the first of many further affirming experiences of my chosen profession, my craft. (pp. 65–66)

Conversely, Weis (2010) describes a negative experience vividly recalled years later. The example again is within the context of clinical supervision, but it could be from any of many new skill areas confronted by practitioners in the caring professions.

> I had just explained to my peers and supervisor how I had started my most recent therapy session. My seasoned supervisor chided, "This is the stupidest thing I have ever heard."
>
> What had I done in therapy that seemed so stupid? I had sat side by side with a client, who had long struggled with bulimia, and had reviewed a list of treatment approaches. She and I compared and contrasted the underlying theories and technical elements of her therapy options. That therapy session helped set a tone for an intentional, transparent, and open-minded collaboration. Reflecting on my supervisor's disdain, I concluded that my supervisor expected me to be the authority on matters such as selecting a treatment option. (p. 52)

The novice seeks a person senior in experience, credentials, position, or expertise. Someone with all of these would work fine. This acute need for positive mentoring is an elevated stressor for the novice practitioner because it often does not happen in the measured-out degree and intensity desired by the novice exactly when needed. The difficulty is often related to the narrow match needed by the novice and the lack of structural or financial considerations built into this novice need. The orphaned novice or the novice with an indifferent, incompetent, or hostile mentor suffers an elevated level of stress. Other novices are more fortunate because they have terrific mentor relationships at this point in their development

Glamorized Expectations

> A vast deal may be done by those who dare to act.
>
> **—Jane Austen (As cited in Maggio, 1997, p. 176)**

One of the classic distinctions in career decision making is the separation between being interested in "people" and in "things," with things related to jobs like engineering and people related to jobs like counseling. Being drawn to working with people often involves the daydream of making a difference in the lives of others. Tom remembers reading as a child about the work of doctors in developing countries—Albert Schweitzer in Africa and Tom Dooley in Southeast Asia—and also hearing stories of his Uncle Erling, a doctor in rural India. All of these stories, in his mind, were about heroic efforts to dramatically reduce the suffering of impoverished people. They were inspiring. He wanted someday to work hard and make the world better.

The models we use for inspiration to enter a career field seem to excel at miracles. They may be a teacher who cared so much for us and taught us so much, a nurse who seemed so exceptional, an addictions counselor who helped us to stop the addiction, a physical therapist who brought the legs of a loved one back to full use, or a professor who was so good at the work. Idealized, highly competent models can really motivate us. They also help us to see that idealistic may be realistic. They feed the idea of glamorized expectations as realistic.

It is natural, when drawn to helping people, to want to enter a career where one's efforts produce wondrous results. It propels the individual to study the content of the counseling, therapy, teaching, or health field in an endurance contest of tests, papers, and reports, and to read hundreds of pages of textbooks and listen to many lectures. In the caring professions, novices are highly motivated to find a way to help others.

Without full awareness, the novice often is more hopeful about the impact of one's efforts to counsel, teach, or heal than is warranted. This overoptimism coexists with fear about one's skill level. They connect in the goal of magnificent change. If this occurs, the work is impactful, and the novice is a successful practitioner. The novice may reason: If I am able enough, skilled enough, warm enough, intelligent enough, powerful enough, knowledgeable enough, caring enough, present enough, then the other will improve. If the other does not improve, then I am not these things, and my entrance into this career field is precarious.

The unclear expectations for the work occur in part because the change process is occurring with the most complex of all species and the beginner hinges practitioner competence to client improvement. Success is mostly measured by direct change of the client, student, or patient in the equation: improvement of the other equals practitioner competence. The novice is often not fully aware of this self-focus strand in the unrealistic expectations: "If the client really gets better, expresses appreciation, or likes me, I'm really good at helping."

The following first-person account illustrates the tie between practitioner self-evaluation and client reaction within the vulnerable world of the novice:

> Pam was my first client as a professional counselor. I looked forward to meeting her with such unbridled anticipation that I didn't even notice that the air conditioner was broken and the temperature had climbed into the 90s. I fantasized about sitting quietly and listening to Pam

with great understanding and much compassion. I just couldn't wait to hear her story.

Pam was already in my office when I arrived. As I stepped through the door she frowned at me, shaking her head. "Excuse me," she said, "nothing against you, but I'm not talking to anyone but Florence." Florence was her previous counselor who had left our clinic for another job.

I was stunned by Pam's rejection of me. Although I attempted to squelch my feelings, it did not work. I was lost. ... We sat quietly as I looked at her, waiting for her to make sense of her feelings. I, too, had to come to terms with my own feelings. I was ill-prepared to deal with the assault of my emotions. Despite the pain, I almost wanted to thank Pam for creating this experience for me. If I was going to grow in this field, to find my own way, I had to learn to recognize my interfering feelings and deal with them.

The silence felt more oppressive than the weather. I began to feel anxious, almost faint. ... My relationship with Pam began to grow. She was speaking to me, even though she was singing the praises of another counselor, and I no longer felt devaluated or rejected.

I continued to see Pam for a while, though somewhat sporadically. Many of our sessions focused on Pam's mother. She told me how her mother gave her to foster care when she was very little because her new stepfather was so abusive. I could see the anguish in Pam's face as she talked about her foster home. Often I wanted to take her in my arms to comfort her. "No one should have had to go through your kind of torment," I said.

"You know," she said, "I like you better than Florence."

"Why is that?" I asked.

"Because you seem to understand me better than she did."

I wanted to hug her. (S. Pincus, 1997, pp. 59–60)

The crash occurs and the stress level goes up for the novice when the expectations, often unarticulated, are battered and broken. This occurs when the client, student, or patient does not show much improvement. At this point, the human change process, directed by the novice, often seems bland and unspectacular. The result seems to be no client, student, or patient growth equals practitioner incompetence.

In time, the novice becomes more experienced, in part through a "series of humiliations" while doing the work, and develops much clearer, more realistic and precise, and less glamorous expectations, which tend to lower stress. No longer is one able to cure the other quickly and easily. Rather, human change is seen as a complex, often slow process in which the practitioner plays only a part. This helps to reduce practitioner stress. But it takes time to get to a place where "realistic" replaces "idealistic."

Only later will the novice really comprehend how so many factors, such as readiness by the other, play such a role in client, student, or patient success. Lange (1988) describes her emerging understanding of readiness:

> [Growth] in my professional development has increased my sensitivity in several areas. First is my appreciation of client readiness to change. No matter how brilliant my insights and strategies, the ability to change rests with clients, who will hear what they need to hear and know what they need to know. What may seem insignificant to me may be the critical incident for a particular client. I am a facilitator and an encourager, but the client decides how and when to create a new identity. (p. 109)

In addition to being attracted to a field in which one dreams of magnificent work, with a connection by the novice between client success and practitioner competence, there are other factors that tend to help inflate and glamorize expectations. One factor is the many factors of successful people work. What is success? For example, is a doctor successful if the patient lives? Then how about those doctors who work with high-risk patients with deadly diseases? Right away, with just a few sentences about one occupation, we can see that measuring success within each of the caring professions can be difficult. When it is hard to measure something, expectations can get glamorized without the novice realizing it.

Another factor is the confusion in the literature regarding professional experience and practitioner success. For example, Ericsson (2007) argues that experience does not ensure expertise. Yet, there is no clear connection between more professional experience and more expertise. In fact, high expectations fueled by enthusiasm can produce impressive results by novices. Every year, thousands of counselors, therapists, teachers, clergy, and health professionals in training, individuals still in school, help many people. In an analogous study of helping, college professors did as well as trained counselors (Strupp & Hadley, 1978). These results fuel an element of enhanced hope, a trace of glamour attached to the work, and a sense that if one is really good at the work, big, magical client, student, or patient improvement will occur. For the veteran practitioner, the paradoxical reality is that significant change is possible when one is not so grandiose and unrealistic.

Our own personal experience leads us to evaluate some counselors, teachers, and doctors as better than others. And others say the same thing: "Good teachers matter more than anything; they are astonishingly important. It turns out that having a great teacher is far more important than being in a small class, or going to a good school with a mediocre teacher" (Kristof, 2009, p. 11).

For the novice, the problem with glamorized expectations is, of course, that they add to the mountain of elevated stressors. It is just not possible to have a major impact each of the thousands of times that one meets with the other during a career. When the novice thinks, "I need to have a big impact in every session, every class, every health consultation," then there is pressure and stress. Wanting to do really good work is one thing. Using the client, student, or patient as the only criteria for success is different.

Intense Evaluation and Illuminated Scrutiny by Professional Gatekeepers

> You supervisors dance
> on the rim of
> this machine
> certain of your
> power, your values
> clear and calm in your purpose
> I
> trainee
> am tumbled and
> tossed
> caught in the spin
> jerked about by the hierarchy's
> agitation
> my vision
> clouded by products
> that whiten and soften the dark edge
> of reality
> And you and I know
> that
> the spinning always stops when
> you open the lid to
> check.

> **—L. Moreland (1993, p. 13)**

For trainees, acceptable levels of practitioner skill seem like a "moving target with an elusive criteria."

> **—W. N. Robiner, M. Fuhrman, and S. Ristvedt (1993, p. 5)**

Practitioners involved with every field within counseling, therapy, education, the ministry, and health care—occupations where there are interactions with people when they are at vulnerable levels—are ethically obligated to regulate their own practitioners. Even after passing through numerous gates, a small percentage of incompetent and unethical practitioners damage clients, students, or patients. The profession responds to these events by only admitting qualified candidates. However, because intensive professional work with human beings is, at the core, complex and ambiguous in nature, the process of selection is quite complicated, confusing, and convoluted.

Enter the novice who must pass through numerous gates. Evaluation is a large factor in the elevated stressors of the novice practitioner. For example, teaching researchers Morton, Vesco, Williams, and Awender (1997) state, "It is clear that evaluation anxiety is paramount for student teachers" (p. 85). As evidence, lack of control is often cited as a major component in occupational stress and burnout (Maslach & Leiter, 2008). Evaluation by others is certainly a "lack of control" factor.

Part of the level of evaluation stress in the helping fields is the lack of task clarity. For example, there is no clear formula for the exact performance of expert practitioners in counseling and psychotherapy. Theoretical differences wash out, and common factors seem to emerge in outcome research (Bergin & Garfield, 1994; Wampold, Mondin, Moody, & Stich, 1997). Yet, there is more murkiness than clarity in defining expertise (Skovholt et al., 1997). A classic quote from Raimy (1950) illustrates this: "Psychotherapy is an undefined technique applied to unspecified problems with unpredictable outcome. For this we recommend rigorous training" (p. 150). Similarly, we have heard thoughtful teachers lament the lack of clarity in defining good teaching.

How then can the field evaluate novices when the road to expertise is unknown? Evaluation happens anyway, and must, because the public and the profession demand it. So the novice, with as much choice of his or her supervisor as his or her parent, and with ambiguous standards to meet, lives under illuminated scrutiny. The difficulty is magnified by the following reality: "Supervisors are not only admired teachers but feared judges who have real power" (Doehrman, 1976, p. 11). Now, that's stress!

Evaluation is often provided by a senior member of the field who may be a seasoned professional but may not be adequately trained in supervision. For example, a senior member of the profession may find it difficult to be the supervisor rather than the practitioner. She or he may be more comfortable with practitioner tasks such as the academic advisor helping a student move toward increased clarity about a major, the teacher aiming for increased student fluency in a second language, or the physician helping a patient move toward reduced blood-pressure readings. In contrast to these process goals, supervision involves other skills such as evaluation.

Borders and Brown (2005) offer remedies to move beyond the natural role, such as counseling, to the supervision role. One conflict is between the helping self and the gatekeeper self. Supervision has more of a pass–fail mindset, one that practitioners often do not use in their regular work. The supervisor is often ambivalent about the grading demands in the supervisor's role (Bernard & Goodyear, 2008). In addition, evaluation by a supervisor may be an added responsibility given, without choice, to the senior practitioner. All of these factors contribute to possible difficulties in the evaluation process and may heighten the evaluation stress experienced by the novice.

Porous Emotional Boundaries

The pain stayed with me residually when returning home.

—A novice counselor

When I first taught, I thought constantly about my classes.

—An experienced high school teacher

What passes in the world for tragedies … I hear about them, I see them. I can't be knocked against the wall by each one. I have to construct a coping technique that allows me to survive.

—C. Kleinmaier (As cited in Garfield, 1995, p. 6)

The word *boundaries* has entered the lexicon of the contemporary helping professions and is used mostly to describe the not-to-be-crossed line between proper and improper human contact between the practitioner and the client or student or patient. In the shifting sands of culture and the historic times, it is a valuable term in defining the difference between "appropriate" and "inappropriate."

Although the novice is often helped in training and supervision to develop clarity for appropriate physical boundaries (i.e., to touch or not to touch), less attention is paid to emotional boundaries. The term *emotional boundaries* refers to the internal feelings and accompanying thinking of the helper.

The ability to strategically detach and reattach is a difficult, advanced skill. Novice teachers often think constantly about their classes while not at work; novice nurses wonder if they did the right thing when working with a patient; novice counselors and therapists can be very preoccupied with the emotional pain of the client. This "off-duty" penetration of the emotional boundaries is one more elevated stress factors for the beginner.

This emotional and cognitive preoccupation can be educational. It serves, in fact, to provide the material for reflection, a central method of professional development (Neufeldt et al., 1996; Rønnestad & Skovholt, 2003; Schön, 1987). The task here, however, is to learn how to establish and regulate useful emotional boundaries. The novice, flooded with impressions, images, feelings, ideas, worries, and hopes, often has no established dike to withhold all of this.

In studies of practitioner stress, less experienced practitioners report more stress (Ackerley, Burnell, Holder, & Kurdek, 1988; Farber & Heifetz, 1981; Rodolfa, Kraft, & Reilly, 1988; Rønnestad & Skovholt, 2003). One caution with some of these results is a possible cohort effect. It may be that the most stressed practitioners leave the field so that, at the senior level, the stress profile is lowered, in part, for this reason. Ackerley and colleagues (1988), for example, reported more stress for less experienced practitioners in their psychologist sample. Results were measured by the emotional exhaustion and depersonalization subscales of the Maslach Burnout Inventory (Maslach & Jackson, 1981). Overinvolvement was a variable that accounted for some of the variance on both emotional exhaustion and depersonalization. Overinvolvement produces porous emotional boundaries that result in elevated stress.

Novice practitioners working with acute human problems, such as trauma, experience difficulty with porous emotional boundaries. Pearlman and MacIan (1995) found that sexual assault counselors with less than two years of trauma experience had higher overall general distress and more disrupted cognitive schemas on issues such as interpersonal trust and safety. Perhaps most intense of all is the flood of emotions that hits the novice trauma therapist who has a personal history of trauma, such as the female therapist at a sexual assault center who was a victim of such assault herself (Pearlman & MacIan, 1995). This is an extreme example of porous emotional boundaries, one of the factors contributing to the elevated stress of the novice practitioner.

Developing a variety of boundaries takes time. This skill involves learning to constantly monitor the self, like the car owner monitors the fluid levels

of the car—oil, power steering, transmission, brakes. One looks for a positive interplay between empathic attachment to the other and one's own very
important self-care needs. It takes time and experience, something the novice
does not have.

Ethical and Legal Confusion

The novice practitioner is focused on being competent in a professional role.
Depending on the career field, this activity focuses on an emotional, intellectual, spiritual, or physical domain. The goal is to be helpful to the other,
to be therapeutic in the broadest sense of that term, that is, to help the client,
student, parishioner, or patient. At the same time as the therapeutic route
is being pursued by the novice, there is another route that is important but
often out of the novice practitioner's awareness. It is the ethical and legal
route. Of course, the goal is to be ethical and legal when following the therapeutic route. With the ethical–legal route we are talking about a very explicit
focus on ethical rules and legal procedures.

The therapeutic and the ethical and legal routes are, in fact, quite different
and must be thought about differently. The ethical and legal route has a strong
dose of self-protection, yet this is not the illuminated part of the stage for
the novice. The caring professions—counseling, therapy, teaching, and health
careers—all socialize beginners, while in training, to care for the other. The
caring is expressed by focusing on increasing the competence of the client, student, or patient. The ethical and legal route asks the novice to be self-protective.
Along this route, the concern must also be for others, such as potential victims
of a client's anger. This too is not part of the therapeutic route.

The two-route dilemma is stressful because it makes difficult work even
more difficult. Here is an example. In Tom's supervision of a novice counselor,
he was listening to her self-report about a session. The supervisee was describing the interaction between herself and a teenage client, telling elements of
the client's story, which consisted of struggles with self, friends, and family.
She told how she worked so hard to fully understand the client and of trying
so hard to help by using the right method at the right time in the right dose.
She was motivated to help, especially when sensing the client's anguish.

Midstream in a sentence, she told how the client wanted to kill her stepfather. Without pause, she told how she processed this angry feeling with
the client. The goal was to help the client feel less anger and to find a more
constructive approach to the problem. The counselor was fully engaged

in driving down the therapeutic route. When Tom heard "wants to kill her stepfather," he jumped the median and immediately started driving on another road, the ethical and legal route. The client's anguish and the counselor's intense efforts were no longer dancing in Tom's head; Tarasoff was (*Tarasoff v. Regents of the University of California,* 1974).* Suddenly, the task was "duty to warn."

The route mindsets are different. The legal–ethical focus is on rules and procedures, not therapy. The practitioner changes from being an engaged therapeutic presence to a person of action. No longer is the client, student, patient everything; now the welfare of others, including the practitioner, takes center stage. Knowing and using the two routes adds complexity to the work of the novice. This is an unwelcome addition because things are already complex. Analogies are being bicultural or being a switch-hitter in baseball. One of the two is hard enough; doing both well and switching back and forth quickly and with grace are more difficult. Yet, competent practice demands both. This adds another stress factor for the novice.

In addition, legal and ethical road signs are often fuzzy because there is so much confusion within the practitioner professions about many important ethical and legal issues. For example, the communication technologies are quickly being used before we have clear ethical principles about their use (e.g., texting, e-mail, voice mail). One wants to act in an ethical and legal manner but often does not know what that means in certain situations. That is when the practitioner goes to conferences on ethics or consults with colleagues; however, often this input increases one's anxiety rather than decreases it.

Together, the need to integrate the two routes into one profession and the fuzzy and changing nature of many ethical and legal issues makes for novice confusion. As if the novice is not already confused enough.

Acute Performance Anxiety and Fear

> As a young teacher, I yearned for the day when I would know my craft so well, be so competent, so experienced, and so powerful, that I would walk into any classroom without feeling afraid.
>
> **—P. J. Palmer (1998, p. 57)**

Tarasoff is a case in which the client threatened to kill someone and the practitioner did not warn that person. After the person was murdered, the court said that the practitioner was wrong not to warn.

Fear stops all forward movement.

—Axiom

Anxiety about the unknown and fear about the known are like a one-two punch. The novice can feel so inadequate when stepping into the professional role. The result can be acute anxiety cascading upon the person. These moments can be unforgettable. As if it were yesterday, although it was decades ago, Tom remembers entering a college classroom with the students, and as the students sat down, he went forward, turned around, and saw 46 eyes in close proximity staring at him. Thus, with no professional training, his college teaching career began.

Usually, the acute anxiety occurs when the novice is trekking on a mountain path that is too narrow and the situation is novel (i.e., doing a specific professional task for the first time). Perhaps there is a strong evaluation climate. The situation often becomes arduous because the anxiety of self-consciousness and focusing on oneself makes it more difficult to attend to the complex work tasks. A moderate level of anxiety can improve performance, but high levels of anxiety reduce performance by directing the individual's attention to both reducing the external, visible effects (e.g., trembling and wet hands, unsteady voice) and lowering the internal anxiety level so that one can think effectively.

Opposed to pervasive performance anxiety, hovering like a menacing rain cloud, are fears about specific things. The list can be endless, although there are some specific favorites, for example, being speechless with no idea what to say to one's client, losing control of a classroom of active students, or using a health procedure that causes unpredicted pain. Together, anxiety and fear can seriously heighten the stress level for the novice.

The Fragile and Incomplete Practitioner Self

At the beginning of any new human role—walking a bridge along the mountain path from the known and secure competence of the past to the unknown and insecurity of the future—we usually feel unsure. Examples abound: the first time with a new date, landing at the airport of a city on a foreign continent, the first day at a new job, or the early days of parenting. The novice is trying on new clothes and new ways of being in the world to create a *practitioner self*. We are using this term, related to one used by Ellwein, Grace, and Comfort (1990), to describe the vigorous interior construction work of the novice in creating a practitioner identity. Trying on clothes takes many forms over many days, weeks, and months. With the awkwardness of a new adolescent play-acting in the adult world, the novice is trying to act like an advanced practitioner. All of us as novices, like all of us as adolescents, go through it. A classic method used here is what we call "imitation of experts" (Skovholt & Rønnestad, 1995).

Like an adolescent, the fragile and incomplete practitioner self shifts through a series of moods: elation, fear, relief, frustration, delight, despair, pride, and shame. This raw mixture of emotions is a predictable outcome when the novice practitioner self steps into the practitioner world. Although this world produces valuable food for the slow development of practitioner expertise, it is also the context for the "series of humiliations" experienced by the rookie in the practice world. The novice self is fragile and, therefore, highly reactive to negative feedback. There is not much muscle, and the immunology system is stressed. Age and experience in allied jobs tend to mute the various novice effects. For example, the 40-year-old counseling student who has worked as a hospital aide tends to have a less intense reaction to this elevated stressor than does the inexperienced 23-year-old counseling student.

The following accounts from new student teachers, taken from student diaries by Galluzzo and Kacer (1991), show the emotional reactivity we are discussing here:

> The students began asking me questions over my head. Questions that I found no material on. I handled it wrongly. … I was embarrassed and getting worked up. The students laughed at me and that really hurt. (p. 15)
>
> It was the dullest, driest lesson that was ever recited … the students were bored out of their minds … I felt like crying. The lesson was over in about a half hour. I thought that it would last two days. Worst of all the students were saying I was boring. That was the worst insult of all. They didn't like me. (p. 16)
>
> I felt very disgusted and almost indignant toward the kids because they could not grasp the things I was trying to explain. (p. 21)

These preoccupations, both with self by the novice and the sense that the practitioner self is on stage, are analogous of the adolescent sense of being exposed and illuminated while on stage. There is then, of necessity, a self-focus for the novice because of a need to protect and nourish the fragileness. The difficulty is that this occurs at the same time that one is preparing for a career where the needs of the other—the client, student, or patient—are the central focus of the work. A supportive senior practitioner as mentor can mute the self-protective, defensive focus and help keep the novice open to learning and growing while focusing on the needs of the other. This clash between a self-focus and another-focus while creating a practitioner self produces another elevated stressor for the novice.

Summary

Two phrases in high-touch work, "talking about the elephant in the corner" and "finding a voice," describe the value of articulating the unarticulated. This powerful curative result within groups has been called the "universality of experience effect" (Yalom, 1985). The aim of this chapter is to produce this universality of experience effect by describing a landscape peopled by each of us when a novice. More specifically, the intention is to provide a positive trinity of validity, clarity, and hope for current novices, their teachers, and their supervisors. The goal is a recognition reflex to terrain descriptions, like of the valleys and hills, the rocks and soil, and the watering holes. Hopefully, the map of terrain descriptors will help in navigating the journey that all of us, as novices, must take.

Self-Reflection Exercises

As you read this material, you may be a beginning practitioner in counseling, therapy, teaching, or health care. Perhaps you are a student in a training program at the graduate or undergraduate level, or you may now be more experienced; but, like everyone, you were once a rookie.

1. Regardless of your experience level, how do you react to the description of the elevated stressors experienced by the novice? Do they ring true or not so true for you?

   _____

   _____

   _____

   _____

   _____

   _____

_____

_____

2. Perhaps of more importance, what could be long-term implications of
   your novice experience on your capacity to be a resilient practitioner?

_____

_____

_____

_____

_____

_____

_____

_____

6

Hazards of Practice

I am interviewing my new outpatient, Lisa, a fidgety young woman with darting eyes that avoid contact with my own. She perches on the edge of her seat, seemingly ready to bolt, her left leg jiggling fervently as she describes to me the circumstances leading up to her most recent psychiatric hospitalization.

"I sat on my bed in the dark with a loaded gun to my head, completely numb, just getting the courage to pull the trigger. And then, out of nowhere, my cat jumped on my lap! I dropped the gun and just started crying. And then I called my boyfriend. I couldn't even talk, but he just knew it was me. He came right over and drove me to the hospital."

When I suggest that her cat could have just as easily startled her into pulling the trigger, Lisa's leg motions cease and, for the first time, she meets my gaze head-on.

"That would have been OK, too."

My adrenaline gives a mild surge, but my eyes meet hers unflinchingly. We have our work cut out for us, I think. "So what do you imagine would have to change in your life for you to feel differently about that?" I say out loud, alert to every nuance, verbal and nonverbal. She meets this question with a long, thoughtful pause.

As Lisa ponders her response, I marvel at the social and historical forces that have propelled the two of us together: she the help-seeker, semiattached to her life as if it were a half-severed limb, and I, the salaried healer, paid to be committed to her life, at least within the allotted time, until the next patient takes her place and I focus on that person's anguish. A clock silently logs the minutes on my desk, its glowing red numbers managing the procession of patients in and out of my office in this busy HMO health center, where a multitude of lives in turmoil intersect with my own. My time is a semiprecious commodity to the insurance company that pays for it. My patient's time? She clearly puts no value to it at all.

—G. Garfunkel (1995, pp. 148–149)

The Difficult Nature of the Work With Clients, Students, and Patients

High-touch work means making a highly skilled professional attachment, involvement, and separation over and over again with one person after another. To really matter to the other, these must be I–Thou relationships, not I–It relationships to use Martin Buber's (1970) term. This means these relationships are full of respect for the other, understanding of the other, energy for the other. As Skovholt and D'Rozario (2000) found in studying students' best teachers, these are caring relationships.

What makes this work so difficult? It often has to do with the reality of these interpersonal encounters. Establishing and maintaining these relationships takes hard work. This means they take enormous energy from the practitioner. This is demonstrated in the 2009 Academy Award nominated French movie *Class*. The movie is about a teacher and the students in one classroom in France, a classroom packed with 13- and 14-year-old students, many from immigrant families. The movie vividly portrays the students' yearnings, confusion, and needs. The movie is based on the teaching experience of Francois Begaudeau, who plays himself. He works really hard to engage the students and their multiple needs, ways, and wants.

The difficulty of the work relates to our hope to make a difference, with our inability to tolerate so much ambiguity, with the distress we vicariously feel from those we attempt to assist. Here are specific hazards that make work difficult with clients, students, and patients.

Hazard 1: They Have an Unsolvable Problem That Must Be Solved

A person may be stuck, as in "can't live with him, can't live without him." Neither approach nor avoidance works. These are the ingredients of hopelessness and demoralization that Frank and Frank (1991) suggest are central when individuals seek help. When we are stuck in life and unable to find a solution, the result is often a feeling of low self-efficacy and high despair. In this situation, it is usually difficult for helpers to have a strong, quick impact. If it was easy, the person would have solved it already. And, if the person could have avoided it, it would have been avoided. We all do both of these: solve or avoid problems. When neither is possible, we ask for professional help.

And the professional helper can help. Our experience as therapists and counselors is that answers can come but they usually take time and a certain amount of agony for the client along the way. Often these situations mean a choice between two options, both involving doors opening and doors closing in one's life, like a bittersweet option. The person's life can move forward but the process of getting there is not like life on a cruise ship.

Examples here include the counselor's work with a parent of a very rebellious teenager. The parent will not abandon the teenager but is unable to reach the team to stop the angry, rebellious activity. A counselor can be effective here but not in the sense of finding an immediate, positive solution. A teacher of children with learning disabilities struggles to help them get up to grade level, a difficult task given the children's abilities. The physical therapist works to increase the mobility of a patient with osteoporosis who needs to get past a hip fracture. The possibility for improvement is limited. All of these practitioners are operating within the common arena of an unsolvable problem that must be solved.

Hazard 2: They Are Not "Honors Students"

Honors students can get better, improve, and learn anywhere. Harvard professors may do little for the students who come in brimming with resources and skills. If the professors do not harm them, the students will be successful, and the professors can later bask in their success. In the past, Schoefield's (1974) term *YAVIS* (the acronym for young, attractive, verbal, intelligent, and socially skilled) was a way to describe desirable psychotherapy clients, that is, those who could improve rapidly. As a practitioner, if one does not get in the way, one can feel successful. There is a natural tendency for practitioners in the helping fields to want clients, students, or patients who have resources (e.g., motivation, ability, limited problems) that will fuel the success of the practitioner's helping effort. This way, there is improvement, and the practitioner, feeling competent, can bask in the positive change. For example, one of the ironies of the modern university is that there is more status attached to teaching honors courses or advanced doctoral seminars, in which the students have so many skills, than in teaching basic, developmental courses in which the students are less able and the instructor's work can be more difficult.

Hazard 3: They Have Motivational Conflicts

Motivational conflicts in the helping professions have historically been discussed under the concept of "secondary gains." In some government programs, when one gets better, he or she may lose benefits. For example, a patient at

Veterans Affairs gets money while disabled but loses funding when able to work again. Imagine being a helper there and trying to make an impact.

In the past, Tom had a counseling client who received monthly disability payments because of a mental health diagnosis. Losing the diagnosis meant losing the payments and becoming vulnerable to the legal demands for funds from a former business partner. As a younger practitioner, Tom would not have understood the profound impact this situation had on his ability to help the client change. He would have charged ahead, being naive about how much the client had to lose to change.

Tom remembers the grieving of an economically poor African American woman who was finally getting her BA degree. Grieving when a great success was at hand? It was confusing because success meant triumph over long odds in an oppressive environment. Success, however, also meant losing her former peer group, a rich source of friendship. Suddenly, she was not so accepted by the rest of the group.

In one research study, Hagstrom, Skovholt, and Rivers (1997) interviewed advanced undergraduates who were unable to decide on a college major. They were often frozen in the decision-making process, not by simple issues such as lack of information or decision-making skills, but by a highly complex set of conflicts that was difficult to resolve.

Motivational conflicts also refer to being sent by others, such as parents or the court system (e.g., for remedial classes, domestic violence counseling, nutritional information). The motivation is outside oneself: outplacement—*sent by others;* driving while intoxicated and chemical abuse classes—*sent by others;* academic probation and mandated work with an academic advisor—*sent by others;* dragged to marriage counseling by one's spouse—*sent by others.* One of the classic red flags predicting limited success in human services is external, not internal, motivation for seeking help. And this, as we discuss in Hazard 4, is why motivational interviewing has become popular (Miller 1983).

Hazard 4: The Readiness Dance; There Is Often a Readiness Gap Between Them and Us

The newly trained firefighter rushes out of the station, with the siren blasting and lights flashing looking for the fire wherever it is, ready and eager. The firefighter may be more ready than the fire. Overready is the mindset of the newly minted novice.

Helping, wellness, advising, physical therapy, teaching, therapy—these are all developmental processes. This means that the goal of the counselor, therapist, teacher, or health professional is to facilitate improvement in the person's functioning. The goal is movement on a continuum. How would you have done as a new, first-year college student at age 15? Would 25 be a much better age to begin college because of academic readiness? Ten years can make a big difference. Some 30-year-old new parents would have been overwhelmed at 16, and some 16-year-old parents would be great at 30.

Readiness can also be a matter of first experiencing the "school of hard knocks." As examples: A friend's daughter was more receptive to his ideas after she had been out on her own and *knew more* than when she was home and *knew less*. Helping others as a career counselor may work better—the client may be more receptive—when the client's own career search process has first failed.

In the caring professions, we often worry about our undercommitment, disinterest, and burnout, but overcommitment is also an issue. Readiness is also, therefore, about matching our commitment and readiness to work at change with the client's, student's, or patient's commitment and readiness. This "readiness dance," which in its best form closely matches the helper's efforts to that of the helpee, is especially difficult for the novice who is trying to judge "dose" and "timing" without much practice.

A classic problem in counseling, therapy, teaching, and healing is the offering of programs to people who are not ready. Prochaska and Norcross (2001) summarize research findings on a transtheoretical model of behavior change proposed in earlier writings (Prochaska, DiClemente, & Norcross, 1992). The six-stage model of change has the following stages: precontemplation (no plans to change), contemplation (awareness of the problem but no decision to change), preparation (awareness of the problem and some attempts to be different), action (actively engaged in change processes), maintenance (work to maintain changes made), and termination (ended the change process, no longer have to work to avoid relapse). Prochaska and Norcross's review of research studies on stages of change indicated that pairing knowledge about the client's stage of change with type of therapy and intervention can positively impact the treatment. Prochaska et al. (1992) described a health maintenance organization (HMO) in which 70% of the eligible smokers said that they wanted help with smoking cessation. A program was developed and offered, but only 4% of the smokers signed up. Like firefighters ready to fight a fire, high-touch practitioners often misread smoke for fire.

Charting the gap between client, student, or patient readiness and counselor, therapist, teacher, or healer readiness could look like Table 6.1, which we call the readiness gap.

TABLE 6.1
The Readiness Gap

Stages of Change	Client, Student, and Patient	Counselor, Therapist, Teacher, or Healer
Precontemplation		
Contemplation	⟍	
Preparation		The Readiness Gap
Action		⟍
Maintenance		
Termination		

Sources: "In Search of How People Change: Applications to Addictive Behavior," by J. O. Prochaska, C. C. DiClemente, and J. C. Norcross, 1992, *American Psychologist, 47*(9), pp. 1102–1114; "How Do People Change, and How Can We Change to Help More People?" by J. O. Prochaska, in *The Heart and Soul of Change: What Works in Therapy,* by M. A. Hubble, B. A. Duncan, and S. M. Miller (Eds.), 1999, pp. 227–255, Washington, DC: American Psychological Association; "Stages of Change," by J. O. Prochaska and J. C. Norcross, 2001, *Psychotherapy, 38*(4), pp. 443–448.

Like those health professionals who prepared materials for smoking cessation but were disappointed when few people showed up for help, the helping impulse is thwarted for us, too. Training programs select counselors, therapists, teachers, and healers who yearn to help and share a deep desire to care for others. We can easily be more ready than the client, student, or patient. This is a natural occupational hazard.

Finding the right blend of professional attachment with the helpee is difficult. One can be uninvolved in the attachment, and this, of course, is not good. One can be overinvolved, and this too is not optimal. The underinvolvement impulse among counselors, therapists, teachers, and health professionals is more destructive to clients than excesses of the helping impulse. Examples here include charismatic encounter group leaders (Lieberman, Yalom, & Miles, 1973) and sexually exploitive therapists (Moleski & Kiselica, 2005).

Tom remembers being an academic advisor for high-risk college freshmen. At the time, he was teaching career development theory and practice to graduate students and a career planning class to freshmen. He was an experienced academic advisor and career counselor, and had written articles on career counseling in professional journals. In fact, he was very overprepared for the academic advisor task compared with other faculty member advisors whose only preparation in these specialty such as English, physics, and mathematics.

Tom was really ready to help these high-risk college freshmen advisees, but the task "went South," as former Minnesota Twins' baseball manager Tom Kelly said when things go wrong.

Tom would give these advisees his time, talent, and energy in looking at the big picture of their educational and career futures. After all, we value the work of helpers who assist disadvantaged individuals to find their way through the American reward maze. But in time, Tom changed his behavior when his efforts were consistently met by advisees with only, "Would you sign the paper for the classes?" They did not come for a deluxe version of educational and vocational guidance. They came because bureaucratic regulations forced them to get his signature. The readiness gap! Tom came to see that his own excessive helping impulse produced the gap.

Earlier in Tom's career at the University of Florida, he joined other new faculty members from many parts of the country to start a Department of Behavioral Studies. They were to offer innovative, cross-disciplinary courses to honors undergraduates. The new faculty had spent years in graduate school preparing for the task. At fall orientation, the new assistant professors sat at tables to meet the new students—some of the best and brightest graduates of Florida's high schools. With great animation, the faculty members described the content of new cross-disciplinary courses such as Power and Violence. The new students responded by asking, "What courses do you have before lunch?" Again, the readiness gap.

Readiness is also a matter of cognitive complexity—when the client, student, or patient can understand in a broader, deeper, less egocentric way. Readiness is critical, and sometimes we have little power to affect it. After all, "you can lead the horse to water, but you can't make it drink," and "the teacher will appear when the student is ready." Until then, you, the helper, are *invisible, unrecognizable,* and *inaudible:* "I can't hear a word you are saying, only the echo of my mind."

We cannot all be lucky enough to have the attention and commitment of the airplane passenger listening to instructions on the use of oxygen in the midst of intense turbulence and cabin depressurization. This is exactly why the work can be difficult. Counselors, therapists, teachers, and health professionals want to believe that they make a difference in human life, but sometimes they do not. At times, we feel ineffective; that is why the work is difficult. The key is that, in time, the counselor, therapist, teacher, or healer, like the veteran athlete, learns when to expend energy and when to preserve energy, when effort matters and when it does not.

The practitioner also learns the lesson that too much practitioner eagerness can bring on, in a subtle way, client, student, or patient resistance. And this creating of resistance is something that skilled practitioners learn not to do because it can really derail success. When the client, student, or patient is fighting the professional person, failure is advantaged. Success is hard when the stars are aligned and much more difficult when they are not.

When people are not ready, what can you do? Complicating this whole perspective of readiness, is the work on motivational interviewing, developed by client-centered therapist William R. Miller. Miller (1983) asserted that the way in which a practitioner speaks to a client could grow or minimize their motivation to make changes. Within the context of this counseling style, a therapist employs empathic listening to gain an understanding of the client's problem and to minimize resistance. After rapport is developed the therapist works to explore how a person's goals and values might interact with their desire to change (Miller & Rollnick, 2002).

Hazard 5: Sometimes They Project Negative Feelings Onto Us

> At the best of times, people project on their pastor their fears of judgment, their anger at God, and many other feelings. In moments of severe stress, the tendency to misperceive the pastor is even stronger. (Mitchell & Anderson, 1983, p. 118)

Veteran teachers call this *excess baggage,* a term meaning that the student brings extra, painful feelings from interactions with teachers in the past. Here is a reverse example: In school, did teachers treat you as if you were your older brother or sister? Did they give you his or her name, his or her characteristics? Communication can get worse with new lovers as they get more serious because projections from their past can enter.

These are examples of the dynamic of projection and transference. Our clients, students, and patients can bring intense transference reactions to us with their past pain, hurt, anger, and fear related to helpers and authority figures. We get their unrecognized stubbornness, resentment, anger, and lack of cooperation.

When the helping relationship is very important for the one being helped, that person does not feel much powering in the relationship and the rules of engagement are fuzzy, then transference reactions—projection of feelings—can be activated. This is not the fault of anyone; this is just very human. An unexamined example is the relationship between doctoral advisors and doctoral students in PhD programs. This is a very important part of higher education and the needs in modern society where intellectual property is central for economic prosperity. Yet, professors as advisors, across so many fields (e.g., history, physics, literature, mathematics, sociology), get no training in the art of the doctoral relationship. A negative transference reaction from a student to the professor or the professor to the student can harm the work just as a very positive transference can energize their work together. Many professors are naturally skilled at this relationship work; some are not. None get any direct training in it.

High school teachers often experience angry, disappointed, distressed parents and personalize the parental reaction. It can be difficult to understand the transference element and not be personally hurt. The mark of an expert at attachment and connection may be the ability to do this well even when the client, student, or patient brings hurtful past interpersonal experiences that create very understandable fear (Harmon et al., 2005).

Tom was unaware of his innocence when first teaching disadvantaged, historically unsuccessful students. He thought that they would welcome him as "Tom," the good guy ready to help them. He did not know that he represented all the teachers from the past who had flunked, humiliated, and shamed them in school, the mandatory prison they attended for years. To them, he was often just another oppressive adult.

Hazard 6: Sometimes We Cannot Help Because We Are Not Good Enough

Their needs and our competence as practitioners may not fit. The demographic variables may be wrong. As Tom gets older, he gets more right for some clients, more wrong for others. He is the wrong gender for some women clients who are seeking a female therapist and the right gender for some women clients who seek a male therapist. We may not have the right experiential background or the specific competence needed. For Michelle, sometimes her perceived age, gender, and style fit and sometimes they don't. Maslow's famous quote, "If the only tool you have is a hammer, [you tend] to treat everything as if it were a nail" (as cited in Goldfried, 1980, p. 994), symbolizes the effect of limited competence. In time, practitioners experience a "series of humiliations" when their wrong demographics, life experience, or competence level does not meet the needs of the client, student, or patient. This is difficult for the practitioner because of a basic occupational need to feel that one is making a positive difference in human life.

Hazard 7: They Have Needs Greater Than the Social Service, Educational, or Health System Can Meet

All practitioners have examples of how success would be enhanced with more resources. Tom remembers a high school boy years ago pleading for tutoring help at a school where there were no tutors. In physical and mental health, practitioners are constantly trying to squeeze out resources for patients and clients within the arid world of managed care, HMOs, and limited funds. Difficult clients can be those who fail because the system does not provide enough resources for success.

In contrast, easy clients, students, and patients are those who quickly succeed at the task. They have the motivation, skills, and resources to get better, and we, as practitioners, can bask in their success and are nourished by successfully helping another human being. Even now, let us imagine a world of clients, students, and patients who are easy to assist. Let us dream; bring them on. But of course, the world is not that way.

Managing Major Professional Stressors

Hazard 8: Our Inability to Say No—The Treadmill Effect

> She [the special education teacher] ... felt her enthusiasm ebb in the face of overwhelming problems presented by dozens of students.
>
> **—M. J. Smetanka (1992, p. 1B)**

> Counselors in the sample overwhelmingly thought that job demands and expectations were too great. For many, this meant serving far too many students in one or more schools. For others, it meant required involvement in a variety of duties that, they thought, had little or nothing to do with the professional school counselor's role and may, in fact, seriously detract from it. For still others, the sheer amount of work, even if professionally appropriate, was overwhelming and eventually exhaustive.
>
> **—R. Kendrick, J. Chandler, and W. Hatcher (1994, p. 369)**

The practitioner tries to keep up with constant demands by running faster and faster. Soon the pace is dizzying, and the surroundings blur. The practitioner gets numb and can't think or process experience or feedback. On the treadmill, the pace just seems to increase.

This major professional stressor concerns our desire to help, our difficulty in saying no, and the resulting overload. In "The Heroic Syndrome," Stone (1988)* described his "good intentions and heroic strivings" as ultimately an

---

*Reprinted from *Journal of Counseling and Development, 67,* page 108. Copyright © ACA. Reprinted with permission. No further reproduction authorized without written permission of the American Counseling Association.

Achilles' heel that needed to be changed for long-term professional vitality. His prescription: "The word 'no' belongs in the helping vocabulary." Here is his description:

> My incident deals with a situation I encountered during the first weeks in my new position as director of a university counseling service. My incident provides a useful example of the heroic syndrome, a common neurotic tendency prevalent among counselors.
>
> I received a call from a resident assistant (RA) at about 1:00 a.m. on a Saturday night after a football game. He stated that "a young man was in his room, dripping blood from cuts in his arms and acting very strange." He pleaded, "Couldn't you come down?" I was still somewhere in the twilight zone as I heard this description, yet responded, "Sure." I went to get my John Wayne uniform and wake up the trusty steed. As I was motoring to the rescue, I became aware of how little I knew of the situation. Such things as name of RA, specific residence hall, security issues, medical needs, and so on drew a blank. I finally woke up and lowered my Superman cape, and went to the security office to gather some information.
>
> Although the situation was resolved in a positive manner, the potential for harm was also present, regardless of my heroic although misguided intentions. The incident crystallized for me the importance of becoming informed before blindly attempting to save the world. My good intentions and heroic strivings are no substitute for informed and competent practice. There are limits!
>
> My personal incident also sensitized me to the potential for the heroic phenomenon within the counseling profession and higher education. I have witnessed the heroic drive among counseling center leaders and practitioners as I listen to them describe their responses to their unique campus situations—24-hour on-call duty, treating long-term clients with limited resources, serving as the hero on campus by becoming all things to various campus constituencies. For example, a counseling center may find it difficult to say "no" to a part of the campus community needing long-term treatment, although the center does not have the necessary resources—24-hour on-call service, sufficient staff, and easy access to inpatient facilities. Given the limited resources, long wait lists, and a brief therapy orientation to student developmental tasks, many counseling centers may not be an appropriate treatment facility; that is, use of such a center may be countertherapeutic for long-term clients. Of course, the long-term treatment question for counseling centers is more complex (e.g., a question of availability of appropriate referral sources), but to the degree that heroic intentions of counseling centers are not matched by adequate resources and competent practice, they become prone to the heroic syndrome.
>
> On our campuses, the heroic trend also seems to be present. It seems that the social progress expectations of the "Great Society" of the 1960s

have been transferred to the "Great University" of the 1980s. We hear about the expanded mission of the university as it is frequently called on to address the social ills of economic hardships, racism, and war. For instance, the role of the university in fostering economic development has become a hot topic.

The heroic symptoms seem to be everywhere—personally, professionally, and institutionally. I wonder if Karen Horney might be right; namely, the feeling of being outside the camp, feeling inferior, and isolated instigates the need to "search for glory." Horney's insight seems on the mark for a counseling profession perpetually seeking an identity, counseling centers trying to justify their existence, higher education struggling with criticism and new mandates, and even the larger society that has lost some of its moral and economic leadership in the world; there seems to be a focus on heroic actions. Each of these entities seems preoccupied at the moment with its perceived inferior status and related heroic aspirations.

I am not troubled by heroism, but I have relearned that the heroic drive needs to be tempered by realizing the necessity of limits. The word no belongs in the helping vocabulary.

My discussion has to end here because I just received an emergency call. I've got to roll. The struggle continues. (p. 108)

Stone's dilemma is the dilemma of all of us in human services, education, and health care. It concerns the tension between two elements: good intentions/heroic strivings and the "no" of turning one's back on human need. These two pulls on the heart and mind of the practitioner are extremely difficult to reconcile, especially for the novice counselor, therapist, teacher, or health professional who is often confused about how hard to try in the helping role. Practicum, clerkship, practice teaching, and internship sites often receive excessive services from students in training whose strong intentions and heroic striving naturally lead to overextension. This process occurs year after year, like the swallows returning to San Juan Capistrano, with each new wave of students in training. It happened with us and our classmates; did it with you and your classmates? Learning boundaries and saying no seem to come later.

There was the public health nurse in Chicago (L. Smith, personal communication, 1982) who had a 550-person caseload, and the school counselor in New York (R. Severson, personal communication, 1987) who tried to be fully available for 400 students and to please all the relevant groups—the school administrators, his counseling colleagues, the students, and the parents. Often, the ability to set limits and say no only occurs with exhaustion and the realization that the individual cannot physically or emotionally maintain the pace over the long haul of 30 to 40 years or even a shorter haul of months or weeks. For Hill (1988), it came only after she had become totally overwhelmed as *the* college counselor for hundreds of students. She wrote:

> Nine years ago I accepted the position of college counselor at a private liberal arts college of 800 students. I entered with 4 years of community counseling experience but was new to the needs and expectations of a college system. Seventy percent of the position was designated for directing and providing personal counseling and programs, and 30% was designated for teaching one psychology course each semester and serving on departmental committees. In addition to the college counselor, there was one career counselor.
>
> My first year was chaos. Ongoing, and at times simultaneous, situations occurred that required immediate attention be given to students, staff, and faculty. For example, class lecture preparations and test design and evaluations were left to the late evenings because of the high demand of 35 to 40 hours of psychotherapy per week. (There were times when 3 or 4 students were simultaneously needing immediate counseling.) I was called out for approximately two middle-of-the-night emergency calls per weekend because a poorly trained housing staff was unable to identify, respond to, and refer students with problems in their early stages of development.
>
> Needless to say, I felt exhausted, angry, hurt, and numb. I wanted the college system to reward me for my hard work and to rescue me from the overload. Neither occurred. I went to an extreme, working lunches, evenings, and weekends before I was willing to say to myself; [sic] "I have done all I can do and it's not enough." At the end of the first year I faced a cathartic moment, which became a turning point in my life. I realized that I had the choice of quitting or rescuing myself and the position. I chose the latter. (p. 105)

How does one learn to say no yet avoid indifference and apathy? For many, as Hill said, the proper point of tension only occurs after becoming overextended and exhausted. This process inspired the first work on burnout by Freudenberger (1974) and the subsequent work by many others. In the years after Freudenberger first used the term *burnout*, many books have addressed this topic including Baker (2003), Larson (1993), Norcross and Guy (2007), Rothschild (2006), and Wicks (2008). We now have many other warning words like *emotional depletion, secondary trauma, compassion fatigue,* and *vicarious traumatization.*

Hazard 9: Living in an Ocean of Stress Emotions

> The capacity for compassion and empathy seems to be at the core of our ability to be wounded by the work.
>
> **—B. H. Stamm (1995, p. ix)**

> The incidence of stress-related problems for teachers has been dramatic in studies that have investigated this phenomenon. Surveys have demonstrated that up to 90% of all teachers may suffer from job-related stress and 50% of all teachers indicate that stress is a serious problem for them.
>
> **—M. T. Schelske and J. L. Romano (1994, p. 21)**

Practitioners often work with those who are experiencing some kind of difficulty. It may be a physical, academic, or emotional problem. Often a component of the need is emotional distress. Confusion, frustration, discouragement, anxiety, and anger are common. Unable to solve their own problems, helpees often experience a strong dose of the distress we can call *demoralized hopelessness.* Frank and Frank (1991) state that it is the job of the professional helper to work with demoralization. Hopelessness is a strong predictive sign of suicidal ideation. We use the term *demoralized hopelessness* to communicate the level of human distress that we are often asked to address.

One reason it is important to describe the intensity of client, student, and patient distress is that "forewarned is forearmed" helps us prepare to practice self-care over the long haul. When we understand that the task is stressful, we can prepare for it. The job of the counselor, therapist, teacher, and health professional often involves attaching and being wired emotionally to the other. That is the essence of empathy, being wired as if one's battery is connected to the other's battery to jumpstart it. The wiring often involves the negative emotions, meaning the stress emotions, resulting in the practitioner living in an "ocean of stress emotions." In time, practitioners learn how to be both wired to these distress emotions and separate from them. Learning this skill is intricate and takes time.

Being wired to these stress emotions can be professionally toxic and a threat to the helper's emotional physical health. Support for this idea comes from research on the physical health of individuals experiencing chronic stress, such as caregivers of Alzheimer's patients (Vitaliano, Zhang, & Scanlan, 2003).

While working as a practitioner, which of these client, student, or patient stress emotions is most toxic for you:

Fear
Confusion
Rage
Helplessness
Cynicism
Sorrow
Isolation
Loneliness
Estrangement
Anomie
Lack of motivation
Hopelessness
Anger
Desperation
Bitterness

To understand the poisonous qualities of these negative emotions on you as a practitioner, imagine each of these as a toxic agent attempting to enter your body. Which are most powerful and compelling? What is difficult or debilitating about these emotions for you?

Because working in this ocean of stress emotions is taxing, practitioners sometimes wish to remove themselves. For example, Tom once thought of opening a Joy Clinic, a place for only happy emotions. People would come when everything was going well. Unfortunately, he realized that business might be kind of slow. Later, he thought of a flower shop, an ice cream store, a candy shop, or a plaque and awards store. At these kinds of places, everybody seems happy. There are many positive emotions.

The intensity and scope of human distress that comes to practitioners should not be underemphasized. Human beings are an extremely intelligent, able, and creative species and have the capacity to solve many complex problems. All of us are very skilled at problem solving. As we stated earlier in this chapter, people often seek out helpers *only* when they can't solve their problems by themselves, that is, when they have *unsolvable* problems that must be *solved*. It is the combination of unsolvable and must be solved that leads people to experience demoralized hopelessness.

In the work relationship—in the intensity and vividness of the counseling session, the educational classroom, or the hospital room—what is too much involvement and what is too little involvement in the negative emotions of the other person? We know that lack of empathic involvement in the emotions of the other is often considered poor practice in the helping professions. An uninvolved, callous, disengaged, "burned out" helper is what every counselor, therapist, teacher, and health professional hopes to avoid becoming. Yet, the other extreme, overinvolvement in these stress emotions, may be more precarious and dangerous for the helping process and our own well-being. How then does one regulate emotional involvement in the flow of human data, the life stories, of our clients, students, and patients? What is too much involvement; what is too little in this ocean of negative emotions? Cousins (1979) made a compelling case for the impact of positive emotions and laughter on the health of the individual. In contrast, does the intensity of negative emotions change the helper's emotional immunological system? Are there analogies here to the effect of passive smoke on the nonsmoker or asbestos fibers on the person in the room?

Hazard 10: Ambiguous Professional Loss—Ending Before the Ending

In her book, *Loss, Trauma, and Resilience: Therapeutic Work With Ambiguous Loss*, Boss (2006) says that ambiguous loss produces extreme stress. For example, in families of missing in action (MIA) soldiers or patients with Alzheimer's (Boss, 1999; Boss, Caron, Horbal, & Mortimer, 1990), the family member is missing but not gone, present but not present. This can be extremely stressful. We have modified the term *ambiguous loss* to *ambiguous professional loss* to describe the constant lack of concrete results and closure for those in the counseling, therapy, teaching, and health professions. We have heard many stories of this ambiguous professional loss, the times when there is an ending before the ending. These are actual accounts told to us from people in the caring professions.

- A counselor at a residential treatment center worked very hard with a teenage female runaway, and he and his wife became very committed to this young, troubled teen. They got attached. Then one day, the teenager suddenly left the center, and they never heard from her again.
- A counselor in training told her supervisor that she wanted to have a different supervisor, but the counselor would not say why. The supervisor had to deal with this rejection—this attachment and then separation—without knowing why.
- A teacher spent the year with an at-risk fourth-grade boy, trying amid a room full of 31 children to give him enough attention to improve his poor academic performance. She was very invested in his progress. Just as he started to finally make major strides in April of the school year, after

months of effort by the teacher, he was suddenly removed from his home and put in a foster home in another town. She never saw him again.

- A nurse was working intensely with a seriously ill patient. Upon returning after two days off, the nurse discovered that the patient was discharged because of insurance problems.
- A few years ago, a counselor saw one of her clients at a social event. The client seemed uncomfortable and later did not come back for counseling. Why? Did the social situation make a difference? The counselor never knew.

An elementary teacher told this story of ambiguous professional loss:

Recently I was reminded of a third-grader in my room a few years back. She came to me as a new student the day before Christmas vacation, with no school supplies, late, wearing dirty clothes, and smelling strongly of urine. In a day I learned she had been sexually abused as a preschooler, had severe psychological problems that had never been treated, soiled herself constantly, and had lacking social and motor skills. I attempted to involve school personnel and the parents immediately and continually, with little success. I spent much time working one-on-one with [her], documented daily her behaviors, etc. She was difficult to work with and I was exhausted at the end of each day. After one month, she was put into the psychiatric ward in our local hospital. I was concerned for her but hoped she would receive the care she needed.

She was there for one month, and when she returned to school, she was changed; she appeared to be happy, healthy, and clean. She did better in academic and social areas. I was excited and happy for her! She was with me for one week. One day her parents called on the way to [the West Coast] to say she wouldn't be returning to school.

I remember feeling very uncomfortable, sad, and angry. I had "lost" Cristina when we were just making progress. While she had been a challenging student to work with, her sudden disappearance truly bothered me. I had no opportunity to say good-bye or to wish her well. I felt like I wasn't "finished with her"; we still had more things to do. ... I still occasionally think about her and wonder how she is doing. I believe I am also realistic in knowing that there will be similar incidents regarding lack of closure during my teaching career. (Smith, personal communication, 1996)

Reflecting on ambiguous professional loss, S. Hage (personal communication, February 1994), a counselor in campus ministry, said:

Perhaps here lies one of the most difficult personal challenges of being a counselor. We most likely will never know the fruits of our work.

We are very often the people who sow the seeds or water the soil of the harvest we will never see.

A few years ago, Tom saw a television documentary about an old, illiterate man who, earlier in his life, had a job making bricks one by one in a little machine. Now, decades later, he was walking around his city with great pride, showing his grandson all the bricks that he had made. They were in buildings all over town and obvious for all to see. Tom felt pity for himself, and others in the caring professions, when watching the documentary because the brick maker had solid evidence of his work of making bricks. The work was there for all to see. Where are your bricks? Where are the obvious, concrete signs of your labor?

The constant demand for helping professionals to attach, be involved, and then separate over and over means that this process must be done in a way that is energizing to the individual practitioner. Ambiguous professional loss produces the opposite result; it drains the practitioner. This is analogous to descriptions of how ambiguous loss in the family and the confusion and lack of closure:

> who is psychologically in and who is psychologically out of the family system can block family reorganization and accommodation to chronic stress. ... Caregivers have difficulty accepting the loss of their loved ones (because the loss is only partial) and they cannot grieve and move on to restructure the family as they could if the person were no longer physically present. ... Care-givers' boundary ambiguity and sense of mastery are important correlates in understanding the development of caregiver depression. (Boss et al., 1990, pp. 246–247, 253)

The lack of closure can be quite stressful for practitioners. Being sensitive enough to be affected by such experiences is, we contend, part of the "soft side of the turtle" issue. An exceptional capacity to attach demands emotional sensitivity. A medical doctor described the dilemma this way:

> I suppose one has to have a fairly conscientious type of personality to be a good doctor. It is a caring and painstaking approach which endears doctors to their patients. The problem is that this same personality can make a person very conscious of failure, which in turn leads to depression. I also found that my sensitive nature, which fitted me so well for my profession, caused me to feel hurt over matters I have seen others shrug off without apparent injury. (By a general practitioner, 1985, p. 63)

Hazard 11: The Covert Nature of the Work

The previous hazard suggests that ambiguity and lack of closure can make success feel elusive. This hazard introduces another element that interferes with work satisfaction. Practitioners in the counseling, therapy, teaching, and health professions can't talk about their work. For example, the psychotherapist may have achieved an incredible breakthrough with a client that is life changing, yet the practitioner must return home and maintain confidentiality about the day's success. Imagine that! You want to tell friends and family about your day—doesn't everybody want to do that?—but you cannot because of confidentiality provisions that protect the privacy of the client, student, or patient.

Confidentiality is an important and valuable aspect of these professions and is a catalyst for the work to occur, such as with psychotherapy in which the client reveals very personal information. The privacy and confidentiality provide an environment that promotes client trust and willingness to open up the self for exploration. Although this is a very positive aspect of the work overall, it binds practitioners to put a wall between the work self and the personal self. Therefore, one cannot talk about the work.

Counselors, therapists, and Central Intelligence Agency (CIA) agents share a common bond, a secret life they cannot reveal. The negative side of this is that a practitioner in these fields is unable to share the successes, failures, frustrations, and confusion of the work outside of the professional context; therefore, the value of social support from others, connection to others, and understanding by others as ways to reduce work stress gets greatly compromised in these fields.

Hazard 12: Constant Empathy, Interpersonal Sensitivity, and One-Way Caring

> Empathy is a double-edged sword; it is simultaneously your greatest asset and a point of real vulnerability.
>
> **—D. G. Larson (1993, p. 30)**

> The very act of being compassionate and empathic extracts a cost under most circumstances.
>
> **—C. Figley (2002, p. 1434)**

Individuals in the caring professions or high-touch (vs. high-tech) occupations are successful because they can do "high touch"—relate to others by way of expert people skills. Yet, this work takes effort. The practitioner must concentrate, be involved, and work at it until depletion—not total depletion but relative depletion—sets in. Interpersonal sensitivity demands that the practitioner understand the complexity of human relationships, including concepts such as projection and transference, which mean the feelings that the other projects, like in a movie, onto the practitioner. For example, if you have followed an older sibling in school and the teachers seemed to keep treating you like the sibling rather than yourself, then you have experienced projection or transference.

The psychoanalytic–psychodynamic tradition has been most useful in illuminating transference–countertransference concepts (Corsini & Wedding, 2010). Maintaining a clear awareness of transference–counter-transference issues is not always easy for counselors, therapists, teachers, and health professionals trying to establish positive human relationships with individuals that they attempt to assist. Working in the high-touch professional relationship, amid the transference–countertransference flot-sam is very difficult but of critical importance in achieving excellent human relationships. And, of course, being able to establish excellent human rela-tionships is a marker that sets apart those in the caring professions. But it is swimming upstream and hard work. Working free of our own distortions is a difficult goal because it means that we must take off the layperson's perceptual lens.

As mentioned in Hazard 5, Mitchell and Anderson (1983) describe the stress of the transference reaction in the professional lives of those in an allied helping field, the clergy. They write, "At the best of times, people project on their pastor their fears of judgment, their anger at God, and many other feel-ings. In moments of severe stress, the tendency to misperceive the pastor is even stronger" (p. 118). Members of the clergy, wanting like other helpers to be perceived positively, can often be confused and distressed when those that they seek to help react to them with strong negative emotions.

With countertransference, which is our own distorted reactions to the other (Sexton & Whiston, 1994), we must work to understand the wide array of perceptual filters that we bring to the helping relationship: our personal history; our major demographic variables such as age, race, religion, sex, and socioeconomic status (SES); our family of origin geno-gram and its biases; our trauma and pain; and our cultural encapsulation within geographic and national boundaries. Understanding all of these perceptual filters, and their impact on our reaction to the other, is hard, hard work.

Thus, although transference and countertransference provide rich data for the helper of others, making use of this data means swimming against the current. The temptation is always to turn around and go with the current, with the lay reaction of just being human. Fighting this temptation is both a primary stressor and hard work. Excellent high-touch practitioners, however, maintain the interpersonal sensitivity within the one-way caring relationship.

Hazard 13: Elusive Measures of Success

> Sometimes in this world the best you can do is plant the seed, attend patiently and reverently to a reality you cannot change quickly or even in your lifetime, be present to suffering you cannot banish.
>
> **—K. Tippett (2007, p. 58)**

In the caring professions, it is difficult to gauge success. If the professional impulse is to counsel, teach, or heal, then success must relate to the amount of counseling, teaching, or healing. Or does it relate more to the amount of improvement by the client, student, or patient? Or is it some combination of these qualities—effort by the practitioner plus improvement by the recipient? Is it the quantity of the practitioner's effort or the quality? Is it gain scores—how much the client, for example, has improved compared with oneself earlier or compared with the general population? If the person in need is significantly impaired, do we expect less? If he or she is highly functional, do we expect more? For example, should a doctor who routinely sees terminally ill cancer patients judge success or failure by whether these patients stay alive? If not this criteria, what?

Professional stress comes in part from the elusiveness of concrete results and the difficulty in measuring success. In the ambiguous and murky world of counseling, therapy, teaching, and healing, who is responsible for improvement? A graduate student in the helping professions wrote:

> Related to feelings of success and failure in the helping professions is the issue of responsibility. … My own natural inclinations have been to rescue the client and to work from my own set of assumptions about what the goals and expectations ought to be. The supervision I had … was very useful in helping me see that tendency in my approach with clients. Not only was the overresponsibility sometimes unproductive, or even counterproductive, with the clients, it was horribly frustrating to me to often feel like a "failure" with my clients. I too frequently imposed my view of success, then beat myself up when they couldn't achieve it. (Thorson, 1994, p. 3)

Maybe we are doing a good job if our supervisor says we are, but then maybe the supervisor is in error. Maybe we are doing a good job if our clients, students, or patients like us, but then maybe liking us is irrelevant to having a significant impact on their lives. Haven't we all, with time, come to appreciate and gain from practitioners, such as a demanding teacher in high school, whom we disliked at the time because they were pushing us hard? For example, Tom had an extremely demanding football coach in the past but has come to appreciate having that coach.

Perhaps success is related not to results but rather to skilled effort. In other words, the counselor of acting out, angry adolescents can measure success by how much an adolescent client becomes more cooperative, social, and achieving, or the counselor can measure success by how much he or she practices professional skills to a maximum level. Do we focus on outcome (the client's changes) or process (our own professional effort), or is it a combination of these two? Should one reduce expectations regarding outcome if the level of need, dysfunction, disease, or dis-ease is greater? When do reduced expectations help to fuel the cycle of failure, rather than interrupt it, so that the practitioner colludes in the failure rather than attempting to stop it?

Even if we decide that realism rather than idealism should be a goal, how do we move in that direction? This question often emerges for practitioners from the older dilemma of realizing that one's professional efforts (one's power, influence, commitment, energy, and competence) are not enough. This realization usually occurs through a "series of professional humiliations," which occur when one's best efforts produce only failure (Skovholt & Rønnestad, 1995).

Even when avoiding perfectionistic expectations, the practitioner faces a new dilemma of how to transform expectations. How is the practitioner to distinguish between being realistic and giving up? Giving up is a process in which the counseling, teaching, or healing practitioner colludes in the cycle of failure and becomes, in the end, the official reporter that the system tried but the inadequate client, student, or patient failed. This is when helping becomes toxic, the victim becomes revictimized, and blaming the victim becomes a powerful, destructive enterprise. The liberators have become prison guards who continue on because they like the salary and retirement benefits, the security, and the status, but they no longer care enough to really be powerful helpers of others. They are no longer attached, and without the attachment, the helping relationship, so well documented as an instrument of human change and transformation (Sexton & Whiston, 1994), is unplugged. Powerlessness results. How can this destructive process be distinguished from

the very different process of becoming realistic; that is, gaining a more elabo-
rate, textured understanding of the difficulty of human change and moving
to less grand expectations of oneself as a practitioner?

Hazard 14: Normative Failure

> A common experience of teachers is to feel the pain of opportunities
> missed, potential unrealized, students untouched.
>
> **—W. Ayers (1993, p. 7)**

> [Sometimes] the classroom is so lifeless or painful or confused—and
> I am so powerless to do anything about it—that my claim to be a teacher
> seems a transparent sham. Then the enemy is everywhere: in those stu-
> dents from some alien planet, in that subject I thought I knew, and in the
> personal pathology that keeps me earning my living this way. What a fool
> I was to imagine that I had mastered this occult art—harder to divine
> than tea leaves and impossible for mortals to do even passably well!
>
> **—P. J. Palmer (1998, p. 1)**

One of the most distressing parts of being a practitioner in the caring professions is the often desperate search for concrete standards of success versus
failure. The personal threat is often severe, and one's career search and occupational identity are at stake. Also, there is often a sense of ambiguous but
pervasive anxiety related to this question. One element of this dis-ease is the
need to differentiate normative failure from excessive failure. Resolving this
question is very important for the novice practitioner. Increased professional
experience often brings more clarity to this distinction. This, in turn, tends
to greatly reduce pervasive professional anxiety as one moves from novice
to advanced practitioner (Skovholt & Rønnestad, 1995). After learning to
define normative failure versus excessive failure, the novice must begin to
clarify whether he or she is on the normative failure rate or high failure rate.
Being able to place oneself on the normative side also reduces one's free-
floating worries about professional skill.

A second element here is the term *normative failure.* It is a startling term.
People most often enter counseling, therapy, teaching, and the healing arts
with an intense desire to make a significant impact in the lives of others—to
heal, educate, reduce hurt, stop pain, increase competence, provide insights.
Accompanying this desire, there is often an only partially understood sense
of using a powerful method of change, a feeling of one's own potency in helping others make positive changes. Related to this, there can also be an urgent

attempt to rescue the other. Thus, the concept of normative failure can be a startling jolt.

Those in the caring professions can be extremely distressed when they feel that they have failed in helping. Linville (1988) describes such an experience*:

> I was in my first position as a school counselor and soon found that I was expected to do much more than talk with students who had problems. I learned that I was also the director of the school district's home-bound program. I tried to be conscientious, but my world seemed to be a jumble of interviews with students, parents, and teachers; of trying to deal with classroom and playground emergencies; and of jumping from one thing to another. I was not quite sure who or what I was supposed to be.
>
> One morning I found a note on my desk. A boy in the upper grades who had leukemia now required home-bound instruction. He was only a name and an added responsibility for me, part of my duties. I shook my head. I had begun fitting students into categories, "Problems" and "Duties," and I slipped Tim, the boy with leukemia, neatly into the "Duties" category.
>
> I made my telephone calls. I called the teacher who worked with home-bound students and asked when she and I could visit the boy. I called Tim's mother, and we set up a time for the visit.
>
> The teacher and I visited the home. I didn't know what to expect, but Tim was dressed and he was up and around, a little pale perhaps, wearing a brown sweater to keep warm, but happy to see the teacher.
>
> "I'll be back on Friday," the teacher said. "Maybe you can have all of your assignment done by then."
>
> Tim came up to me. "When will you be back?" he asked.
>
> "I'll come back a month from today," I said cheerfully. "That will be Tuesday, the 28th. I'll see how everything's working out."
>
> "What time will you be here?" Tim's mother asked.
>
> "About one o'clock," I said.
>
> "Come back," Tim said.
>
> He stood just inside the door, holding one of his books.
>
> Arrangements had been properly made. Another of my assignments had been completed. When I was back in the office, I made a note in my appointment book about the visit on the 28th.
>
> I was soon involved with Parents' Night, with some boys who were leaving school at recess, and with two teachers on a teaching team who had stopped speaking to one another. The month went fast. The day I was to visit Tim came, but the school superintendent came by to talk to me, and I forgot to check the appointment book. Then the

---

*Reprinted from *Journal of Counseling and Development*, 67, page 87. Copyright © ACA. Reprinted with permission. No further reproduction authorized without written permission of the American Counseling Association

superintendent asked me to go to lunch, and when I got back to the office it was two o'clock.

"Tim seemed all right," I said to myself. "I'll stop by another day when I'm in the neighborhood."

Another day became another day, and Tim was a forgotten note in an appointment book. The days were blurs of conferences and telephone calls and bits and pieces of advice and admonition, all shaped by duty and expectations. A month passed, and I stopped at a grocery store on my way home from school. It was an evening in early winter, and I was glad to walk down the brightly lit aisles of the store after walking through the evening darkness outside. I stopped by the produce counter and picked up a head of lettuce.

I looked up and there was Tim's mother, pushing a grocery cart. She pushed it slowly, and her lips moved as if she were trying to remember something. There was a large orange box of cereal in her basket with a picture of a baseball player hitting a home run on the side.

I said cheerfully, "Hello. Do you remember me?"

"Yes," she answered.

"How's Tim doing?"

This time she didn't answer. She only looked at me.

"I hope ..." I started talking because everything seemed so quiet.

Suddenly she spoke. "He died," she said in a harsh voice.

I gathered up the usual words of sympathy and smoothed them out. She kept looking at me, and I shifted the head of lettuce in my hands. I stepped back a little. I thought she was looking at me as if she hated me.

"He thought you were coming," she said. "He waited for you. He had his work ready to show you."

I still remember every sharp detail of the scene—her face with the tight lines of grief by her mouth, the stacks of produce, the bright lights of the store. Her hands were gripping the round handle on the grocery cart. She looked at me and said softly, "You hurt him."

She pushed the cart hard and walked away. I stood there. I put down the lettuce and walked out of the store. It was dark outside, no touch of evening left. The lights fell across the parking lot in pale and wavering lines. I waited a while before I opened the door of my car. I felt as if I had turned my back on another human being.

Since then I have kept duplicate appointment books, but, far more than that, I began to think about what I was really doing. I realized that I had a responsibility to others, that I could not keep people waiting through long afternoons, that being busy (often idle busyness) was no excuse. My essential function was to be there and not leave people all alone, waiting for a word from me. I saw that failure in my work could go far beyond not meeting job specifications. I realized that children were not Problems and Duties, that human contact was more than making proper arrangements, that beyond the performance of assignments were human needs reaching toward me—and I had not been there. A little boy in a brown sweater had been waiting, and the afternoon was long. (p. 101)

We may know at one level that the patients of expert doctors sometimes die, but this profound understanding of the reality of professional success and failure doesn't penetrate our own professional self-concept. Somehow, we believe that we will succeed in our own healing of others, and our clients, students, patients will change and get better. With further experience and a clearer reality, practitioners must realize that they are like doctors whose patients die. All our will, all our work, all our competence will sometimes not be enough. This means that, in time, the practitioner must develop the capacity to accept lack of success—normative failure—as a component of the work. Being able to come to this realization, accept it, and incorporate it into one's professional self-concept is important for long-term, high-quality professional functioning. In our research, experienced practitioners often were, in effect, talking about acceptance of normative failure when they described their own shift in expectations as they moved toward being "realistic" (Skovholt & Rønnestad, 1995).

Hazard 15: Regulation Oversight and Control by External, Often Unknown Others

A medical doctor told me of being scolded by an administrative clerk the day after admitting an adolescent to the hospital. The evening before, he had seen the adolescent while he was on emergency room duty. He made a medical decision, based on 20 years of practice, that inpatient care was warranted. The next morning, the administrative clerk, an anonymous person in another state, told him that the admission was unwarranted.

This new layer of administration between the practitioner and the client, student, and patient in human services, education, and health care has a positive goal—to reduce excessive costs and increase quality of care. From the practitioner's point of view, however, the main result is often increased stress. The ingredients for the increased stress are less control but increased responsibility by the practitioner, more detailed paperwork without pay for the additional work, and contradictory messages to increase and decrease services at the same time. There are many difficulties. For example, should the mental health practitioner highlight the client's problem areas when asking for authorization of more treatment? A yes might increase the stigma of emotional illness; a no might decrease the chance for authorization.

Hazard 16: Cognitive Deprivation and Boredom

The novice, at sea in heavy waters, tries hard to maintain the craft and avoid sinking. It is often an anxiety-filled voyage, composed of quick changes, new challenges, occasional calm, and a veneer depth of professional confidence. Like a powerful, churning sea, the novice is never sure of the professional challenge to be faced in the upcoming minutes, hours, and days. It is often intense, involving, and engrossing and sometimes very exciting in a positive vein. It is *not* boring.

For the senior practitioner in the high-touch fields, the challenge can be 180 degrees from that facing the novice. For the veteran with years of experience, the sea is calm, the route predictable, and the work tasks, now mastered, the same as before and before and before. This situation is especially true for a practitioner working in a very prescribed arena in terms of the scope of the work and the job environment. Sure, the payoff is reduced anxiety and increased professional confidence. That counts for a lot. The problem is that the intellectual stimulation is lessened, the routine has become boring, and task repetition grates like an old wound. The stimulation of novelty, with its sugar coat, is gone. The obnoxious, unpleasant, unwanted, and routine tasks, which do not seem too bad for the novice who is simply trying to stay afloat, can be felt as very deadening by the veteran practitioner.

This drama for the veteran practitioner occurs in the bigger drama of the dance between the practitioner and the client, student, or patient. The client, student, or patient is, of course, fully invested in his or her personal needs, as should be the case, and wants very much to have a practitioner who is fully invested too. The unwritten, unspoken contract desired by the one in need is that the practitioner be strongly engaged in the cycle of caring of empathic attachment, active involvement, felt separation, and re-creation. For example, remember in Chapter 3 the research study of teachers that found that, most of all, people want a caring teacher. They want to feel they matter to the practitioner.

With boredom, there is a lack of novelty to stimulate the practitioner. One kind of novelty relates to the practitioner as a cultural anthropologist. One vocational choice inventory asks if the person is more interested in people or things. For counselors, therapists, teachers, and health care workers, it is people. People—their lives, choices, thoughts, feelings, and ways in the world—enchant them. It can be exciting, like a big tip for a taxi driver. Being with people, therefore, is very rewarding because the practitioner keeps learning about these beings called people. When one knows enough about one aspect of human life and the curiosity factor is satiated, then the cultural anthropologist reward disappears. Tom remembers working at the University of Florida Counseling Center as a psychological counselor for 18-year-old college freshmen. He found it interesting to try to understand all the permutations and combinations of these students' lives. Yet, after four years of it, Tom felt that he knew more than enough about being 18. He was getting bored with the same thinking, struggles, worries, and developmental vistas. He wanted out and was lucky to expand his client's load to include a bigger variety of people.

Aside from learning about people through involvement with them, practitioners are stimulated in their search for more professional competence. Good practitioners always want to find ways to work effectively with those that they serve. Using one's own mind to search for ways to improve can be immensely stimulating intellectually.

For example, imagine that there is a seventh-grade boy in front of you. He is in school but not doing well. You, the teacher, are charged with charging him up. What route will you take? Or imagine that you are a physical therapist with a patient who fails to do critical exercises at home. What will you do? Or you are a school counselor leading a group of children from divorcing families. These children have never been together before to discuss this difficult topic. How will you lead the group so that the children will benefit?

These challenges stimulate the practitioner; however, at some point, especially with a narrow population or problem, the practitioner has seen and done it all before, and *boredom sets in*. The counselor has heard the story many times before; the teacher has taught the subject over and over; the physician has repeatedly performed the medical procedure. The rub is that the client, student, or patient needs an energized practitioner, but the practitioner is bored. The practitioner can be engaged by new work but may be trapped by "golden handcuffs," the financial benefits given to those who stay in a position for many years. In short, this problem of cognitive deprivation and boredom is a significant hazard in the counseling, therapy, teaching, and health fields.

Hazard 17: Cynical, Critical, Negative Colleagues, and Managers

> It is not unusual to see faculty in midcareer don the armor of cynicism against students, education, and any sign of hope. It is the cynicism that comes when the high hopes one once had for teaching have been dashed by experience—or by the failure to interpret one's experience accurately.
>
> **—P. J. Palmer (1998, p. 48)**

The work can be hard, and those that we try to help can stress us. Yet, with a supportive work group and a good boss, the job can be positive and fulfilling. When colleagues are negative or the boss is incompetent, reality is more burdensome. Cynical colleagues spread a highly infectious disease. This disease, negativity, is easy to catch. It is also a seductive disease because, when one first gets it, he or she feels better. Venting helps. But like other seductive diseases (those caused by smoking, for example), the long-term result brings on a grimmer reaper. Cynicism, in the air, is especially dangerous in the high-touch occupations. Members of the people occupations need the stress-buffering effect of positive colleagues, which is a long distance on a continuum from the nonbuffering effect of negative colleagues.

A second factor relates to the needs of those we serve. The caring desired by the other, whether client, student, or patient, is most empowering when it contains the active ingredient of hopefulness. In fact, Frank and Frank (1991) argue that helpers are sought out when a person feels demoralized, with the chief curative agent being hopefulness. But how can one offer hope within a critical, cynical work environment?

Bosses get paid more because they help create the important work environment. We are reminded of the work of Carkhuff (1969), whose research suggests that the client cannot function psychologically at a higher level than the helper. In a parallel fashion, it is hard for a worker to function at a higher level than the boss. With a great boss, everyone can sail; with a poor boss, the environment leads to no sailing or poor sailing by all on board. In the caring professions, bosses are incompetent if they are very critical or unfair. They also are poor if they do not support ideal conditions that enable counselors, therapists, teachers, or health workers to use the caring cycle with those that they serve. And remember that only energized people can continually care for the other in need and do it over and over again.

Hazard 18: Legal and Ethical Fears

> We used to be on our toes of concern for the kids, now we are on our heels of worry about ethical and legal threats.
>
> **—25-year veteran teacher and counselor participant
> in other-care and self-care workshop (1996)**

It is important to start by noting that legal and ethical complaints have been nurtured by illegal and unethical behavior of practitioners in the caring professions. Misuse of power to meet one's own needs, general incompetence, and other unethical behaviors are not to be tolerated. But here we are talking about the wider arena of potential legal and ethical complaints, and instances where the practitioner is wrongly accused.

Hazard 19: Practitioner Emotional Trauma

> Last week on one day I had eight appointments, all with people who had been terminated from their jobs. After that day I wanted to crawl in a hole [to escape the painful feelings].
>
> **—Matt Johnson, counselor of newly "downsized"**
> **employees (August 1996)**

We have described the practitioner dilemma of needing to connect with the other by using one's "soft side of the turtle" rather than the hard shell. Yet, unfortunately, doing this produces a side effect—practitioner emotional trauma—as surely as strong medicines produce side effects. Terms used to describe the impact on the practitioner are *vicarious traumatization, countertransference, compassion fatigue,* and *secondary traumatic stress* (Sabin-Farrel & Turpin, 2003).

This construct overlaps the earlier described ocean of distress emotions, but it goes beyond that to experiencing the reality of difficult events in the lives of our clients, students, and patients. These include vicariously experiencing and understanding sexual assault, chronic physical pain, unexpected failure in school, betrayal in friendship, student neglect by parents, severe financial loss, a child's death, physical attack, sudden job loss, deceit within marriage, a fatal car accident, onset of a serious illness, and severe existential anguish. Over the years of a practitioner's career, many of these events and others are described by clients. Often, for history taking and diagnostic purposes, the counselor, therapist, teacher, or nurse must hear the details of the experience. Later, in counseling or therapy, for example, the desensitization protocol may entail countless times of recalling the experience to help the client reduce the traumatic elements of it. The therapeutic process for the client can, over time, produce a vicarious traumatization or secondary trauma experience for the counselor or therapist. Therapist Sussman (1995) describes it this way:

> Prone to overidentifying with clients, I tend to experience much of their emotional pain and internal struggles as if they were my own. The permeability of my ego boundaries may facilitate empathic contact, but it also leaves me vulnerable to emotional overload. Especially when working with more disturbed individuals, hearing and digesting their stories of past and present abuse can be highly disturbing. (p. 21)

A parallel process can happen for health professionals who repeatedly hear of the vulnerability of the human body to disease and injury. The human body in front of them that has been attacked by disease or injury is not unlike the body that they themselves possess. Educators also experience versions of this vicarious stress when they interact with struggling students unable to learn and with little family support. Vicarious traumatization, or secondary trauma, means processing this knowledge and the realization that "there but for the grace of God go I."

Another kind of practitioner emotional trauma involves "taking in" the hostility of the client, student, or patient toward the practitioner. For example, there is the angry reaction of a parent to a teacher at a parent–teacher conference, the intense affect liability of a teenage client to a youth counselor, or the hostile behavior of a patient to a nurse. This negative reaction from those that we try to help can be quite stressful because it can hit the "soft side of the turtle" part of us with which we attach and negates our primary occupational need of being helpful.

Hazard 20: Practitioner Physical Trauma

Sometimes things go beyond severe overload, the ocean of negative emotions, ambiguous professional loss, and normative failure so that the "underside of the turtle," the soft defenseless part, the area that attaches the caring professional to the other gets physically hurt.

The most frightening form of practitioner physical trauma for psychotherapists is direct attack by clients. In the *Boston Globe* on August 21, 1999, a headline stated, "Social Worker Slain Outside Client's Home." The first paragraph reads, "A social worker whom colleagues described as dedicated to his job counseling troubled youths and trained to deal with violent situations was shot dead yesterday, allegedly by a member of a family he had gone to visit" (Milbouer, 1999, p. B1). And so the nightmare came true for a 30-year-old practitioner, married with children, just trying to do his job.

In research on this topic, Guy, Brown, and Poelstra (1990, 1992) discovered that 40% of their sample group of 750 predominantly full-time psychological practitioners had been physically attacked by clients during their careers, and 49% had received serious verbal threats against their health and safety. These kinds of traumatic events led to many different concerns about safety. For example, 28% often or sometimes were concerned about the verbal threats toward their physical safety, 17% were often or sometimes concerned about physical attacks on their loved ones, and 7% were often or sometimes concerned about being murdered. This in turn led to a variety of protective measures against client threats. For example, this sample group frequently refused to treat certain clients (50%), discussed safety issues with loved ones (30%), installed a home security alarm system (13%), or kept a weapon at home to protect themselves against present or former clients (5%). This study provides sobering data regarding this issue of counselor or therapist primary trauma.

Both Kinnetz (1988) and Zeh (1988) describe highly traumatic experiences while they served as counselors. Both were physically attacked by their clients and traumatized by these events. For Kinnetz, it occurred while she worked in a maximum security psychiatric unit; for Zeh, it was in a shelter for runaway adolescents. Kinnetz describes her experience*:

> At the beginning of my counseling career, I was employed as an art therapist in an adult male, forensic, maximum security psychiatric unit. The job was difficult because I had never before worked with an all-male population, let alone one that was explosively violent. Angry patient outbursts were common. For example, in one scuffle a patient cracked the jawbone of a hospital aide, and, on another occasion, a patient knocked his doctor nearly unconscious in an unprovoked attack. Nearly paralyzed with fear during the first few days, I stayed in the protective nursing station away from the patients, leaving only to come and go from work. My fear of being harmed lessened considerably, however, when I realized that the hospital staff was very tightly knit and could be counted on to work as a team, especially in emergencies. So, despite the limitations imposed by the strict safety requirements, I began to feel challenged to stay on the ward and to establish an art therapy program.
>
> My discomfort did not completely disappear, however, as I sensed tension in the patients as well. Although I never actually observed a blatant example of staff abuse, I became aware that some of the staff's behavior was less than professional. It seemed to me that, at times, their methods of patient restraint were too strong and bordered on abuse. Certainly, the patients were both verbally and physically abusive to staff as well [as] to each other, and any staff intervention was aimed at rapidly defusing a potential fight and reestablishing compliance with hospital routine. A client-centered approach would have been ludicrous in this situation, because immediate control had to be externally imposed to protect other patients. It was obvious that very strong measures were needed. But how strong, and what kind?

---

*Reprinted from *Journal of Counseling & Development*, p. 87. Copyright © ACA. Reprinted with permission. No further reproduction authorized without written permission of the American Counseling Association.

My dilemma was this: Do I report my suspicions in an effort to stop overly aggressive restraints, and risk being told that the force was really necessary? Or do I continue to observe the strong-arm control and be ensured of the protection of the staff? I could depend on the staff to promptly come to my aid should a fight threaten to break out, and was afraid that if I reported my suspicions, I might upset some of them and lose their protection. My fear won out; I did not report anyone until I left the unit for another position.

One of the factors that helped me to decide to leave was when a patient attempted to rape me. I had been escorting him to another part of the hospital when he suddenly grabbed me around the neck and twisted my arm behind my back. He held a contraband razor to my throat and dragged me into an empty room. Fortunately, I was able to free myself and run back to the unit for help. But I continue to wonder whether help would have come so quickly if the staff knew that I was considering reporting them for excessive force.

Years later, I still have not come to terms with the issue of whether I should have reported the possible abuse earlier. This incident has sparked many internal dialogues on the general issue of how I can best take care of myself without sacrificing my client's care. I have found that it sometimes becomes necessary for me to pull back momentarily from the continually intense and demanding emotional needs of a client. This is essential to preserve my own emotional reserves and to prevent eventual burnout. These client needs are less life threatening than the attempted rape, but my time-out response to them is no less important over the course of therapy. Certainly, if I withdraw every time the client becomes emotionally demanding, it would be a major therapeutic error, and my effectiveness would be severely compromised.

The ability to be fully engaged with the client in his or her struggles is a powerful curative factor. But if I allow myself to become emotionally overwhelmed and burned out, the long-term result is a compromised effectiveness. Not only is one client affected, but all my clients and even family and friends suffer. Although the strong-arm measures on the unit were extreme, perhaps (but perhaps not) they were justified to preserve the unit's functioning and ultimately to benefit the patients. Similarly, without taking care of myself emotionally, I cannot help clients learn to take care of themselves.

The unresolved nature of this question continues to keep me searching for balance. Too much therapist emotional withdrawal is not in the client's best interests, but continual emotional availability to the client is draining and dangerous, particularly in the absence of sufficient external therapist support. It is imperative that I monitor my own internal state as well as attend to my clients' emotional well-being. I judge my immediate internal state as a balance of present emotional and physical reserve, counterbalanced with the amount of support and replenishment that I can count on in the near future to replace the outgoing supply. This self-monitoring can be considered an extension of caring for my client. Although self-monitoring is not sufficient in itself to prevent therapist burnout, it goes a long way in helping me remain effective in both the short-term and long-term. Nonetheless, it is an ongoing, elusive dilemma—where is the balance between my needs and the needs of those I serve? (p. 87)

This is a gripping story by counselor Kinnetz. Both her experience and that of Zeh, mentioned earlier, are examples of practitioner physical trauma. These are acute wounds to the "underside of the turtle" part of the self from work as a practitioner. They include experiences that produce the stress emotions of anger, fear, and despair.

Hazards Summary

Work in the high-touch and caring professions can be positive. It is important to emphasize this point, to you the reader, because it can be easily lost after reading about these 20 hazards. It is also important to note that the sting of the hazards can be lessened if we face them directly. That is our intention with this chapter.

For veteran practitioners, there often are difficult incidents over the years of practice that lead to a loss of innocence. The most traumatic incidents, such as the suicide of a client, are stressful and, at the time, bring on daydreams of other, hopefully more positive, occupational choices. What are the lessons from these incidents? For one, practice can wound the practitioner. Often the vulnerability is unknown. The person may not have known before that a field that can do so much good can also wound its practitioners. Innocence is not knowing how the "soft side of the turtle" can produce practitioner vulnerability.

Reading this chapter of 20 hazards may lead a person to question the wisdom of entering any of the caring professions. Bodily experiences can include a pit in one's stomach, an increase in anxiety felt, or the beginnings of a headache. This is our intent. We also tried to communicate the opposite feelings that one can get in Chapter 2, "Joys, Rewards, and Gifts of Practice."

The overall goal of this whole book is to portray first the wonderful qualities of the work, then in contrast, the stressful qualities of the work, and consequently, the need for professional self-care on an ongoing basis.

Self-Reflection Exercises

In this chapter, we discussed many difficulties that can affect the work of the practitioner. We suggest that you review the chapter and then pick five from the list of hazards. As a next step, fill out the following:

1. Hazard number _____ Name: _____

   Why has this been a significant practice hazard for you?

   _____
   _____
   _____
   _____
   _____
   _____
   _____
   _____
   _____
   _____
   _____

   What methods have you tried to alleviate its impact? How successful have you been?

   _____
   _____
   _____
   _____
   _____
   _____
   _____
   _____
   _____
   _____
   _____

2. Hazard number _____ Name: _____

Why has this been a significant practice hazard for you?

_____

_____

_____

_____

_____

_____

_____

_____

_____

_____

_____

_____

What methods have you tried to alleviate its impact? How successful have you been?

_____

_____

_____

_____

_____

_____

_____

_____

_____

_____

_____

3. Hazard number _____ Name: _____

Why has this been a significant practice hazard for you?

_____
_____
_____
_____
_____
_____
_____
_____
_____
_____
_____
_____

What methods have you tried to alleviate its impact? How successful have you been?

_____
_____
_____
_____
_____
_____
_____
_____
_____
_____
_____
_____

4. Hazard number _____ Name: _____

Why has this been a significant practice hazard for you?

_____

_____

_____

_____

_____

_____

_____

_____

_____

_____

_____

What methods have you tried to alleviate its impact? How successful have you been?

_____

_____

_____

_____

_____

_____

_____

_____

_____

_____

_____

5. Hazard number _____   Name: _____

Why has this been a significant practice hazard for you?

_____
_____
_____
_____
_____
_____
_____
_____
_____
_____
_____

What methods have you tried to alleviate its impact? How successful have you been?

_____
_____
_____
_____
_____
_____
_____
_____
_____
_____
_____

7

Burnout
A Hemorrhaging of the Self

After working in community mental health for five years, I was burned
out, or burned up, by a sense of hopelessness after overextending myself
to help people and no one seemingly appreciated my efforts.

—M. E. Young (1997, p. 45)

You may wonder where the term *burnout* came from. In the early 1970s,
Herbert Freudenberger was a practitioner in New York City at a community agency focusing on drug abuse. At the time, drug abusers were often
called "burnouts." Being called a burnout meant that the person no longer
cared about anything except drugs. As a consequence of a slow erosion of
motivation and competence, the person was not capable of much or interested in anything that was not related to being high. Hence, one became
a burnout.

In 1974, Freudenberger published an article titled "Staff Burnout" in a
psychology journal. Freudenberger attempted to describe a loss of will among
the practitioners who worked with these addicted clients. He used the word
burnout in this way for the first time, and the term was born. This first article
on burnout began:

> Some years ago, a few of us who had been working intensively in the
> free clinic movement began to talk of a concept which we referred to as
> "burn-out." Having experienced this feeling state of burn-out myself, I
> began to ask myself a number of questions about it. First of all, what is
> burn-out? (p. 159)

In the 1980s, the term burnout hit a cord. It quickly became a popular way to consider exhaustion and disquiet at work. It had what measurement people call face validity, meaning that it captured something that practitioners could identify as real. Soon, a number of authors wrote books on burnout in various occupations, such as human services (Cherniss, 1980), teaching (Cedoline, 1982), nursing (McConnell, 1982), and medicine (Wessells et al., 1989). From 1980 to 1985, there was an outpouring of 300 academic articles on burnout (Roberts, 1986). Schaufeli, Leiter, and Maslach (2009) estimate that over 6,000 journal articles, books, chapters, and dissertations have been published on the topic of burnout in the 35 years since the term was identified.

Searching the literature, Söderfeldt, Söderfeldt, and Warg (1995) found many descriptions of the term. Although the descriptions were different, key words reveal commonalities. These key words are fatigue, frustration, disengagement, stress, depletion, helplessness, hopelessness, emotional drain, emotional exhaustion, and cynicism. These words point to a profound weariness and hemorrhaging of the self as key components of burnout. This profound weariness and hemorrhaging of the self makes the concept of burnout one that is understood by counselors, therapists, teachers, health professionals, and clergy, too.

Compassion Fatigue

In the helping profession, practitioners may experience difficulties from continual exposure to hearing clients discuss trauma in their lives. A term parallel to burnout in some ways, Figley identified the concept of *compassion fatigue* defined as "the natural consequent behaviors and emotions resulting from knowing about a traumatizing event experienced by a significant other-the stress resulting from helping or wanting to help a traumatized or suffering person" (Figley, 1995, p. 7). In his later work, Figley expands his initial definition to include "a state of tension and preoccupation with the traumatized patients by re-experiencing the traumatic events, avoidance/numbing of bearing witness to the suffering of others" (Figley, 2002, p. 1435). Figley asserts that compassion fatigue results in higher levels of helplessness and a feeling of being isolated from a support network. In contrast to burnout, compassion fatigue results from exposure to hearing about a specific event or supporting a client who has suffered from a traumatic event.

Lack of Clarity

Paradoxically, although the concept of burnout seems understood by all, it does not seem to really be one specific thing. One could ask, what does it really mean, and what is the research summary at this point many years later? The answers are murky. It has been hard to find strong, consistent statistical relationships regarding burnout. Söderfeldt et al. (1995) wrote, "Overall, there are weak indications of any pattern in the associations, except that they generally seemed job related" (p. 642), and concluded that "burnout should be considered a multidimensional syndrome" (p. 644). In their review of burnout in research and practice, Schaufeli et al., (2009) report that the concept of burnout has different meanings across international contexts. For example, in Sweden and the Netherlands, burnout is a medical diagnosis. A wide variety of variables have been found, in at least one study or another, to be associated with burnout. Table 7.1 is an example from the field of social work.

TABLE 7.1
Factors Associated With Burnout in Social Workers

Work Related
Low work autonomy
Lack of challenge on the job
Low degrees of support
Role ambiguity
Work in public sector
Low professional self-esteem, low salary
Dissatisfaction with agency goals and minimal use of coping strategies at work
Difficulties in providing services to clients
Negative attitudes toward the profession, high degree of work pressure, bad agency functioning

Client Related
Negative impressions of the clients
Empathy
Personal involvement in clients' problems
Involvement in the client–worker relationship

Worker Related
Chronic minor hassles of daily living
Family income, attitudes toward the profession, years of experience, low education

Source: "Burnout in Soical Work," by M. Sölderfelt, B. Sölderfelt, and L. E. Warg, 1995, *Social Work, 40,* p. 641. Copyright © National Association of Social Workers, Inc.

Work of Maslach

Christine Maslach, a psychology professor in California, is considered one of the leading burnout researchers. (This is opposed to being a burned out researcher. Tom heard her speak at a professional conference and she was quite energetic.) The Maslach Burnout Inventory, a popular research instrument (Maslach & Jackson, 1981), and her books, *The Truth About Burnout* (Maslach & Leiter, 1997), *Burnout: The Cost of Caring* (Maslach, 2003), and *Banishing Burnout: Six Strategies for Improving Your Relationship With Work* (Leiter & Maslach, 2005), have been well received.

Maslach and Leiter (1997) give their definition of burnout: "Burnout is the index of the dislocation between what people are and what they have to do. It represents an erosion in values, dignity, spirit, and will—an erosion of the human soul" (p. 17). They go on to describe three key work dimensions in which a person could be fully engaged or burned out (p. 24):

Fully Engaged	Burned Out
Energy	Exhaustion
Involvement	Cynicism
Efficacy	Ineffectiveness

Regarding the causes of burnout, Maslach and Leiter (1997) take a strong work-climate view. Instead of focusing on the individual practitioner, they say "burnout is not a problem of the people themselves but of the social environment in which people work" (p. 18). They cite six specific work environment sources of burnout: work overload, lack of control, insufficient reward, unfairness, breakdown of community, and value conflict. As an example of their view of burnout, we are using a long citation from Maslach and Leiter—their description of the case of Julie, a public school teacher*:

> *Julie taught history and literature to eighth graders in a public school and had a reputation as an outstanding teacher. Students loved her, parents called to get their child enrolled in her class, and the principal rated her as one of the best. Young and successful, Julie was expected to have a long and distinguished teaching career. But this year, Julie decided to quit. Her decision came as a shock to everyone; some of her colleagues cried when they heard the news.*

---

*Reprinted from Maslach & Leiter, *The Truth About Burnout*. Copyright © 1997. Reprinted by permission of Jossey-Bass, Inc., a subsidiary of John Wiley & Sons, Inc.

At one time Julie was completely dedicated to the job because it allowed her to do things she valued highly—to make a difference in the world, to have a positive impact on other people's lives. But today she doesn't feel the job is worth it. At one time she brought enormous energy and commitment to her work, putting in long hours and agreeing to do all sorts of "extras" above and beyond the call of duty. Now she is exhausted just going through the motions and doing the bare minimum. At one time she was deeply involved with her students, attentive to their progress and achievement in learning, sensitive to their individual needs. Now she is more negative and cynical about their motivation and skills. At one time she was confident that her efforts would pay off, that the kids would get a better education and a better start on life because of what she and other teachers were able to accomplish. Now she questions whether the students are really getting what they need; she even worries that children are getting damaged by overworked teachers like herself. To Julie, trying to do good came at too high a price.

What is noteworthy about Julie's case, and many others like it, is that the negative slide to burnout started from a position of strength and success rather than from one of weakness. Julie was not an incompetent, lazy individual who didn't know how to teach. She brought to the job an impressive set of credentials and personal qualities and was able to use these to produce high-quality teaching. In terms of skills and motivation, she was at the top of her class—one could hardly ask for more. As one of her colleagues said, "Julie was 'on fire' from the beginning, not like some of those teachers who never even 'light up' in the first place. She had a passion for teaching, and it is so depressing to see that disappear." Indeed, losing the best and the brightest—people like Julie—is the most devastating cost of burnout.

Seven Sources of Burnout

What led to the erosion of Julie's engagement with teaching? A close look at her case reveals the presence of the mismatches between job and person that we described in Chapter 1. Maslach and Leiter (2008) identify seven domains of the workplace environment: workload, control, reward, community, fairness, values, and job–person incongruity.

Work overload was a major factor from the beginning. Julie spent intense 8-hour days in the classroom and extra hours—after school, in the evening, and on weekends—to prepare for class, grade homework, and attend meetings. Although she had a great deal of control over how she taught her class ("When I close that door, the class is all mine—just me and the kids"), she had a *lack of control* over the district policies that led to increased class sizes and decreased teaching resources. Like other teachers, she received a low salary that was clearly *insufficient reward*; she didn't mind so much when she was young and single and just starting out in the profession, but later it posed a severe financial burden. Furthermore, low salaries are the most visible symbol of the lack of respect for teaching. Julie's wages fueled her sense that there was an inherent *unfairness* in the system ("Why am I working so hard, doing so much, and yet getting so little in return?"). The bickering, political infighting, and competitiveness between the teachers in her school made her feel alienated from them, and thus there was a *breakdown of community*. There was a growing *value conflict* between what Julie was trying to achieve in the classroom and the "extras" she was being asked to do by the school. As she put it, "The last straw was when they wanted me to spend a lot of time pulling together all this material to prepare an application for a 'good school' award— there was far more concern about getting the award than actually doing the things that would make us a good school!" (Maslach & Leiter, 1997, pp. 25–26). Finally, Julie experienced *job–person incongruity* as she determined that trying to do good in this setting cost too much in terms of personal sacrifice and lack of unambiguous rewards. In other words, the organizational environment no longer fit for Julie.

Maslach and Leiter's (2008, pp. 500–501) correlates of burnout and engagement address each of the seven problem areas described in the case of Julie. We have put the alternatives in a table and labeled them burnout creation and burnout prevention.

Burnout Creation		Burnout Prevention
Work overload	vs.	Sustainable workload
Lack of control	vs.	Feelings of choice and control
Insufficient reward	vs.	Recognition and reward
Breakdown of community	vs.	A sense of community
Unfairness	vs.	Fairness, respect, and justice
Significant value conflicts	vs.	Meaningful, valued work
Lack of fit (incongruence) between the person and job	vs.	High job–person fit

There is strong research support for the Maslach and Leiter (1997) belief that the cause of burnout is often in the organization, not the individual.

Their interventions, therefore, are to change organizations. We think that this approach has merit, but it is also myopic and dangerous for practitioners. Actually, Maslach and Leiter (1997) support this caution in their description of the contemporary work environment:

> The workplace today is a cold, hostile, demanding environment, both economically and psychologically. People are emotionally, physically and spiritually exhausted. ... The idea of the workplace as an efficient machine is returning to undermine the ideal of the workplace as a safe and healthy setting in which people may fulfill their potential through intrinsically rewarding work for which they are given fair compensation. (pp. 1–2)

What if one's work environment is not a place that constantly addresses the psychosocial stress of the staff? It reminds us of the play *Waiting for Godot* (Beckett, 1997), in which two individuals waited and waited for a man named Godot to show up so that they could go on with their lives. He never did, and the play ended. The moral of the play for practitioners: Be careful about waiting for others to care for you.

Consider the two work settings described by Molassiotis and Haberman (1996) in their research on bone-marrow-transplant nurses. This is a caring profession group at high risk for stress and burnout. They have the grief work that accompanies engaging in the cycle of caring with dying patients and their families. In one setting, there was a supportive environment that addressed staff psychosocial needs. This was not present in a second setting, and the stress and burnout level was higher there. Hopefully, in the second setting, some of the nurses took charge of their own self-care and did not "wait for Godot."

We are reminded of many settings in which we have worked. Some were burnout creators and some burnout preventers. In the bad settings, no one rescued us. It was up to us to create an environment that worked. In the absence of psychosocial support, counselors, therapists, teachers, or health professionals must create it for themselves and "create a professional greenhouse at work," a concept identified in the chapter on sustaining the professional self.

There are some exceptions to this rule. One successful, systemic, organizational intervention is that of Gysbers and Henderson (2005). Instead of waiting for others to create a positive work environment, they have taught school guidance counselors how to do it for themselves.

Meaning and Caring Burnout

The term *burnout* has helped us lift a shade and see more clearly through a window to the realities of the practitioner's world. The symbolism involved with the word burnout relates to the extinguished flame, which is the motivational force in the caring professions.

It is helpful to distinguish between two styles of burnout; one is meaning burnout, the other caring burnout (Skovholt, 2008). Meaning burnout occurs when the calling of caring for others and giving to others in an area such as emotional development, intellectual growth, or physical wellness no longer gives sufficient meaning and purpose in one's life. Individuals in the caring professions derive much "psychic income" from helping others. In religious terms, such occupations are often labeled a calling, a calling to something of great value. When the meaning of the work disappears, an existential crisis can develop, and meaning burnout can result. Meaning burnout occurs when the meaning of the work has been lost and the existential purpose for the work is gone.

This may occur for any number of reasons. It may be that the activity—such as counseling adolescents, teaching children to read, or nursing the frail elderly—becomes routine, boring, and seemingly insignificant for the practitioner. It may be that the practitioner entered the occupation in part to satisfy his or her own personal needs. This in itself is not a negative factor in job choice. Yet, when it is a predominant factor and the need is filled, then the meaning of the work can decrease. Here are some examples. There is the "wounded healer" who feels healed after counselor training and work in the field. A teacher may have entered education to prove that he wasn't dumb, after feeling that way in high school. Now, years later, he feels intellectually competent and no longer has to prove himself. How about the wellness nurse who was attracted to the field because of her own body image distress earlier in life? Now, she has better feelings about herself. Each of these individuals has lost some of the original meaning and purpose in their occupational choice. However, new meaning in the work can emerge. If it does not, meaning burnout can grow.

Another kind of meaning burnout occurs when the practitioner no longer feels that the work is helpful to the client, student, or patient. This can be a "crisis in meaning" time because if the work is not useful, and the point is to be useful, then why continue. Examples here are a job in (a) an agency where too many cases and too much paperwork make good work impossible, (b) a school that seems to promote a "revolving door" of failure rather than student success, and (c) a health setting where the finances do not permit the practitioners to operate in a competent manner. One colleague working with substance abuse talks of the relapse problem bringing on meaning burnout for him. He wondered how the work could be meaningful when relapse seemed to be more of a reality than recovery.

The second type, caring burnout, is the most popular way of describing burnout. This type focuses very strongly on the professional attachment–involvement–separation process that all counselors, therapists, teachers, and health professionals engage in over and over again with their clients, students, and patients. As described in an earlier chapter, the quality of the attachment to the person in need is of central importance for client, student, or patient gains. (For example, think of your favorite teacher. Was his or her interest in you *as a person* a central element of what you treasured about this teacher?) This idea corresponds with research in the helping professions described in Chapter 3. "Indeed, of the multitude of factors that account for success in psychotherapy, clinicians of different orientations converge on this point: The therapeutic relationship is the cornerstone" (Norcross, 2010, p. 114).

If the inevitable separation with the client, student, or patient does not too severely deplete the practitioner, then he or she can attach again. But if the process drains the person, perhaps each time just a little—just as the plaque in arteries builds up little by little—then the life force, the blood flow for the counselor, therapist, teacher, or health professional, is gradually choked off. This is the caring burnout process. One could also use the analogy of a battery. The battery keeps getting energized or drained. When drained enough, there is no spark, no life.

Professional attachments and separations that deplete the practitioner, such as too many ambiguous professional losses, can lead to a subsequent inability to attach. The three subscales of the Maslach Burnout Inventory (Maslach & Jackson, 1981) seem to capture this process—emotional exhaustion, depersonalization, and lack of personal accomplishment. Okun and Kantrowitz (2008) provide a description that fits with this description of burnout:

> You may be suffering from burnout when you feel exhausted and are unable to pay attention to what someone is saying; you find yourself reacting more impatiently and intolerantly than you have in the past; your sleeping and eating habits change or you experience a new physical symptom; or you find yourself dreading the beginning of the workday and lacking enthusiasm, motivation, and interest. (p. 302)

An older reference shows that burnout has been a problem for a long time (Corey & Corey, 1989):

Continuous contact with clients who are unappreciative, upset and depressed often leads helpers to view all recipients in helping relationships in negative terms. Practitioners may care less, begin to make derogatory comments about their clients, ignore them and want to move away from them. Dehumanized responses are a core ingredient of burnout. (p. 167)

The most important point that we are making here is that the presence of losses and the absence of gains in the caring cycle of empathic attachment → active involvement → felt separation → re-creation contribute to burnout. This definition of caring burnout, as opposed to meaning burnout, is focused specifically on the most important work task in the high-touch occupations. Caring burnout is the result of a decreased ability to professionally attach with the next client, student, or patient because of the cumulative depletion and negative energy generated over many previous episodes of work between the practitioner and the client, student, or patient. We define caring burnout as disengagement of the self from the caring cycle of empathic attachment → active involvement → felt separation → re-creation. Hopefully, there are bountiful joys, rewards, and gifts of practice. It is best when the work itself, active engagement with the other, produces energy rather than depletion. When depletion occurs more than a positive effect, energy is drained from the battery. Without a spark, burnout occurs.

Both meaning burnout and caring burnout are destructive realities because the end of active engagement by the practitioner means the end of competent practice in counseling, therapy, teaching, or health work. Mediocre work can occur, but expertise in these fields needs the active engagement of the self. You ask, what is one to do about burnout? Our attempt to answer that question can be found throughout this book. We hope that you will find some answers or at least some strategies in different places in the book.

Self-Reflection Exercises

First, consider all of the different meanings of burnout discussed in this chapter.

1. Of all the different meanings of burnout, which definition speaks most directly to you?

_____

_____

_____

_____

_____

_____

_____

_____

_____

_____

2. Using your understanding of burnout, how much does this definition define you at this time? Circle the number.

1	2	3	4	5
Not at all	A little	Some	A lot	Totally

Describe the key factors in your rating.

_____

_____

_____

_____

_____

_____

_____

_____

_____

_____

Part Two

8

Balancing Caring for Others and Caring for Self

In life, it is important to first take good care of yourself. If you don't, you can't take care of others.

—**Tom Skovholt's mother, Elvera Meyer Skovholt**
(August 1994; still true, at age 93, 2002)

If I am not for myself, who will be for me, if I am only for myself, what am I, and if not now, when?

—**Hillel (As cited in Neusner, 1984, p. 32)**

Overall, we recommend that therapists do for themselves the self-nurturing, self-building things they would have their clients do. Increasing our awareness of our needs and remaining connected with our bodies, our feelings, and other people will strengthen us as individuals and allow us to choose to continue to do this important work.

—**L. A. Pearlman (1995, p. 62)**

Losing One's Innocence About the Assertive Need for Self-Care

The following describes the work of mental health practitioners in the military (Carey, Cave, and Alvarez, 2009):

Many of the patients who fill the day are bereft, angry, broken. Their experiences are gruesome, their distress lasting and the process of recovery exhausting. The repeated stories of battle and loss can leave the most professional therapist numb and angry. (p. 1)

This statement about the work of military therapists helps us see the importance of assertive self-care. Remember the career is to thrive within the deeply meaningful and valuable work of the helping, healing, teaching, and spiritual/religious professions.

The focus of the early chapters of this book is on some of the difficult elements of the work. Hopefully, with foresight, we can be forewarned. Too often in the helping fields, we focus on the immediate tasks at hand and the intense human needs before us, rather than thinking of how we must take care of ourselves if our self, the healing agent, is to thrive for the decades of our work.

In addition to realizing that the work is difficult, and often very rewarding, one should remember that helping practitioners, teachers, healers are people too, with their own lives that often contain the normal stress and strain of life during these early years of the 21st century. That often means time and money pressure, multiple-role demands, and high workplace expectations to perform. The result is often a series of stress-related problems. This can be understood by examining the results of a study (Table 8.1; Mahoney, 1997, p. 15) in which helping practitioners were asked about a variety of personal problems.

The table lists a variety of stress-related conditions, some job related, some personal-life based. When one combines the hazards of practice in Chapter 6

TABLE 8.1
Mental Health Professionals' Previous Year Personal Problems Endorsed by 20% or More of the Sample (N = 86)

Problem	Percent
Concerns about the size or severity of their caseload	48.2%
Episodes of irritability or emotional exhaustion	46.5%
Problems in their intimate relationships	41.2%
Doubts about their own therapeutic effectiveness	40.7%
Insufficient or unsatisfactory sleep	39.5%
Chronic fatigue	37.2%
Feelings of loneliness or isolation	33.7%
Episodes of anxiety	31.8%
Feelings of disillusionment about their work	27.1%
Episodes of depression	25.3%
Frequent headaches	20.9%

with personal-life stress, it is clear why there is an assertive need for practitioner self-care.

Ingredients of balancing include:

1. *An attitude of altruistic egotism*—Selye (1974), the pioneer researcher in body–mind medicine, described the helper of others as needing to also be concerned with the welfare of the self. He called for a stance of altruistic egotism. Given Selye's credibility as a pioneer of the concept of stress and its toxic effects, his ideas warrant attention. Veteran psychology practitioners J. Buchanan (personal communication, 1995) and E. Nightengale (personal communication, 1995) coined similar concepts—holy selfishness and self-attentiveness. By holy selfishness, Buchanan means that the individual must hold his or her own welfare as a holy or sacred obligation. For Nightengale, self-attentiveness means having a focus on one's needs and concern for others. Here, we are talking about an obligation in attitude that involves a constant allegiance to one's own well-being as necessary for competent other-care.

2. *Continual behavioral monitoring of one's other-care–self-care balance*—Buchanan's holy obligation to oneself is more than attitudinal. It also involves an obligation to monitor oneself and constantly be nurturing of self. Robinson (1992) describes "brownouts," episodes of forgetfulness and inattention, among helping professionals as early warning signs of insufficient self-care. Veteran helping professionals often develop personal signs indicating that they are approaching a point of danger. When the practitioner works in a highly stressful environment, this means monitoring and nourishing oneself, just as diabetics monitor their insulin levels. This describes actual behavior engaged by the practitioner to check for signs—physical, emotional, social, spiritual, and intellectual—that one's self is seriously depleted. For example, Stevanovic and Rupert (2004) studied behaviors that psychologists employ to sustain their careers and found that the second highest career sustaining behavior was maintaining balance between professional and personal lives.

Hage (2010) describes the importance of balancing self-care and care for clients in her work:

> I learned how important it was to provide a consistently caring presence with Peter to let him know I would be present with him unconditionally,

no matter what pain or hurt he shared with me. I also learned, as time progressed, that I needed to keep a certain level of emotional distance, to maintain a separate space for reflection and self-care, to be effective in my work as a counselor.

... The "lesson" and the challenge of my experience with Peter is one that I continue to deal with almost daily in my work as a teacher, mentor, researcher, and clinical supervisor. How do I truly and fully care for my students, mentees, supervisees, and their clients, while setting appropriate limits, to ensure that the work is truly empowering instead of disabling and also doesn't leave me depleted? It seems that as professional helpers we need to learn to live with the tension of this paradox-caring and simultaneously letting go. A danger is that, to avoid the tension and ambiguity of this paradox, we may turn to self-protection and project a "hard shell" with our clients and students. (p. 183)

The Need for More Self-Care at Times of Personal Crisis or Excessive Stress

Self-care is always important. At times of personal crisis or excessive stress, when ability to function well may be severely compromised, it is even more important. There are, as we all know, bountiful examples of either personal crisis or excessive stress (e.g., the serious injury of one's child, a sudden loss of family income, a major geographic move, the death of one's parent, the emergence of a chronic disease for oneself, the loss of one's intimate partner, destruction of one's property because of the force of nature). Following are two examples of a serious family illness that have had an impact on the practitioner. First, Schorr (1997) discusses how the personal crisis affected his ability to listen to his counseling clients:

> In my sessions with clients, there would be frequent reminders of our black cloud [my wife's diagnosis of leukemia]. One man complained about a woman he knew—she was weird but that was because she had cancer. Another client had a son who killed himself after he was diagnosed with leukemia. Another came in numb with grief over the recent cancer death of a housemate. When clients would tell stories in which the mention of disease was a minor note, I had to restrain myself from asking questions merely to satisfy my own insecurity. Or to let my mind drift off into worrisome tangents. (p. 57)

Pollack (1988) describes her own experience as a person in the caring professions who experienced extreme stress*:

> The timing was right when I entered graduate school. The youngest of my three children had reached age 10, my husband's career was stable, and I was 37 and ready for a new challenge. I was going to explore my long-time goal of working with adults, with an emphasis on older adults. Two years later, during my spring break, I found myself facing the severest challenge of my life. At first we thought it was the altitude of the Colorado ski resort that was making my husband ... ill. When the doctor said it was colon cancer we were totally shocked. ...
>
> Immediate surgery provided temporary relief. Although we were far away from family and friends, the hospital had become like a cocoon, with its kind and caring staff. I felt a sense of terror when we left. Back at home in Maryland, I felt nearly unbearable anxiety while waiting for the results of further surgery. I will never forget my feeling of devastation when the surgeon told us the cancer had metastasized and the prognosis was poor.
>
> The next 11 months were an emotional roller coaster. Why him? Why me? I felt shock, sadness, and disbelief. I was angry at the doctors who took away our hope, joyful during experimental treatments that shrank the tumor, distressed at the appearance of another malignancy, happy with his recovery from the second surgery, depressed as it became clear that it was only temporary, encouraged by the good days, cheered by the jokes we shared about the situation, and distraught at my impending loss. ...
>
> As his condition worsened, I tried to prepare the children, urging them to read books about death and to talk with us. ... My grieving started long before his death. Never before did I realize the strength I had. Indeed, I had never before been put to the test.
>
> ... As I look back and reexamine my experience in facing his death, I am keenly aware of what helped me to integrate it, of what may similarly help my clients to come through devastating transitions successfully. According to the Transition Model (Schlossberg, 1984), there are three components in how one copes with any transition: the situation, the environment, and oneself. All of these contributed to my understanding of what I was going through and my eventual adaptation. In terms of the situation, I knew what it meant to be an "off-time" or early widow. There were no rules or role models, no one to guide me, and no one who would understand my feelings at a gut level. Consequently, I learned to become more self-reliant, independent, and capable of making decisions.

---

*Reprinted from *Journal of Counseling and Development*, 67, page 117. Copyright © ACA. Reprinted with permission. No further reproduction authorized without written permission of the American Counseling Association.

Not only was the transition off-time, but it was unanticipated and outside my control, so there was a high degree of stress. This was balanced by an environment of tremendous social support from family, friends, and my department at the university. I could not have survived without the constant telephone calls, concern, and continuous offers of help. I was surprised at my initiative in creating a support group of single women to share common concerns.

In terms of myself, I discovered that I used many coping strategies. Giving in to my sad feelings helped me get through them. I jogged every day, which helped me reduce the stress. I talked to myself, reassuring myself that things would get better and that I could handle the situation. I also talked to trusted others and learned it was more helpful to be listened to than rescued. The emotional pain made the world look gray and bleak, but I felt that the pain lifted, and with it, my spirit, when I was able to have a sense of humor. Although not changing anything, it did provide temporary relief. The process took time; there were many setbacks. I discovered that there is no "best" coping strategy that works in all situations, but no matter how difficult the situation, I will eventually find a way to cope with it.

By working through my own loss I feel better able to help others, particularly the elderly population, for whom loss is a common theme. Facing death has enabled me to grieve, to learn, to grow, and to be a better counselor. (p. 117)

For short periods of time, one just tries to hold on and get through it. For example, an intern was trying to hold on for 3 more months before she could leave her internship in a distant city and return home. At the time, though, she was coping with the stress of a major geographical move, the sudden death of her brother in a traffic accident, and an inadequate internship stipend, as well as the demands to perform at a high level to meet the expectations of internship supervisors.

The balancing equation can be especially precarious in times of extreme stress. How do we do adequate self-care during these disequilibrium periods, these times of exhaustion, pain, despair, and disquiet? A short answer to a difficult question is that we must continue self-care but do so at an accelerated pace.

Codependency and Self-Care

When considering how a practitioner might balance self-care and other care, the term *codependency* is helpful for counselors, therapists, teachers, and health professionals in pointing out factors in excessive self-sacrifice. It is also a concept that should be used sparingly because much of the self-sacrifice and giving in the caring professions is central to the work, helpful to others, and meaningful to the giver.

Helping professionals at risk for excessive codependency-type behaviors would do well to address the short-term seduction and long-term destruction of an excessive other-care orientation. A core aspect of the term *codependency* is an abandonment of self, and this ultimately has severe implications. Abandonment of self, however, like all strong seductions, can have great appeal. The appeal is often in avoidance of the self and its own growth. There may be unresolved grief, strong ambivalence, or great risks that are avoided through abandonment of the self. It can draw one in like a strong magnet.

Severe codependency, as abandonment of self, is a behavior that should be a warning to high-touch practitioners. Years ago, Tom worked with a client. After her husband was killed, she totally invested herself in her children. After a long period, she stopped running, faced the reality of her grief, and started the healing and moving on process. Yet, for us helpers, running from ourselves and our needs can be a temptation because denial of reality can solve short-term problems. Helldorfer (as cited in Robinson, 1992) describes the clergy, a helping profession, as composed of many individuals engaged in such "addictive caring."

Women writing about women's lives often describe female socialization as focused on an "ethic of care" and nurturing human life, with concern for others as a strong value. This is a major theme of Gilligan's *In a Different Voice* (1982), Ruddick's *Maternal Thinking* (1989), and Chodorow in *The Reproduction of Mothering* (1978). Montagu (1974) expressed a similar sentiment in *The Natural Superiority of Women*. This ethic of care may be a very positive trait. After all, how can helping professionals not endorse it? But it may also produce extra risk for a high other-care, low self-care focus among those who are oriented this way by the three elements of personality, gender, and membership in a helping profession (e.g., females who are elementary or secondary teachers, social workers, nurses, rehabilitation counselors, psychotherapists, or physical therapists).

The opposite option, too little other-care and too much self-care, also tips the balance. Although understandable, self-absorption carried to an excessive level is also out of balance. To abandon clients, to meet only our needs, to do excessive self-protection, to listen to their struggles and solutions and apply them to us and our problems, or to use the "hard side of the turtle" to avoid involvement, is excessive self-care. We can listen to client, student, or patient concerns—their struggles and strategies—and use them excessively to bring us back to our own lives. For example, a client loses a job and reacts to it with disbelief and inaction. We say to ourselves that we would handle the situation better if it happens to us. We use the client's behavior to focus on our own well-being. Without knowing it, we are focusing on ourselves.

The ability to naturally turn one's focus onto the other is, we must remember, a wonderful attribute for those we serve. The opposite focus for counselors, therapists, teachers, and health professionals—self-care at the expense of other-care—is potentially unethical and destructive to the well-being of the often vulnerable individuals who we help. Unethical, exploitive helping professionals are often focused on the needs of the self. One example comes from the encounter groups of previous decades where charismatic, self-focused leaders often produced deterioration in group members (Lieberman et al., 1973). A second example comes from the unethical, exploitive therapists who violate professional boundaries to satisfy personal needs (Pope & Vasquez, 1991).

Psychological Wellness as an Ethical Imperative

Barnett, Baker, Elman, and Schoener (2007) describe ongoing self-care to promote psychological wellness as an ethical imperative for psychologists. They emphasize that self-care is important both for our personal lives and as an essential ingredient for our work as practitioners. When the practitioner is not mindful of the consistent need for self-care, other-care, in the form of professional helping may suffer. Barnett, Johnston, and Hillard (2006) assert, "Self-care is not an indulgence. It is an essential component of prevention of distress, burnout, and impairment. It should not be considered as something 'extra' or 'nice to do if you have the time' but as an essential part of our professional identities" (p. 263).

Self-Reflection Exercises

One of the themes of this chapter and, in fact, the whole book is the need both to lose one's innocence about the grinding nature of the work and to actively practice resiliency development. We use the term *innocence* to describe the belief by practitioners that they can escape either insidious or overt burnout effects without active prevention efforts. Let us ask you: How is your practitioner innocence quotient, your PIQ? How do you react to this idea that actively practicing resiliency development is important?

_____

_____

_____

_____

_____

_____

_____

_____

_____

_____

9

Sustaining the Professional Self

When you open your life to the living [your clients, students, or patients], all things come spilling in on you, and you're flowing like a river, the changer and the changed … it's an endless waterfall, like the rain falling on the ground, all around.

—C. Williamson (1975, side 1, track 1)

I am grateful to have the opportunity to hear my clients' stories and learn from them. I look forward to having more clients to smile about, squirm about, and wonder about.

—S. Chambers (2009, personal communication)

Sustained by Meaningful Work

Occupation is essential.

—V. Woolf (1990, p. 503)

The only ones among you who will be really happy are those who have sought and found how to serve.

—A. Schweitzer (1975, p. 87)

Do all the good you can,
By all the means you can,
In all the ways you can,
In all the places you can,
At all the times you can,

To all the people you can,
As long as ever you can.

—John Wesley (Oxford Dictionary, 1979, p. 568)

Practitioners often choose their work because they perceive it to be of great value. The work to benefit other members of the species *Homo sapiens* can provide enormous meaning and purpose. You may remember the George Bernard Shaw quotation earlier in this book: "This is the true joy in life, the being used for a purpose recognized by yourself as a mighty one; … the being a force of Nature instead of a feverish selfish little clod of ailments and grievances" (as cited in Larson, 1993, p. 2).

Tom knows a remarkable public school teacher whose work is infused with meaning. Coming from a home with a shaky foundation, she received needed transfusions from teachers during the difficult hinge days between childhood and adolescence. Now, with great energy, enthusiasm, and competence, she helps young people. Her work, of great help to them, is rich in purpose and meaning for her. This inoculates her from burnout. All win.

The sense of purpose and meaning is most at risk when, for example, a caseworker senses that her work accomplishes little good and that her clients are caught in destructive, bureaucratic systems. It is when the counseling, therapy, teaching, or healing seems to have little effect that we reach despair because our *raison d'etre* for choosing this work—to make a difference in human life—is threatened. We call this meaning burnout.

The problem is not the choice of the work itself, like it is with some other jobs. We could all name occupations that do little to further the development of our species and others that are very destructive to human life. That is not true of our work; at least, it is not true of our intentions. We are trying to make the world a better place, each in our own small way (e.g., to ease the physical pain of a postsurgery patient, to provide safety to mothers and children in a shelter, to reduce the anxiety of a college freshman away from home for the first time, to assist in reducing the shock of sudden joblessness). This means that the search for meaning and purpose in life, such a major life crisis for so many individuals at this time in history, can be less of a crisis for us because our work intrinsically gives us meaning.

For some practitioners, formal religion offers a rich structure of beliefs that provide meaning and purpose and help them confront mortality with answers and assurance. For many others, formal religion seems not to offer assurance or answers for the larger life dilemmas. In either case, we are suggesting that our work can provide meaning because we often sought this work to make a difference. Victor Frankl, in *Man's Search for Meaning* (1946/1959), addresses this concern, as do many powerful existential writers such as Rollo May, Paul Tillich, Soren Kierkegaard, Irving Yalom, Albert Camus, and Jean-Paul Sartre. Ernest Becker has produced one of the most impactful books of the last half-century in its focus on the meaning and meaninglessness in modern life. In *The Denial of Death,* Becker (1973) suggests that we, as a species, spend an enormous amount of time and energy in denial of our own mortality.

Many of us know stories of individuals who, in later life, radically changed their life's work to engage either professionally or as a volunteer in work that nurtures human life. The search here is often for more meaning or purpose and is an attempt to tie oneself more directly to the species and its survival. It is a kind of immortality, an identification with our species' history or future and is analogous to the way that grandparents partake in the future through the lives of their grandchildren.

As practitioners, our crisis of meaning burnout concerns the sense that we are not being very effective. If we can feel effective, we can obtain the kind of meaning that can offer great sustenance to the self. For the sustenance of the self, therefore, we must find a way in our counseling, therapy, teaching, healing, or religious occupations to feel that we are succeeding, even if it is in very small ways.

Maximizing the Experience of Professional Success

> One generation plants the tree, another gets the shade.
>
> **—C. Warner (1992, p. 301)**

> Having an impact ... is crucial to [practitioner] career satisfaction. Jobs that allow active, skillful involvement that produce tangible results are inherently sustaining and rewarding. ... Constant giving in a one-way relationship, without feedback or perceived success, is hard on anybody. ... Unrealistic expectations may be especially manifested in terms of expectations of client growth. The same urge to help and to be seen as helpful that propels many into the therapeutic professions often fosters grandiose notions of completely turning people's lives around.
>
> **—W. N. Grosch and D. C. Olsen (1994, pp. 8, 15, 16)**

What is success in the helping professions, education, and the healing arts? How can we judge our success? We discussed this problem earlier. Here, we are suggesting a perspective that attempts to reduce practitioner stress. There are four different aspects of professional functioning: the changes for the client, student, or patient; external recognition by supervisors, work peers, and others; expert knowledge content; and the professional relationship processes (see Table 9.1). We tend to focus on the first one, whether the person we are helping gets better (e.g., learns more, walks better, is less shy). Our validation of professional competence and self-worth seems to come mostly from this dimension. Because our whole reason for professional functioning is to be helpful, the usefulness of our efforts naturally seems most valid. It is the recipient of our help—the client, the student, the patient—to whom we relate most closely and who also can judge our work. Does not the patient of the physical therapist have the most contact and an investment in judging the professional's efforts? Yet, this is the dimension over which we have the least control. This is an important point.

Students in graduate programs in the caring professions are admitted because they have been very hard working and very successful in their own efforts. The formula is: Success comes from my efforts to push me to succeed. Now, however in practice, success is tied to another person and their efforts. This person is the client, student, patient, or parishioner. We do not control the life of another person. How frightening if the practitioner could do this. So to judge our success by this dimension of client outcome alone is potentially damaging to long-term sustenance of the professional self. In addition, success is so hard to judge. The client, student, or patient may take in the practitioner's help, but like the inside of a dry sponge on water, the absorbed help may go undetected, unexpressed, or unappreciated.

We often choose our supervisors with as much freedom as we choose our parents. Sometimes we are lucky, sometimes not so lucky. Peers too are a

TABLE 9.1
How Much Can the Practitioner Control the Outcome in These Dimensions?

Caring Dimension	Control
Client, student, or patient positive change and/or appreciation	Limited
Supervisor or work peers' support and/or appreciation	Limited
Expert knowledge	Yes
Quality of working alliance; the relationship with client, student, or patient	Yes

mixed bag. They can be friends who give much, but they can also be fierce competition in an arena where jealousy is exchanged more often than support. Excessively tying one's own sense of professional success to any of these external sources—client, supervisor, peer—can make us feel out of control, which can help produce high levels of job stress.

In contrast, we can control two other dimensions: our professional expertise and the quality of our involvement in the relationship process with the recipients. Professional expertise means knowing about our field and keeping up to date on theories, techniques, methods, research, and strategies. All counseling, therapy, teaching, and health fields continue to explode in knowledge. Although hard work, growing intellectually and in professional knowledge is something we can do.

Of equal importance is the relationship, the working alliance, that we create with those that we serve. It is important for us to be fully present with the other in the counseling, therapy, teaching, and healing process. Do we understand the process of involvement in these kinds of relationships, and are we able to be fully involved? This is an extremely important dimension of professional functioning. It is also, as we described in Chapter 3 (Castonguay et al., 2006; Strauss et al., 2006), a key to practitioner success in professional relationships.

For two of the four dimensions (expertise and process), our efforts dictate our success. We can, therefore, have some control over our work and derive some satisfaction from it. For example, when teaching a college psychology course to prison inmates, Tom worked on the subject matter, his teaching style, and his relationship skills with the students. It would have been a setup for professional discouragement if he had expected the inmates as students to write excellent papers, do very well on the tests, or praise Tom as a teacher. Tom looked for small gains for them and expected little positive feedback. However, he did work to be prepared and teach well. Using this approach, the course went well, and he remains excited and pleased about this teaching experience.

The student may fail; the patient may die; the client may continue with substance abuse. We may be distressed by these results, but we must continually reflect about the other two dimensions, relationship and expert knowledge: Did I do the relationship work well? Was I professionally attached and involved? Was my knowledge base sufficient?

Sometimes we get external recognition. Savoring it at the moment can be important for long-term professional vitality. We usually use the term *savor* when discussing food. It means to linger over the food—to enjoy the taste, the smell, the texture—before it is gone. The savoring process gets missed in the mad rush of fast eating. So, too, we practitioners sometimes go madly from one occupational responsibility to another, rushing from one thing to the next without savoring the success.

We have learned, over time, how transitory the moments of satisfaction with our work can be, in part because, at its heart, it often involves the professional–attachment–separation process that has, by the nature of the work, few concrete and permanent results (e.g., the 12th-grade English class goes very well but ends and that same class will never be together again; the cardiac rehabilitation patient completes the program and returns home; the displaced worker no longer needs job assistance and emotional support after finding a new job).

Like all other practitioners in the caring professions, Tom remembers struggling for a long time while trying to become an adequate practitioner. Just in terms of his teaching role, there were many stress-filled hours. He described this in an article, "Learning to Teach":

> I was driving down the freeway from Missouri to Florida, with spouse and baby girl next to me in the Ryder rental truck. Soon I would begin working as an assistant professor at the University of Florida with a split faculty/psychologist position. One thought kept recurring: "How will I be able to teach? I've received no formal training in the art and science of teaching." … [W]here was the training to be a professor? I thought of my sister, an elementary teacher in Minnesota, who had received extensive training before beginning to teach. My mind wandered off to other occupations—hairstylist, airplane pilot, bricklayer, surgeon. Did any of these professions let loose their new graduates without any practical training? How was it, then, that I had received no systematic, organized instruction in teaching?
>
> After days of daydreams and driving, I reached Gainesville, and the academic year began. I spent the first year on a do-it-yourself training program. … My self-training was deficient. … There was no systematic, organized sequence of learning experiences and no feedback from experienced master teachers. … In those first years of teaching, traumas and disillusionment coexisted with a few victories. (Skovholt, 1986, p. 8)

There are many factors that impinge on the recipient's reaction to our practitioner attempts. Once Tom took a time management course. It was difficult for him to really appreciate the instructor's efforts because he was frustrated by all the time demands in life. He felt very strongly that he didn't need time management; he needed more time, less to do, or a culture in which human life was not defined by time-obsessed schedules. None of these were possible.

Only time management was an option, and the instructor did his job. But Tom's evaluation of the course and instructor expressed his frustration with the bigger picture of the rat race and, in that sense, was unfair to the instructor. If he judged his success by Tom's reaction, he would be disappointed. As another example, one time in a mediation situation, one of our colleagues was pleased by the work of the mediator but was too exhausted by the conflict and loss that was mediated to be appreciative. If the mediator depended on our colleague's reaction for validation, she would be disappointed and depleted. Do patients in the recovery room, coming out of anesthesia after surgery, ever really express their appreciation for the gentle, expert care that they receive? Probably not. They are confronting their own disorientation and discomfort and are concerned with little else. If the recovery room nurse judges her success by the appreciation of her patients, will she not soon be discouraged by her professional efforts? If she attempts to receive most of her personal self-esteem validation this way, will these relationships sustain her? And what if the high school teacher relies heavily on student reactions for her self-esteem?

It is important to add that results do matter in the age of accountability, outcome standards, and managed care. But they have always mattered. Here, we are addressing the intensity of this dimension for practitioner long-term vitality. In the dimension of our efforts related to client, student, or patient outcome, it is important to match our expectations to the possibility of positive change.

Avoid the Grandiosity Impulse and Relish Small "I Made a Difference" Victories

When considering results, watching one's expectations can be useful. Sometimes if we expect less in terms of client, student, or patient gains, we can be more satisfied. We do not mean becoming lazy or accepting mediocrity. It can be a paradoxical task. Helping professionals often want so much to help that they get caught up in wanting to make a big difference for many people. Sometimes pushing for big changes actually empowers the client's ambivalence about change and makes improvement less possible. Reduced expectations and focusing on small changes can be more empowering for all—the client, student, or patient and the practitioner's self-care.

Think Long Term

Professional development is a long-term process (see Chapter 4). From the expertise literature of Chi, Glaser, and Farr (1988), Ericcson, Prietula, and Cokely (2007), and Ericcson, Charness, Feltovich, and Hoffman (2006), we know that it takes thousands of hours to develop high-level skill in a complex human craft such as counseling and therapy, high school teaching, or nursing. Breaking down big educational and career steps into small steps is a well-used personal method and motivational strategy; however, considering the long haul is also important. In the wilderness of northern Minnesota, some canoeists start paddling hard in the first hour of the first day. How about the next 5 hours? The next day of another 6 hours of paddling and the day after that and the day after that? Practitioners work 30 to 40 years. Thinking long-term and building professional and personal self-care into this decades-long adventure can change one's perspective and approach. Think of the toddler learning to walk; it is a process, an adventure of attempts, feedback, and more attempts. In time, with experience, the toddler walks and then runs.

Creating and Sustaining an Active, Individually Designed Development Method

To stay alive, one must eat. To stay alive and grow professionally, one must eat voraciously and then digest the new professional food. Not eating or "throwing up" the food—that is, denying it or distorting work-related feedback—can lead to stagnation and pseudodevelopment (Rønnestad & Skovholt, 2003). We discuss this topic here and in Chapter 4.

In contrast to college and university training in which we are told how to develop through class requirements, as practitioners after school we are now in charge of our own development. The use of continuing education credits in many fields is an attempt to ensure development, but the requirement of going to classes reflects an earlier, less developed approach. Highly functioning senior practitioners keep the learning process going over the long run but vary in their development methods (Rønnestad & Skovholt, 2003).

One key element is an openness to new information and to feedback about one's performance. This entails a nondefensive stance, as in Rogers's (1961) description of the fully functioning person and Maslow's (1968) self-actualized personality structure. In both descriptions openness and perceptual accuracy are key. When the individual must distort information or shuts off new information, then development is stifled. This is a reason why experience alone does not seem to increase expertise. We have all met experienced veterans in our field who are seemingly less skilled than newer practitioners. One reason is that the veteran is not growing from the increased experience.

Aside from openness, one must continually feed oneself with data from practice and from the bigger world of ideas and theories. One high functioning practitioner in our community reads five books at once; another works collaboratively with four other practitioners on different projects to keep developing. Both of these senior practitioners are voraciously feeding themselves professionally with new content, new ideas, and new alternatives that they add, modify, and shed with their ongoing professional working method. Highly respected by their professional peers, each has a finely tuned, individually designed development process.

Last, professional reflection as a catalyst for one's development is important. Reflection has recently received much attention as a key developmental process in the professional growth of counselors, therapists, teachers, and health practitioners. Swanson (2010) discusses the use of reflective practice with teachers, while Freshwater and Johns (2005) discuss its use in the nursing field, and Mann, Gordon, and MacLeod (2009) review the literature related to reflective practice in health professional education. Neufeldt and colleagues (1996) identify key elements of the process as starting with an initial problem or point where the individual is puzzled and unsure. The individual's personal and cognitive flexibility, plus a supportive work environment, furthers the reflection process, which is guided by a search for understanding. They write:

> The intent to understand what has occurred, active inquiry, openness to that understanding and vulnerability and risk-taking rather than defensive self-protection, characterize the stance. ... To contribute to further development, reflections are profound rather than superficial, and are meaningful. (p. 8)

The end point, using one's experience and theory, is professional improvement as a practitioner. Benner and Wrubel (1982) describe elements of this process when they say:

> Experience is necessary for moving from one level of expertise to another, but experience is not the equivalent of longevity, seniority, or

the simple passage of time. Experience means living through actual situations in such a way that it informs the practitioner's perception and understanding of all subsequent situations. (p. 28)

These viewpoints are similar to our own three-part view of this essential process for professional development—professional and personal experience; an open, supportive work environment; and a reflective stance. Receiving uncensored performance feedback and ideas from other sources, being open to it, and taking time for it are essential elements of reflection as a developmental process. The closing off or distorting of feedback, with little time given to it, along with an absence of reflection, provides elements for professional stagnation (Rønnestad & Skovholt, 2003).

It may be that the spacious campuses of American colleges and universities, the benches and the grass, serve the serious, intellectual reflective function. After class, these environments encourage students to ponder, wonder about, consider, discuss, and contemplate the content of the past class. This is important because the opposite—experience without reflection—does not produce the same amount of professional growth. The requirement that professional psychology doctoral interns spend at least 25% of their time on direct clinical work, rather than 50% or 75%, represents this stance; professional development entails more than just direct experience ("Internship and Postdoctoral Programs in Professional–Psychology" [Association of Psychology Postdoctoral and Internship Centers, 2010]).

The reflective process is stunted in work environments in human services, education, and health where productivity is measured by volume, and practitioners are kept continually busy and, by necessity, practice in a hectic, repetitive style. The problem is that repetitive practice alone tends to produce the same behaviors, cognitions, and affective reactions, rather than creative professional growth and improved work by the practitioner. There is little evidence that experience alone produces expertise.

Professional Self-Understanding

As important as methods may be, the most practical thing we can achieve in any kind of work is insight into what is happening inside us as we do it. The more familiar we are with our inner terrain, the more sure footed our [work]—and living—becomes.

—P. J. Palmer (1998, p. 5)

Finding healthy ways of maintaining a strong sense of self is a prerequisite for effective functioning as a professional helper.

—W. N. Grosch & D. C. Olsen (1994, p. 31)

Self-awareness is a strongly emphasized value in a variety of high-touch
professions. The psychotherapy professions have especially endorsed one's
own counseling and therapy as a method to develop self-awareness and
increase personal maturity as a way to make one's professional work more
effective. Other helping professions often include training experiences in
self-development as part of the education of helping professionals. Grosch
and Olsen (1994) provide a valuable discussion on the personal background
of helping professionals. For example, they make a surprising declaration
when they say:

> The great paradox revealed by professional burnout is that, although
> helping others can and should be a way to transcend ourselves, many
> of us embark on helping careers not out of a genuine concern for others
> but rather out of a need to be appreciated by them. (p. 170)

Using the work of self psychologist Kohut and family theorist Bowen, Grosch,
and Olsen (1994) suggest that family of origin roles are instrumental in the
excessive needs that some helpers bring as adults into their professional work:

> In dysfunctional families, boundaries may be absent or violated; in fact,
> parent–child roles are often reversed. Rather than receiving the mirror-
> ing [validation] they desperately need for the formation of healthy and
> cohesive selves, children wind up needing to provide mirroring for their
> parents. (p. 93)

Grosch and Olsen (1994) point out that many individuals attracted to
the helping professions received validation and admiration for their helping
attempts early in life. They suggest that these attempts may have occurred
in families in which the helper, as a young person, took on the role of an
adult, perhaps in a highly stressed family, and received this validation rather
than in the normal mirroring and admiration of healthy child and adolescent
development described in self psychology theory (Kohut). If the person then,
as an adult, enters one of the helping professions, the style may continue.

The person enters an occupation in which caring for others is a primary
role. The individual already knows how to care for others—listening, putting
the other's needs first, nurturing the other. These skills are sometimes hard
for others who are not socialized this way, but the helper cannot be sustained

over the long run just by validation from recipients. If the individual centers his or her life on caring for others and does not develop other, more balanced interpersonal relationships, that is, relationships in which the individual is not the giver but also the receiver, then the benefits from the helping role are the only source of the individual's sustenance. This source of sustenance, however, is limited because the client, student, or patient does not have a primary obligation to care for the helper and meet his or her needs. Ethical violations, in fact, occur when the helper's needs become primary in the relationship. In addition, the recipient is often not in a place to help the other because he or she is too distressed to focus on the other.

The essential point here is this: When the child does not receive developmentally appropriate validation from significant adults, the self develops in a different way, seeking self-worth through pleasing, supporting, and understanding others. This need for admiration is then sought in adult work by working extra hard to help others. This deep longing for appreciation is so often thwarted, of course, because the client, student, or patient role is not designed to meet the basic self-esteem needs of the professional helper. For those who need admiration, approval, and validation from clients, students, or patients, the situation is quite precarious. Consequently, "when we do not understand and deal with our craving for admiration and need to be seen in given ways, we tend to get angry and resentful" (Grosch & Olsen, 1994, p. 119). These authors suggest that Bowen's concept of differentiation is useful in suggesting how we need to learn to separate our own sense of self and its basic needs from the professional attachments we make with those we serve. Understanding this family of origin dynamic can be important for understanding unrealistic work expectations and preventing emotional depletion.

Berry (1988) uses the terms *messiah* and the *messiah trap* to describe the extreme helping of others as a defensive interpersonal type. Although this messiah idea may be simplistic, Berry does touch on some important ideas, such as family-of-origin roots and expressions of this style in pleasing, rescuing, counseling, and teaching. She described her own awakening as: "I thought I was doing the 'right' thing by helping people. But by helping others, I avoided being intimate with them. We [other helpers and I] were much more comfortable helping than we were asking for help" (p. x). (See Figure 9.1.)

A related area in which professional self-understanding is important concerns attachment. Within developmental psychology, attachment theory is now widely used to understand, explain, and predict interpersonal relationships, such as success at intimacy. One of the premises of this work, which is now being extended to other relationships such as work collaboration, is

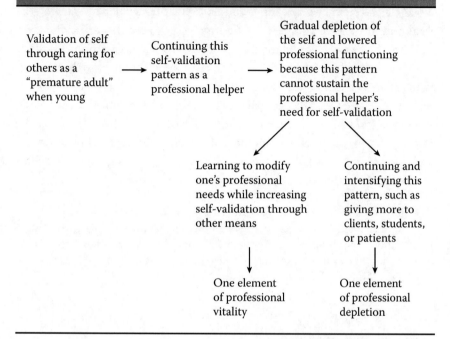

FIGURE 9.1
Possible Outcomes From an Excessive Focus on Helping Others.

Validation of self through caring for others as a "premature adult" when young → Continuing this self-validation pattern as a professional helper → Gradual depletion of the self and lowered professional functioning because this pattern cannot sustain the professional helper's need for self-validation

Learning to modify one's professional needs while increasing self-validation through other means

Continuing and intensifying this pattern, such as giving more to clients, students, or patients

One element of professional vitality

One element of professional depletion

that past relationship patterns have an impact on present relationships. For example, Bachelor and Horvath (1999) summarize the therapist attachment research to suggest that "therapists tend to re-create earlier interpersonal patterns in the therapy relationship and treat clients accordingly" (p. 158).

This research is very important for the caring professions because the important common factor in the high-touch fields is the caring cycle of empathic attachment → active involvement → felt separation → re-creation. If the practitioner has a poor personal history of attachments, the chance of doing good work is at risk. This is another reason for professional self-understanding.

Creating a Professional Greenhouse at Work

No man is an island.

—**J. Donne (1975, p. 87)**

The work is hard. We are constantly asked to increase human competence in areas such as social skills, learning, and health. A stressful work environment can make it even harder. As we discussed in Chapter 7, Maslach and Leiter (1997) make a strong case for organizational factors as the key to burnout. We agree; however, we also urge you as a practitioner not to wait for the organization to serve your needs. We urge you to actively create your own greenhouse at work. A greenhouse, as you know, is an environment where many factors—temperature, soil, and water—are ideal for growth. Five elements seem to create a greenhouse effect at work: leadership that promotes a healthy other-care vs. self-care balance, social support from peers, receiving other-care from mentors, mentoring others, and having fun. These can be hard to find in any work environment. It would be great if all practitioners could describe their work environment like speech pathologist Carole Sellars who works with children who have disabilities. She said:

> It's absolutely the most wonderful place to work. It's spiritually reward-ing and mentally rewarding. I bet I laugh more on my job than anyone I know. The children and families with whom I work have literally sto-len my heart out of my chest. I'll never have a vacancy in my depart-ment. Once you're here, you're here. (Majeski, 1996, p. 5A)

Leadership That Promotes Balance Between Caring for Others and the Self

We pay leaders more because they have the power to create a tone, vision, and direction in an organization. Let's hope that the leader has a symbolic sign that says, "Here, we care for the clients, students, and patients and also the practitioners." Such leadership makes a difference.

Professional Social Support

Many practitioners are social people by nature, and they seek out others. Within the social support research literature, Mallinckrodt and Bennett (1992) found that social support from others can be a stress reducer. The support of one's colleagues can be quite powerful in reducing distress emo-tions such as depression and anxiety. The same principle holds for high-touch practitioners. When we can talk with our colleagues openly and honestly about our work, then the "universality of experience effect," a curative fac-tor in groups (Yalom & Leszcz, 2005), can be a powerful force for our own professional vitality.

One source of self-care is the organizational and group atmosphere at work. Johnson (1994, personal communication), a graduate student in the helping professions, said:

> At my practicum site, I experienced and observed terrific support among staff members. This helped me feel as though I was a significant contributor and was a strong source of professional and emotional support. Through this experience, I better understand that this support is vital in the helping business in order to give the helper a sense that he or she is not alone, a feeling that can occur in this line of work where results are frequently hard to measure. (p. 8)

Another source consists of good work friendships in which one can engage in giving and taking equally with another coworker. These friendships, as we all know, can be rich just in themselves.

Receiving Other-Care From Mentors, Supervisors, or Bosses

The mentoring literature has, of course, developed because of the power of these relationships. Levinson, Darrow, Klein, Levinson, and McKee (1978) describe the power of mentors in men's lives, just as Kram (1985) describes the importance of mentoring in women's lives.

Being Nurtured From Our Work as Mentors, Supervisors, or Managers

The act of mentoring, supervising, and managing others can be very positive in one's own self-care and professional development. For example, a psychologist in his 70s supervising new interns said, "They get brighter all the time. I feel that I learn as much from the interns as I teach them. They have become my teacher" (Skovholt & Rønnestad, 1995, p. 92).

At Work, Learning How to Be Professional and Playful, Have Fun, Tell Jokes, and Laugh

We need to pump positive emotions into a negative emotions environment. One individual approached this task in the following way:

> I continue to try to find ways to make myself laugh and to do small fun things as a way to release tension and to feel more energized. Laughing seems to have a physiological effect. I can feel sad and begin to laugh,

and the tension in my chest dissipates. I like to hear humorous stories from people's lives, I like to tease people and sometimes I like to
be teased. I also keep toys at work to entertain me. I have a rainbow
colored slinky that a friend gave me. I keep it on my desk. The colors
are fun and the slow, rhythmic sound it makes when I play with it is
relaxing. I also have Play-Doh in my desk drawer. I use it in class as
part of a topic on creativity and critical thinking. However, it also is
fun to play with in my spare time. I find that kneading Play-Doh when
I am tense can help relax me. (S. Renninger, personal communication,
February 1995)

Another did it this way:

She kept a tin noisemaker in her pocket, and two or three times a
day, when no clients were around, she'd take it out and make a silly
little "cricket" sound with it. Finally, curiosity got the best of me, and
I asked her about it. "My biggest fault is seriousness," she said, "I need
to remember that there's fun in the world, too. So I take out my little
cricket and give it a couple of clicks, and it always makes me laugh."
(Help for Helpers, 1989, p. 147)

Using Professional Venting and Expressive Writing to Release Distress Emotions

Venting is cathartic, which is an old word out of the psychodynamic tradition. It describes the usefulness of talking about feelings. Professionals in
the caring professions know that human feelings are powerful. They are not
surprised by the study findings that expressive writing, specifically expressing feelings and thoughts about an emotionally impactful experience, can
change a person's mental and physical health (Frattaroli, 2006). In a scien-
tific way, they found what people already know and do. It is called venting, a
wonderfully descriptive term for the process by which people use words and
nonverbal communication to let go of distressing emotions. Venting means,
by analogy, to let the air take away one's emotional distress, as through
a vent.

Professional venting and expressive writing can be especially important
for practitioners who attempt to help people in the human services, education, or health care. Practitioners hear stories of distress. They need to motivate individuals for change when internal motivation is limited, and they

often work in an environment of loss, anxiety, and pain. At work, counselors, therapists, teachers, and health professionals live in an ocean of distress emotions. Their willingness to work in this ocean is a big part of why they get paid.

Let us give you an example. One practitioner told of her job as an employment counselor for the unemployed. She worked for a government agency with a mandate to help clients move from being unemployed to employed. She described the work as very frustrating because of low client motivation. She said that she was "saved" because she could vent to colleagues about the frustration of being unable to reach her clients.

We are describing venting and expressive writing as positive professional methods that help the practitioner stay in the work and continue with intense involvement within the caring cycle. We are endorsing professional venting as a method of helping people do better work. This contrasts sharply with chronic complaining and negativity, which often have long-term negative consequences for practitioners, their colleagues, and the organizational climate. Professional venting improves work functioning; chronic complaining and negativity do the opposite. Negativity weakens one's ability to be hopeful for clients, students, and patients; offering hope is an important element of the practitioner's work.

The "Good Enough Practitioner"

In workshops, presentations, and classes, during the ten years after the 2001 publication of this book, the "Good Enough Practitioner" idea has produced considerable discussion and debate among practitioners. Some people really like the idea, while others dislike it. Those who like it are often responding to their own physical, emotional, and spiritual exhaustion. Those who do not like the idea think of it as an excuse for doing shoddy work that is harmful to those who should be helped. What do you think as you read this?

Practitioners are often afraid of underperformance and want very much to perform at the 100% level, 100% of the time. This is impossible, however, and can lead to the dead end experienced by an elementary school principal who told Tom, "I had to quit after 10 years because after I gave and gave and gave, there was nothing left." Now, after 5 years in moratorium and recovery, she is again trying to do the job, afraid of both underperformance and overperformance.

Some years ago, in a formal mentoring program for new professors, Tom began to talk with these new, untenured assistant professors about avoiding maladaptive perfectionism as a teacher. Essentially, these five new assistant professors in music, chemistry, statistics, business, and history—talented, energetic, conscientious individuals—were facing an impossible job. The life of a university professor has no boundaries. There is always much more to do in the domains of the work: teaching; scholarship and research; and service to the university, one's profession, and the community. In addition, the tenure decision clock begins on appointment, and 6 years later, one either has a job or is fired.

Tom's job as a mentor was to help these new faculty members with their teaching in the context of their larger job that is, by its nature, overwhelming. If they devoted all of their time to their teaching—reading, preparing, presenting, grading, and so forth—they could perhaps do almost perfect work. They could almost reach the practitioner's goal of 100% effort, 100% of the time. Yet, they would be perfect in only one element of the position, avoiding other areas, and would eventually get fired. Tom had seen young professors take this route, a seemingly good choice that eventually leads to bitterness and an occupational dead end. It was hard to see talented, giving faculty members be hit by a toxin to their professional self.

Knowing the seduction of the 100% effort, 100% of the time fantasy, Tom suggested to these new professors that they entertain the style of the veteran athlete who knows when to sprint and when to jog.

The problem is that 100% performance, 100% of the time, is too exhausting to sustain in the work of the counselor, therapist, teacher, and health professional. For example, the paramedic must give all at critical times but perhaps not always. From the child development literature, there is a related concept, the "good enough mother" (Winnicott, 1965). The idea is that the child *very much* needs the parent to be good enough, but the child does not need the parent to be *everything* for *optimal* development of the child to occur. So perhaps our clients, students, and patients also need us to be "good enough," and anything less is unacceptable. Perhaps, however, they do not need us to try for that which we cannot sustain, a 100% effort for 100% of the time. It is a wonderful fantasy, but it also leads to the long-term dis-ease of occupational exhaustion and caring burnout, as well as a loss in creativity and growth. This is expressed by Kushner (1996): "If we are afraid to make a mistake because we have to maintain the pretense of perfection ... we will never be brave enough to try anything new or anything challenging. We will never learn; we will never grow" (p. 85).

Understanding the Reality of Pervasive Early Professional Anxiety

Fear of failure undermines altruism.

—C. Cherniss (1995, p. 7)

One of the most important findings in our research study (Rønnestad & Skovholt, 2003) was the high level of pervasive anxiety among beginners and the great reduction in this anxiety among seasoned veterans. Anxiety is the natural emotion an individual feels when threatened and out of control in an important situation. The novice–veteran contrast in pervasive performance anxiety was startling and affected many facets of the work. The high stress level of the beginning practitioner is supported by other research studies. Cherniss (1995) found an elevated stress level for first year human service workers, and others (Ackerley et al., 1988; Pearlman & MacIan, 1995) have found high stress with new psychotherapists.

Professional experience helps so much in reducing this anxiety because counselors, therapists, teachers, and healers can increasingly rely on their own internalized experience base for professional functioning. The beginner must rely on the expertise of others, such as textbook theories, journal research studies, or the advice of a supervising senior practitioner. These sources can be invaluable. We all are indebted to useful theories and supportive supervisors; thanks, Carl Rogers and others for the theory, and thanks to our many excellent clinical supervisors. Unfortunately, external expertise often does not quite fit the situation, in the way that foreign language instruction in a college classroom does not quite fit with the language usage of the people of a foreign country. Many Turks would get frustrated when Tom, as a visiting professor in Turkey, corrected their English, which they had diligently learned in class, with the comment, "That's really not the way Americans say it." With experience, internal expertise replaces external expertise and pervasive anxiety goes down. A teacher told Tom that she got through her first year by every day asking a veteran colleague, "What should I do today?" Five years later, she never asked the question.

Relevant, fruitful, and illuminating work has been done about novice versus expert differences (Ericcson et al., 2006, 2007). Etringer, Hillerbrand, and Claiborn (1995) summarize the cognitive processing distinctions between novices and experts within the categories of memory and knowledge structures, declarative and procedural knowledge, pattern recognition, reasoning processes and goals, and problem structure. In summary, experts can understand more of the complexity of a situation even if it is ambiguous or unique. They know how to use their more accurate judgments more efficiently; their knowledge is both more differentiated and integrated; and they recognize complex patterns more easily through sensing the most critical features of a problem even if it is ill defined. Examples here include how an expert teacher can more quickly and accurately diagnose student mood level in a classroom and make quick instructional changes or how a nurse can understand the unique expression of a patient's changed pain level and respond with great skill.

This novice-versus-expert work in cognitive science can be highly useful to understanding how pervasive professional anxiety declines with experience in the counseling, therapy, teaching, and health fields because human work often involves complex, ill-defined, and difficult problem situations (e.g., how to introduce court-ordered treatment to a defensive person after a driving-while-intoxicated (DWI) arrest; assessing the maximum level of pain that a physical therapy patient will accept for healing without canceling appointments; finding a midlevel of instruction for a math class widely divergent in ability level). Working with people is so difficult because *Homo sapiens* is the most complex of all living organisms. As we have said in other places in the book, practitioners work constantly in ambiguous, confusing contexts. The veteran practitioner's hundreds of hours of experience can radically reduce daily pervasive professional anxiety.

Increasing Intellectual Excitement and Decreasing Boredom by Reinventing Oneself

In Chapter 6, we discussed hazards including cognitive deprivation and boredom, which can be a very negative force in the lives of veteran practitioners. Now, we discuss an antidote for the boredom.

High-touch practitioners work in the realm of interesting human narratives. Swimming in this reality can be very stimulating for the practitioner. For example, a practitioner may wonder how to establish trust with a guarded, defensive teenager. In time, he or she figures it out and creates an internal plan for such situations. The challenge, excitement, and rewarding qualities of the situation lessen. Now, if the practitioner often works with such teenagers, the intellectual challenge, over a long period of time, may decrease, and boredom can set in. Such a process often happens with veterans who have a narrow set of clients, teach the same subject term after term, or administer the identical health procedure over and over again.

Some veteran practitioners do not get bored in their work domain. When Tom asked a 68-year-old veteran practitioner and beloved clinical supervisor who objected to the boredom idea, she said, "I never get bored because every situation and every person has uniqueness. Like putting a complex puzzle together, the process is always somewhat different. So, this is the uniqueness that prevents the boredom" (H. Roehlke, personal communication, February 23, 2000).

Renewal is a word used to describe a process of freshness. It is like an energy shot that animates the practitioner. Here, we focus specifically on the word renewal viewed as reNEWal. Meaningful new work tasks provide stimulation for the practitioner, and the stimulation, in turn, energizes the practitioner and makes high-touch work possible. How does the NEW work as an antidote and provide renewal? It seems to us that one of the main issues concerns novelty. The key point is that novelty helps to animate the practitioner.

This is not the novice's problem. For the novice, the novelty provides so much stimulation that boredom is never a reality. In fact, for the novice, there is more than enough stimulation. The novice worries more about being anxious and lost while trying to perform work tasks. For the experienced practitioner who works in a fairly narrow domain, the boredom threat is not too much novelty. It is too little novelty.

One of the satisfactions of the work is cognitive. Helpers, teachers, and health professionals work with the most evolved of all species, human beings. These human beings are intricate, complicated, and convoluted. This is a major reason for the attraction to the field. For example, therapists talk of hearing the person's story and how engaging it can be to try to really understand the world of another.

Let us use the case of motivating the other to show the excitement of the work. In all of the professional fields that we are addressing here—human services, education, health, religious/spiritual professions—motivating the client, student, or patient parishioner is a major practitioner challenge. How can a practitioner really motivate the other person to make necessary changes? How can the practitioner motivate the other to become

**TABLE 9.2
Different Ways Experienced Practitioners Reinvent
Themselves**

Ways to Create More Novelty, Challenge, and Energy	Examples
Changing the work tasks	Doing supervision instead of direct service
Changing the methods that one uses	Replacing group process with individual process
Changing the population with which one works	Working with adolescents instead of adults
Changing the time allocation	Doing some administration of research rather than 100% direct service

less angry, study harder, or continue with painful but important medical procedures? It is often a very challenging and intellectually stimulating dilemma.

This is the process whereby the NEW brings reNEWal. Experienced practitioners must keep reinventing themselves. This can occur through different ways (Table 9.2). The goal of all of this effort, of course, is to have the NEW provide renewal.

Minimizing Ambiguous Professional Loss

The lack of closure and concrete evidence of success is a major ongoing stressor for those in the practitioner arts. One way to reduce this stressor is to acknowledge the dimension of ambiguous professional loss. We use this term, *ambiguous professional loss*, to describe the constant series of connections that the practitioner makes with the client, student, or patient that end without an ending. Awareness of this stressor can help us to acknowledge it to ourselves and gain support from colleagues. In addition, we can also try to have as many concrete endings as possible. Termination of the attachment relationship in a formal sense, no matter how brief, is often quite valuable for the professional's vitality.

At the University of Florida Counseling Center, the doctoral interns and the staff are captured in a yearly photo. The photos, year after year, are on the wall of the center in recognition of the training done by the senior practitioners. Year after year, they attach to a new group of enthusiastic and anxious interns. The interns leave at the end of the year and are replaced by a new group of enthusiastic and anxious interns. Is there any evidence of this 15-year effort by the staff? The product, the trained interns, are scattered throughout the United States. Where is the concrete evidence? It is there in the rows of photos of excited and proud interns and staff. What a great idea. What a great way to blunt ambiguous professional loss.

We all need lots of small ways of making the ambiguous concrete. This is the value of concrete achievements, such as a promotion or new certification. Concrete activities such as professional writing can be helpful too. The key words are *tangible* and *permanent*.

Learning to Set Boundaries, Create Limits, and Say No to Unreasonable Helping Requests

> I'm glad that some of the lessons we must all learn as therapists came early in my career: that success and failure are relative, that progress is nonlinear, that there are limitations to what we can offer.
>
> **—Sanger (2010, p. 74)**

As described earlier, learning to set limits only after first exhausting themselves early in their professional careers is a normative experience for counselors, therapists, teachers, and health professionals. Stone (1988) described this process in "The Heroic Syndrome." Veteran practitioners, like veteran athletes, learn to pace themselves, always being ready at critical moments but pulling back some at noncritical moments. For some practitioners, finding the appropriate level of letting go is difficult.

Summary

In this chapter, we have presented a number of ideas for you to consider in sustaining your professional self. Table 9.3 lists factors that practitioners have told me are important in sustaining or depleting the professional self.

Self-Reflection Exercises

A variety of ideas were mentioned in this chapter. They comprise a bag of tricks of the trade. These tips come from seasoned practitioners and the literature on professional functioning.

TABLE 9.3
Factors That Sustain and Deplete the Professional Self

Factors That Sustain the Professional Self	Factors That Deplete the Professional Self
Joy in participating in others' growth	Feeling unsuccessful in helping the other
Feeling successful in helping others	Professional boundaries that allow for excessive other-care and too little self-care
Closely observing human life (creativity, courage, ingenuity, tolerance of pain) and meaningful human contact	Low peer support
Finely tuned professional boundaries	Low supervisor support
Peer support	High organizational conflict
Supervisor support	Excessive seriousness in purposes and style
Low level of organizational conflict	Little attention to long-term professional development
Sense of humor and playfulness	Inability to accept any ambiguous professional loss or normative failure
Constant focus on professional development and avoidance of stagnation and pseudo development	Neglecting the importance for self and others of a positive closure experience at the time of professional separation
Tolerance of some ambiguous professional loss and normative failure	Insufficient salary and benefits or educational credits if the practitioner is in training
Attempting to have a closure experience at the time of professional separation that is positive for both parties	Realism and idealism as one
Sufficient salary and benefits or educational credits if the practitioner is in training	Distinguishing between idealism and realism

1. Which of these ideas do you already use in your own work? Perhaps you have a refined and improved version of one of these ideas. If so, please describe it.

_____

_____

_____

_____

_____

_____

_____

_____

2. Are there any new ideas in the chapter for you? If so, write about one or two that may offer something to you as a practitioner. How do you imagine these idea(s) might be helpful in your life?

_____

_____

_____

_____

_____

_____

_____

_____

_____

_____

10

Sustaining the Personal Self

This capacity to be deeply involved in the cycle of caring of empathic attachment → active involvement → felt separation → re-creation is the core skill for effective work in the high-touch human fields such as counseling, therapy, teaching, and health care. The opposite reaction—an inability for deep involvement in giving of the self and the cycle of caring —is, in our view, the strongest indicator of caring burnout. Without deep involvement of the self in the cycle, effective high-touch work cannot occur.

This chapter flows directly from this central premise. Sustaining the personal self is a serious obligation because the work, giving of the self, cannot successfully proceed without it. Many practitioners in the caring professions struggle with feelings of selfishness when they think of trying to meet their own needs. Their own conflicts about feelings of selfishness versus needing some self-focus can be very intense. You may be one of these people.

Our goal here is not to increase a person's capacity to be self-centered. The goal is to help the practitioner, over decades of work, to be able to engage in caring for others. Maintaining oneself personally is necessary to function effectively in a professional role. By itself, this idea can help those in the caring fields feel less selfish when meeting the needs of the self.

There are many methods of personal renewal. In this chapter, we suggest some of them. You may have developed others.

Constant Investment in a
Personal Renewal Process

Constant renewal is essential so that our "pond" does not become stagnant. Being fed by "springs" and "streams" is important so that we can continue to attach professionally as practitioners who assist others with emotional, educational, and physical needs. Self-care means finding ways to replenish the self. The result is more important than the method. The point here is to find ways to produce constant self-renewal.

A major goal for professional self-care could be described as adrenaline-boosting. This means searching for and finding positive life experiences. By this, we are suggesting that personal self-care should focus in part on producing feelings of zest, peace, euphoria, excitement, happiness, and pleasure. These are adrenalin boosters.

Awareness of the Danger of One-Way Caring
Relationships in One's Personal Life

Individuals in the caring professions are experts at one-way caring. Others are attracted to them because of their expertise and caring attitude. This can lead to interactions like when a doctor is asked to diagnose a mysterious ailment in the middle of a festive party. What to do? One therapist decided to shed two friendships that were too much like work to her; she was the giver in these one-way caring relationships. A teacher made sure that the caring was two-way by assertively telling the other his problems while also being a good, supportive listener. As an overall self-care strategy, practitioners must be careful about the number of one-way caring relationships in their personal lives. In our lives, it is important for us in the caring professions to have a distinction between our personal relationships and professional relationships. The hope is that caring goes back and forth in our personal lives, as other people care for us, we care for them. As others discuss their personal dilemmas, we discuss ours.

Nurturing One's Self

One could describe the self as composed of parts, with each part needing nurturing by the counselor, therapist, teacher, or health professional.

Here, we describe the parts as the emotional self, the financial self, the humorous self, the loving self, the nutritious self, the physical self, the playful self, the priority-setting self, the recreational self, the relaxation–stress reduction self, the solitary self, and the spiritual or religious self. Each of these elements of the personal self can use nurturing for ongoing sustenance.

Nurturing the Emotional Self

> Problems do not go away. They must be worked through or else they remain, forever a barrier to the growth and development of the spirit.
>
> **—M. S. Peck (1978, p. 30)**

> When I do not know myself, I cannot know who my students are. I will see them through a glass darkly, in the shadows of my unexamined life—and when I cannot see them clearly, I cannot teach them well. ... The work required to "know thyself" is neither selfish nor narcissistic. Whatever self-knowledge we attain as teachers will serve our students and our scholarship well. Good teaching requires self-knowledge; it is a secret hidden in plain sight.
>
> **—P. J. Palmer (1998, p. 23)**

We need to acknowledge that what is good for others is good for ourselves. Psychotherapists have led the way in emotional self-care through the concept of "therapy for the therapist." Geller, Norcross, and Orlinsky (2005) explore this topic in-depth in their book *The Psychotherapist's Own Psychotherapy: Patient and Clinician Perspectives.* In an earlier study by Pope and Tabachnick (1994), 476 psychologists described their own therapy and the vast majority of this group (86%) found it to be very or extremely helpful. Many reported positive changes in self qualities such as awareness, understanding, esteem, and confidence. Because helping professionals often use the self as the work instrument, these positive changes are notable. Perhaps psychotherapists, in their use of therapy and supervision for themselves, are setting a valuable self-care example for other helpers, teachers, and healers. Yet, it is even difficult for psychotherapists (the shoemaker has no shoes problem) according to senior practitioner E. Nightengale (personal communication, 1995), who said, "Too many therapists fail to take the 'medicine' they prescribe for others."

Another concept that is helpful in caring for the emotional self is developing practices that help to foster self-compassion. Self-compassion is defined as "being kind and understanding toward oneself in instances of pain or failure rather than being harshly self-critical; perceiving one's experiences as a part of the larger human experience rather than seeing them as isolating; and holding painful thoughts and feelings in mindful awareness rather than over-identifying with them" (Neff, 2003, p. 1). The practice of self-compassion promotes the ability to forgive oneself and understand that imperfection is a part of the human experience. Neff, Kirkpatrick, and Rude (2007) indicated that self-compassion is linked to psychological well-being. Developing a sense of self-compassion can help us respond more productively to the highs and lows of the work.

Nurturing the Financial Self

> Culture can have a profound effect on the causes of happiness by influencing the goals people pursue as well as the resources available to attain goals … selecting compatible goals may be a critical aspect of achieving [subjective well-being].
>
> **—E. Diener, E. M. Suh, R. E. Lucus, and**
> **H. L. Smith (1999, p. 285)**

How does the practitioner manage the stress that comes from being paid modestly while living in a consumption-saturated culture? This is our question in this section.

For many of its citizens, the United States is a place of affluence (i.e., there is only one person in most cars). The percentage of consumption of the world's resources vastly exceeds the United States' percentage of the world's population. Living, however, within a cultural bubble of unending messages to consume more means that most people do not feel wealthy. The unrelenting saturation of advertisements and pleas to buy are successful. See *The Overspent American* by Schor (1998) for a description of this reality. In America, many people spend all that they make. The irony is that in a rich country "the personal savings rate is zero. In the aggregate, Americans are spending every dollar they take home" (Cassidy, 1999, p. 88). A note to students: Beginners usually feel that, after school is over, they will have money and save. The record, however, is different. When they get money, many people spend all of it and more.

In the United States, consumption is a major value that drives many decisions. The great recession of 2007–2010 has brought hardship to many and altered some of this behavior. Yet, having lots of good, new stuff is a basic value for many. Many are trying to keep up with the Joneses.

Why, you may ask, do we speak here about this issue? We do so because the high-touch occupations pay well but not in cash. The pay comes in the immense satisfaction and pleasure one gets from the work at the deeper level of human existence. The pay comes from making a significantly positive difference in the lives of many other people. It is the joys, rewards, and gifts of practice effect. A major practitioner stress factor comes from being paid modestly yet living in a consumption-saturated culture. Controlling this dominant cultural voice is a key to sustaining the financial self.

Most jobs within human services, education, and health pay modestly. The starting salary gets the attention of most beginners. That number is often low, but it is not the really important statistic; salary range is. High-paying occupations can start low but have a large range. Low-paying occupations start low and have a narrow range. The range is more important because, in the high-touch fields, the narrow range means a person will never be paid a lot. Of course, there are some exceptions, like psychotherapists for the wealthy, industrial psychologists to large corporations, professors with lucrative consulting contracts, and physicians in many specialties. These, however, are exceptions. Most counselors, therapists, teachers, and health professionals work in jobs that start low and cap within a narrow range.

For practitioners, the key to developing the financial self is to spend less and invest more. It is impossible to do this if one is strongly influenced by the intense advertising propaganda in the culture.

Three factors can help mitigate this effect. Living in a developing country gets one out of the cultural bubble and makes it easier to really see the wealth in the developed world. Then one can see that many in the United States live "high on the hog." Knowing that one is already high on the hog makes for less motivation to live higher and higher on the hog. To aspire to higher consumption levels seems to make less sense. Because of the power of the cultural bubble, a person is usually encapsulated and feels that overconsumption is a worthy goal. Outside of the bubble, it seems less sensible.

A second factor is the literature, which shows that an individual's financial well-being has a stronger association with modest spending and moderate risk investing than it does with income. It is common to think that one's income is the central determinant of financial prosperity. This focus is misguided. Some good academic research on this topic is described in *The Millionaire Next Door* (Stanley & Danko, 1996). The central finding of this academic study is a surprise because it violates two basic ideas of the American ethos—that millionaires are very different from the rest of us and that buying a lot now and paying with credit is a reasonable thing to do. The central premise is that millionaires are people who could be living next door and are millionaires in part because they live well below their means and invest the difference.

A similar thrust comes from the simplicity movement. Dominguez and Robin (1992) argue in *Your Money or Your Life* that frantically living to pay for overspending, which they say is the basic American approach, is a very unwise use of time, which they call a person's most precious resource. Their book title spells out this option—chasing money for spending or having time for a life. Their answer is found in the charts they use, where they offer evidence for how low consumption and high savings can lead, at midlife, to living off one's investments. This, they suggest, then dramatically reduces the time and energy one needs for work to pay the bills. Instead, they say, people can use their time for richly meaningful life activities.

One other factor is worth mentioning concerning the financial self of the counselor, therapist, teacher, or health professional. In these jobs, the pay is usually mediocre, but sometimes it is even more mediocre than necessary because the practitioner has poor assertiveness skills regarding money. Let us tell you a story. We know of a person who worked at a university on a 9-month contract. Usually he found work in the summer. One summer, it was especially important because his salary had to support two adults and four children. He was told that there would be summer work, but he was passive about the whole process. Then, a few weeks before summer was to begin, he was told that there was no summer money. It was a good lesson for him. He told himself that it would never happen again and that he had to be more active and assertive about financial needs. The point of this story is that financially unassertive practitioners in the low-paying human services, education, and health jobs can become very demoralized because of financial stress.

If a practitioner has poor money skills or is financially unassertive, and also has been seduced by the consumption culture, then the financial self can be highly stressed. In time, this can affect the practitioner so that he or she can no longer make the necessary emotional connections with clients, students, or patients. If that happens, competent work is no longer possible.

Nurturing the Humorous Self

Maintaining a sense of humor was the number three career sustaining behavior (behind spending time with partner/family, and maintaining balance between professional and personal lives) in a study of professional psychologists' coping strategies (Stevanovic & Rupert, 2004). Actively laughing, being playful, telling jokes, and being humorous are very positive activities for individuals whose work environment is often filled with serious human problems. How then does one laugh in a serious environment? It takes time to learn the "art and science of laughter" at work. Students in training often lose their humor because they worry that it will be perceived as unprofessional. In time, one's sense of humor often emerges from hiding, and gradually there is, in the best situations, a proper place for humor in the environment of the caring professions. Laughter sustains practitioners. Learning how to be serious and having fun can help sustain the self.

Nurturing the Loving Self

Here we are addressing the problem of the nurturer has no nurturing (like the shoemaker has no shoes). Affection in the practitioner's personal life can be such a powerful source of professional vitality, enabling practitioners to sustain themselves amid significant professional stress. Over and over again, year after year popular songs speak to this human need. For many people, this means a strong primary relationship with one other person who is loving, affectionate, nurturing, and fun to be with. It often means having and raising children. For many practitioners, a family is a very rich source of the best ingredients of self-care. For others, loving and being loved takes a different form. The overall effect, however, is a sense of well-being that radiates from the practitioner's personal life.

Those in the caring professions are occupational experts at addressing the needs of others. Often, they have a long personal and professional history of successfully nurturing the mind, body, soul, and heart of others and getting praise for doing so. They may also have hopes, fantasies, and dreams of others anticipating and addressing their own needs. The nurturing dream often involves a sense of anticipation by the other and may sound like this: "The other will know what I want and gracefully—in timing, method, and style—care for me." The dream may end with a sense of frustration and resentment because no one seems to notice. Where is he or she or somebody or anybody for the professional nurturer? Too often the dream ends with a disappointing reality.

The terms used earlier in Chapter 8, *altruistic egotism, holy selfishness,* and *self-attentiveness,* suggest that professional nurturers must learn how to do more than dream. Nurturers having no nurturing means—the shoemaker has no shoes—that they can make shoes for others but not so easily for oneself. In moments of reflection, they realize that their feet are bare. Part of the conflict for counselors, therapists, teachers, and health professionals is their own ambivalence about putting their own needs versus the needs of others under the spotlight. Perhaps it is important to realize that, according to the attachment process described earlier as an essential element of practitioner success, care of the self is a sacred responsibility. Being loved by another, or others, is a wonderful method of self-care for those in the high-touch fields. The personal life caring can be very sustaining and is often greatly appreciated by the practitioner.

Nurturing the Nutritious Self

Psychologist and performance specialist Kate Hays (1999a) addressed practitioners at a "Taking Care of Yourself" symposium. There, she provided eight nutritional recommendations for high performance. The commentary under each one is from us. Though written over 10 years ago, her basic recommendations still apply.

1. *Happiness is a steady rhythm of blood glucose.* The steady idea speaks against skipping and binging patterns of eating such as "sugar hits" and supports regular eating. The idea of eating small meals combined with snacks (Schafer, 1996) is one way to maintain a steady glucose stream. Consultation with a dietitian can be a valuable way to discover what foods provide each practitioner with a steady glucose stream.
2. *Provide yourself with a regular routine of eating.* Routine provides structure and stability, and encourages planfulness. It helps us to avoid the impulsive eating that serves as admission to the "paved with good intentions" double lane, filled with traffic, road to hell.
3. *Breakfast is the one meal a day not to skip.* In a world of mixed, contradictory, and confusing messages about nutrition, this one is consistently recommended. Why? It seems that breakfast is used as gasoline to get the body going. Without food early in the day, the body runs out of gas late in the day and screams for food. It is a timing

problem because food late in the day tends to go into storage, perhaps forever.

4. *Your body needs water.* Back to the basics. Water, and lots of it, seems to be one of the top nutritional secrets. Because over 70% of the body is water, it makes sense that the hose should keep running. On this note, Balch and Balch (1997) state, "To keep the body functioning properly, it is essential to drink at least eight 8-ounce glasses of quality water each day" (p. 30). Products containing water, such as cola and coffee, are not part of the secret because the caffeine acts as a diuretic, stealing water from the body.

5. *Befriend food and be flexible.* Eating disorders are at war with food when they use and abuse food to serve other gods and goddesses. It is better to enjoy the friendship of food, just as one enjoys, but does not abuse, other friends. Flexibility speaks to the failure of fad diets whose inflexibility means that they desist rather than persist. Flexibility also means that small indulgence is a positive trait for long-term success.

6. *Learn how to distinguish true hunger signals from other bodily or emotional signals.* Bad feelings such as anxiety, loneliness, anger, fear, confusion, hurt, and sadness trigger eating for lots of people. The problem is that the person may not be hungry.

7. *Learn for what your body is hungry and thirsty.* Self-awareness can be a valuable people skill. Listening to oneself can provide lots of important information. Knowing the language of hunger and thirst can lead to efficient responses to the message of the body rather than useless utterances in another language, which may be telling the person to eat unnecessary foods.

8. *Develop a long-term perspective with regard to eating habits.* Eating is forever, and for most people, that is a long time. This means that all kinds of short-term schemes (e.g., losing 20 pounds before the reunion) don't cut the mustard. Going from a bad relationship with food to a good one is more than adding a little veneer. Sometimes it's a major remodeling job. The payoff is that, after major remodeling, one has something.

In a review of studies focusing on the outcomes of calorie-restricting diets as a treatment for obesity, Mann et al. (2007) conclude that diets don't lead to lasting weight loss. Smith and Hawks (2006) offer intuitive eating ("an anti-dieting, hunger-based approach to eating"; p. 130) as an effective tool for weight management.

The aforementioned nutrition recommendations give the practitioner another attractive piece of fabric when making the "sustaining the personal self" quilt.

Nurturing the Physical Self

> The vast majority of studies examining the role of exercise on psychological well-being and mood support the notion that exercise will improve well-being and mood states such as anxiety, stress, depression, tension, and fatigue.
>
> **—T. G. Plante (1993, p. 362)**

> Exercise has so many benefits in combating depression and improving brain chemistry that the following advice—while true—may sound like a cliché: Find a form of vigorous movement that appeals to you, practice it three to five times a week for twenty to forty minutes, and watch your mood improve.
>
> **—Henry Emmons, MD (Emmons & Kranz, 2006, p. 93)**

We repeatedly hear that we are supposed to get exercise. Often, this is said as a way to improve general physical health; however, we are bringing up this topic for a different reason. As Emmons says in the quote above, there is strong evidence that vigorous physical exercise is beneficial in regulating mood (Penedo & Dahn, 2005). It is only a short step to suggest that intense physical activity is an antidote for the emotional toxins in the practitioner's work life. Given the benefits of exercise, it is easy to speculate that, if it came in pill form, exercise would be *the* most popular pill taken on a daily basis.

The work in the caring professions is emotionally demanding and draining. Remember that the term *burnout* originated in these professions. For a reminder that practitioners' work is stressful, we ask you to look again at the content in earlier chapters: "The Cycle of Caring as the Practice Essential," "The Elevated Stressors of the Novice Practitioner," and "Hazards of Practice." These chapters, read together, present a view of the work as overwhelmingly difficult. For example, there is the hazard of living in a world of distress emotions. One needs methods to combat the depression, anxiety, and pain that the practitioner feels when closeted with the distressed client, student, or patient. This is why helpers, teachers, and health professionals must seriously consider intense physical activity as a piece of the "sustaining the personal self" puzzle.

In addition to knowing that intense physical activity is good for us, we also know how hard it is to maintain a highly active physical life. Why is it so hard for practitioners? For one thing, competent practitioners in the caring fields tend to put the needs of others before their own. It is an occupational characteristic. A great example occurs in the practitioner's personal life when he or she is a parent. Of course, good parents do focus on the needs of their children; however, the result is a reality where the practitioner's needs get squeezed. Then, there is the time problem in modern life, or shall we call it the lack-of-time problem? Also, there is the way that we have starched out almost all physical activity from modern life. This happens in building design (the elevator is available, but where are the stairs) and attitude (at the health club, people try to park close to the door).

It seems that one of the greatest self-care challenges for many practitioners is the challenge of creating and maintaining a highly active physical life. Research suggests that physical exercise can be highly effective in combating the emotionally stressful parts of the work. Unfortunately, it does not come in pill form.

In addition to exercise, sleep is an essential component of overall health. According to research compiled by the National Sleep Foundation (2006) lack of sleep is linked to decreases in cognitive performance and mood difficulties such as anger, anxiety, and sadness. The amount of sleep a person needs varies by individual, though researchers tend to agree that adults need between 7 to 9 hours per night. As practitioners in the caring professions, you are likely aware of strategies that promote healthy sleep referred to as "sleep hygiene." If not, try these simple techniques to help develop a more regular sleep schedule: (1) go to bed at the same time each night and wake at the same time each morning to help your body develop a routine; (2) develop an evening routine that encourages your body to relax and prepare for sleep; (3) reserve your bedroom for sleeping and intimacy, refrain from doing work or watching television in bed.

Knowledge of sleep science has even shaped how practice times are determined for players on some teams in the National Basketball Association (NBA), Beck (2009) reports in *The New York Times*. In consultation with Harvard Medical School sleep expert Dr. Charles Czeisler, the director of the Division of Sleep, some teams have opted to cut their morning practices (called morning shootarounds) in favor of allowing players to get more sleep. Czeisler recommends 8.2 to 8.4 hours of sleep per night for players, to promote the ability to learn new information and perform their best. If sleep is important for basketball players' performance and learning, it is equally as important for practitioners to care for themselves in this way.

Nurturing the Playful Self

Practitioners are serious people trying to do good work under stressful conditions. To have a long, happy career, there is an ironic prescription for these serious people. That prescription is play. Listen to these words: "The world of play favors exuberance, license, abandon. Shenanigans are allowed, strategies can be tried, selves can be revisited. In the self-enclosed world of play, there is no hunger. It is its own goal which it reaches in a richly satisfying way" (Ackerman, 1999, p. 6). The emotional world of the practitioner is filled with words like *earnest, hard, stressful, challenging*, and *serious* and more intense words like *sad, anxious, fearful*, and *angry*. The words of play are different. These words include *fun, zest, relish, delight, enjoyment, gusto, enthusiasm*, and *exuberance*. The world of play helps make the world of work possible.

In transactional analysis (TA), it is the child ego state that does the playing. So how does one nurture this part of the self? In popular language it is called babying oneself. What does it mean to baby the self? It usually means to attend to, to pamper, to be tender. Why is this important? Because it is the self of the professional that must work very hard. So how can the practitioner baby the self? Lots of ways—bubble baths and chocolates, playing golf or watching a great basketball game for others, walking aimlessly in the woods, lunch with girlfriends, and on and on. The choices are endless. Finding something that babies the self and doing it are the essentials.

In her book *Deep Play*, Ackerman (1999) describes deep play as an ecstatic form of play. She says that there is an unconscious engagement with the world and an exalted zone of transcendence. In the book, she travels through multiple examples: scuba diving, mountain climbing, wearing a mask, studying animals in the wild, and visiting exotic sites. Describing one form of deep play, she says, "While cycling, I tend to commune with nature, feel life's elements, and repeat a simple mantra of sensations that I experience separately: blue sky, white clouds, green trees, apple scent, bright sun, warm breeze" (p. 33).

Her discussion of the Grand Canyon reminded Tom of his own deep play nine-day rafting trip on the Colorado River through the Grand Canyon. At the time, he was very tired from all of his own high-touch work. Every day, he sat on the raft and watched the beauty unfold all around him. Looking through this kaleidoscope of color, shape, and form brought pleasure and peace. He was sitting there doing nothing but transcending the reality of the work life and being renewed by his own playfulness. One member of the raft group found out after a few days that he was a psychologist and asked Tom if we was observing the group process. Tom said: "Are you kidding? What group process? I'm on vacation watching the water and the rocks?" May we invite you as a practitioner to inventory your playtime. Perhaps it is there; perhaps it needs to be added.

Nurturing the Priority-Setting Self

Let's start with this premise: There is always too much to do. Why is it so? Modern life is a decent answer, with information overload (it comes from the north and south, east and west, from everywhere), the disappearance of boundaries, and accessibility by cell phone, e-mail, text messing, video conferencing, and social networking everywhere. The "Berlin Wall" of our lives has disappeared, a blessing and a curse.

We must make our own boundaries around our work and lives. Where is the compass for this task? It is our own values, job and boss demands, and our personal lives. It is important for all of us to set priorities for our time—an irreplaceable, precious commodity. Then, the chance improves that each of us will get to the primacy, our own hot center of importance, and never have time for the flotsam of our life. This can be a good outcome.

Setting priorities and time management are, first of all, a recognition that there is always too much to do. Secondly, they are a realization that the locus of control for the person's agenda can be internal or external. As they say in Alcoholics Anonymous (AA), "Who is driving your bus?" The task can be difficult for those in people occupations who readily want to assist the other. The struggle to stand upright and follow one's own compass gets hard on the slippery floor of trying to be there for the other. The bells and whistles of time management—put an A next to the important tasks for the day—are easily mastered when the bigger issue of setting priorities is directly faced and managed. Good luck. We are still working on it.

Nurturing the Recreational Self

Hobbies can be great for self-care because they have so many elements of renewal. An element of this is what C. Wambach (personal communication,

1989), a college teacher of high-risk students, calls "positive significant distractions." We control the involvement and outcome; the domain is manageable; and the task is fun, interesting, and absorbing.

Being a collector, of whatever, captures so many of these positive elements, and it is concrete—one can see and feel results. Concrete is the opposite of the practitioner's world where multiple realities and unclear patterns of results are central in the work. Is it any wonder that collecting is a popular activity in the stress-filled world of other-care practitioners? E. Nightengale (personal communication, 1995), a senior Veterans Administration hospital psychologist, responded to these comments by saying, "The value of a hobby, with concrete results, clear beginnings and finished 'products,' is important for the helping professional. The need for completion, for progress, and success can be channeled or 'found' by these kinds of activities." One of our friends, an other-care practitioner in a high-stress job, collects rocks. For her, it is a low maintenance, concrete hobby with no care or watering needed; even after a long Minnesota winter, the rocks left outside emerge from the receding snow undamaged. She can look at them, touch them, move them around, and add to her collection. No nurturing is needed. The key with collecting or other hobbies is to be taken away from the focus on one's own professional work demands. The result can be a healthier perspective on work, the world, and oneself. There are so many possible hobbies and fun activities—gardening, photography, movies, playing music, building birdhouses. These are the enjoyable activities of some practitioners we know.

Nurturing the Relaxation–Stress Reduction Self

Do members of the helping, teaching, or health fields manage stress by using techniques developed from their own professions? Sometimes. Many of us in these practitioner fields are familiar, through our professional work, with stress-management methods such as relaxation training, meditation, biofeedback, yoga, and self-hypnosis. Yet, we often do not personally practice these methods to reduce our own physical body response of overarousal, although we know that overarousal is the key to many current lifestyle-type physical problems and diseases.

There are many sources of stress that lead to overarousal. There is the constant need for practitioners to focus on the needs of the other. There are, of course, many other sources of stress, such as organizational politics and policies that may greatly affect the individual practitioner who often has little voice in major decisions. Big bureaucracies can be hard places to feel control over one's professional life. Electronics and technology can be so great and also so frustrating. Another source of stress is internal in the practitioner's own thoughts and appraisal of self in a variety of contexts.

A century ago, overarousal was termed the *fight or flight response* by Cannon, a professor at Harvard. Cannon suggested that, in response to threat, the human body goes into an emergency mode to either attack the threatening object or escape from it. The attack mode produces physical changes in the body that can help in the attack or escape. Modern life produces the same physical reaction but within a different context, for example, a traffic jam. The long-term consequence is the onset of stress-related disease turning into a disease. Current diseases, which sometimes have a stress component, include high blood pressure, heart disease, depression, cancer, arthritis, and gastrointestinal system disorders.

Nearly one hundred years after Cannon, another Harvard professor, Herbert Benson (1975), stated that the best antidote to overarousal is a simple procedure he called "the relaxation response." The Benson-Henry Institute for Mind Body Medicine (2010) states that relaxation, as an antidote to the chronic overarousal of modern life, can be done through two simple steps. Within a context of quiet and comfort, and a period such as 20 minutes, the individual is to:

1. Repeat a word, sound, prayer, thought, phrase, or muscular activity.
2. Return to number 1 whenever other thoughts or activities intrude.

These two steps, along with slow, deep breathing, are the elements of the relaxation response. Benson (1999) states that increasing oxygen consumption is a powerful yet easy part of stress reduction. He also maintains that all of the world's major religions have incorporated these elements into their religious prayers, rituals, and practices.

Learning through practice and overpractice to reduce the stress response of overarousal can be of great value in the practitioner's personal and professional life. *The Relaxation and Stress Reduction Workbook* by Davis, Eshelman, and McKay (2008) is one of many sources of useful techniques. Some of the stress reduction methods they emphasize are body awareness, breathing, progressive relaxation, and visualization. They describe body awareness as a first self-assessment step regarding stress management and breathing as a central part of stress reduction. They say, "Improper breathing contributes to anxiety, panic attacks, depression, muscle tension, headache, and fatigue. … Breathing awareness and good breathing habits will enhance your psychological and physical well-being, whether you practice them alone or in combination with other relaxation techniques" (p. 23). They emphasize the importance of deep abdominal, diaphragmatic breathing as opposed to shallow chest, thoracic breathing.

First developed by Jacobson in 1929, progressive relaxation is an old method of relaxing the body. It has been a central part of therapist-directed anxiety management for many years. It essentially consists of tightening and then relaxing different muscle groups in the body. The theory is that a person cannot be tense and relaxed at the same time. By relaxing, the person is teaching the body to respond differently during periods of overarousal.

Visualization is the practice of seeing something in the mind's eye. It is a way of using one's imagination and creativity to enhance one's life. Similar terms are *imagery* and *guided fantasy*. Skovholt, Morgan, and Cunningham (1989) have described the use of visualization in career and life planning. In managing stress, Davis and colleagues (2008) say that guided visualization can be used by imagining a place where you can be very relaxed. For many people, this involves an outdoor scene such as the ocean, a lake, or the wilderness. The individual can develop this picture in the mind and then imagine it during high-stress times.

Mindfulness

> From the outset of practice we are reminded that mindfulness is not about getting anywhere else or fixing anything. Rather, it is an invitation to allow oneself to be where one already is and to know the inner and outer landscape of the direct experience in each moment.
>
> **—J. Kabat-Zinn (2003, p. 148)**

Mindfulness is defined as "paying attention on purpose, in the present moment, and nonjudgmentally to the unfolding of experience moment to moment" (Kabat-Zinn, 2003, p. 145). Mindfulness takes many forms in therapeutic offerings. Namely, programs such as dialectical behavior therapy, mindfulness-based stress reduction (MBSR), and acceptance and commitment therapy teach mindfulness as the key component of the therapy. Mindfulness has been shown to be an effective intervention for issues such as treatment of chronic pain (Kabat-Zinn, Lipworth, & Burney, 1985), depression and anxiety (Reibel, Greeson, Brainard, & Rosenzweig, 2001), and chronic stress (Chang et al., 2004).

In addition to having clinical significance, mindfulness is a useful tool for practitioner self-care. For example, the practice of mindfulness meditation (MM) is based on a simple strategy of bringing mindful attention to the present moment experience. Formal practice of mindfulness mediation involves focusing on the breath as an entry to the practice.

You may wish to try these simple instructions for mindfulness meditation. Sit in a comfortable position in which your body is alert and relaxed, allowing the breath to flow freely. Take a deep inhalation through the nose and a deep exhalation through the mouth. Often people have a tendency to breathe into their upper lungs, thus the chest rises and falls as they breathe. Consider an image of a baby sleeping, you see her belly rising and falling as she breathes. Hold this image in your mind as you work to breathe into your belly. You may choose to bring attention to your belly by placing your hand there and watching it move as you begin to learn this breathing. The mind will naturally wander onto other thoughts; you can simply bring your awareness back to the sensations of the breath. Each time the mind wanders, simply return to your breathing.

Another helpful practice, taught through the MBSR program, is the body scan. Participants in the course are taught to bring awareness to different parts of their body and notice any body tension or tightness, pain, lack of sensation, or relaxation. This practice is typically done lying down and in a quiet space. Busy practitioners can get at the essence of the body scan by working to develop more awareness of how the body feels throughout the day. For example, in between meeting with clients, patients, or students simply take a moment to scan your body from head to toe and notice any sources of tension or strain; mindfully relax these parts of the body.

MBSR programs offer formal training in mindfulness meditation, body awareness (through the use of the body scan), and gentle hatha yoga. As a practitioner, participating in such a program can be a useful self-care endeavor. Michelle has participated in an MBSR program as both a student and a co-facilitator. She found that the practices had a powerful impact on her life both personally and professionally. Additionally, Michelle's dissertation research explored the effects of participation in a 12-week MBSR course on college students' psychological well-being, psychological distress, self-compassion and health status (Trotter, 2009).

Another therapist writes of how mindfulness practices promoted self-care (Christopher, 2010):

Mindfulness practices also provided me with way of taking care of myself and preventing burnout. I learned through meditation that I could just allow experiences to move through me. I do not mean "moving through" in the sense of moving through to get rid of. Rather, moving through in the sense of not resisting, not putting up walls around seemingly negative experiences and emotions, but giving them space and being a good host, to use the mystic poet Rumi's metaphor from "The Guest House" (Barks, 2005). At the end of those days or session that felt tiring, burdensome, deadening, I would allow myself some time for the residuals that seemed stuck in my body to manifest themselves and to have access to my consciousness. Often this would be accompanied by tears, but then a sense of having been cleansed, of the heaviness lifting. Through yoga I learned when I was "efforting" or unnecessarily expending energy or tension to accomplish something. Noticing the state of my body when sitting with clients gave me indicators of when I was becoming tense, when I was trying too hard in session, when I was getting attached to a particular outcome. (p. 39)

Nurturing the Solitary Self

It is a difficult lesson to learn today—to leave one's friends and family and deliberately practice the art of solitude. … I feel a limb is being torn off, without which I shall be unable to function. And yet once it is done, I find there is a quality to being alone that is incredibly precious. Life rushes back into the void, richer, more vivid, fuller than before. It is as if in parting one actually did lose an arm. And then, like the starfish, one grows it anew; one is whole again, complete and round—more whole ever than before, when the other people had pieces of one.

—A. M. Lindbergh (1975, p. 42)

Solitude, an antidote to people intensity is important for professional givers of the self. Solitude can nurture us in a profound way. Learning to enjoy solitude can be a difficult process for practitioners. Solitude is increasingly difficult to find and nurture. For one thing, lots of television viewing has become central to most people's lives. There is so much about the technology of television that is deeply appealing to people. Conversely, television is so overstimulating that solitude becomes even more foreign and uncomfortable.

Solitude means removing oneself from the known channel of life (e.g., being plugged into the electronic world, intense contact with others in need) to an often unknown channel (silence, no human voices, aloneness). Those in the caring professions often have to fight through the disquieting elements of the quiet—the loneliness, the self-focus, an alienation from nature.

They need to learn how to change loneliness into solitude. In time, however, the sounds of the natural world, the wilderness, can fill up the self in a way that refreshes. So too can just plain quiet. We suggest *The Singing Wilderness* (Olson, 1997), a wonderful book on this topic.

A negative byproduct of technology has been noise pollution; noise is everywhere. The cell phone is wonderful, as are texting, Skype, and other ways of connecting. Yet, they imprison as much as they free. The phone rings; cars drive by; people are talking all around. The life-enhancing machinery around us, such as washing machines and lawn mowers, also are life nonenhancing because of noise. In solitude, silence is the gold. Spiritual and religious practices also offer a bed for solitude. One can meditate and pray alone with the focus often being the connection between the self and the eternity.

The typical K–12 teacher is exposed to overwhelming numbers of living, breathing, needing things called students Monday through Friday. Was it a genius who invented a professional teaching year of 9 months? This permits a teacher to recover and be ready again after 3 months away from the people intensity. Maybe the 9 month–3 month cycle of intensity and distance was created by a very wise student of professional development rather than by the agrarian pattern of early American life. We prefer to think that the calendar came from someone who knew decades ago that the cycle of caring demands an on and then off of human contact. After the phases of empathetic attachment with the new children in the fall, active involvement during the school year, and then the felt separation of May and June, there is the summer of time away. This is the solitude of the re-creation phase, so necessary so that when the children fill the school again in the fall the teacher can vigorously enter the empathetic attachment phase.

Yes, of course, teachers do not go from work to 3 months of hermitlike existence. In fact, many take classes and work during the summer. However, at least the occupation is structurally set up to permit removal from the intense human contact at work. The 9 month–3 month rhythm permits something else that is very valuable. It permits the felt separation phase to occur within the structure of the occupation. Listen carefully to elementary teachers talk about their work. They often use the words "my children" when describing their students, and they often describe end-of-the-year rituals that they say are to help the children make the transition to summer. We hope that the rituals are also for the teachers to help them grieve the loss of their caring attachments, attachments that will change forever. Positive loss experiences permit a new round of attachments for teachers when August and September come again.

With too many unresolved and painful losses, we cannot attach again in our personal lives. With too many unresolved and painful losses at work, we cannot attach in our professional lives. Unlike K–12 teaching, most careers in the high-touch fields do not have an involvement–distance structure built into the occupation.

Nurturing the Spiritual or Religious Self

> The mystery of life, cloaked so guilelessly in day and night, makes the search for God the enduring human drama. We know so little, we feel so much. We have only the shape of our lives, experienced in the cycle of light and dark, to guide us toward meaning.
>
> **—P. Hampl (1995, p. xxvi)**

Friends have said that *The Denial of Death* by Ernest Becker (1973) is the most profound book, the one with the greatest depth, they have read. In the book, Becker describes death as the great human fear, a fear so great, he says, that people construct their whole lives to manage its intensity. Becker suggests that denial of death's reality is a central coping strategy for this intense fear.

It seems to us that the reality of death is a major motivation in the human quest for a spiritual or religious life. This quest is both cross-cultural and historic. Concerning which spiritual or religious path is the right one, Tom has personally had difficulty believing that "all the marbles" are possessed by one narrow, highly dogmatic belief system. In houses of worship, he has celebrated the sacred and God's presence with Muslims in Turkey, Buddhists in Thailand, Lutherans as a child growing up in Minnesota, Catholics at the Vatican, Jews when his father was a resident of a Jewish nursing home, Chinese Baptists in Singapore, and at his grandfather's church in Norway. He has also experienced the power of the Christian God in the beautiful wilderness of Minnesota's canoe country.

We have come to believe that a spiritual or religious life is an important part of how one sustains the personal self. This has many meanings for different people. It is not our role or right to tell others what to believe.

For us, there are two reasons why being active spiritually or religiously is important. First, an active spiritual or religious life acknowledges the reality described by Becker. Death can be terrifying, and facing the reality directly through a spiritual or religious life is a reaction of more depth than the use of denial. Also, an active spiritual or religious quest addresses the central mysteries of life: What is the meaning of life? Is there an active divine presence?

What is God's plan for my life? Are people basically good or evil? How does one achieve forgiveness, atonement, and peace? What moral rules should govern my life? Is there eternal life?

Second, workers in the caring professions are actively present in the drama of human tragedy, disappointment, and pain. Examples include a counselor hearing of betrayal of one person by another, a teacher seeing a student try but fail, or a nurse watching while a severely injured person struggles with intense pain. An active spiritual or religious life can help the practitioner search for meaning and understanding of these painful human realities seen at work on a daily basis. For example, it is important to ask questions such as: Why does God permit acute human pain and suffering? An active spiritual or religious life seems for many practitioners to be an important part of sustaining the personal self.

Summary: Keeping in Focus One's Own Need for Balanced Wellness—Physical, Spiritual, Emotional, and Social

Professionals in the caring fields need to be assertive about their own wellness. One way of conceptualizing this involves four dimensions of health and the balance between them (Figure 10.1). The diamond and its four

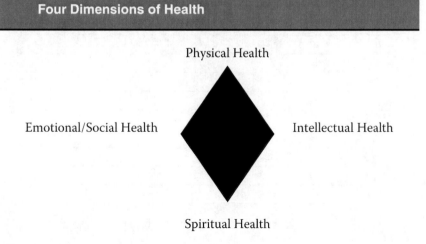

FIGURE 10.1
Four Dimensions of Health

Physical Health

Emotional/Social Health

Intellectual Health

Spiritual Health

dimensions help one to see the need for a focus on the dynamic interplay between them. The diamond symbolizes the reality that the whole is greater than the sum of the parts. Yet, the whole is strong only by attending to each dimension.

Self-Reflection Exercises

Here, versions of the personal self were considered. In terms of a self-care action plan for you, which parts of the personal self are in "good shape" in your life, which ones need a "tune-up," and which ones need a "major overhaul"?

1. Parts of the personal self in good shape:

_____
_____
_____
_____
_____
_____
_____
_____
_____
_____

2. Parts of the personal self in need of a tune-up:

_____
_____
_____
_____
_____
_____
_____
_____
_____
_____

3. Parts of the personal self in need of a major overhaul:

_____

_____

_____

_____

_____

_____

_____

_____

_____

_____

11

Burnout Prevention and Self-Care Strategies of Expert Practitioners*

Mary Mullenbach and Thomas M. Skovholt

This chapter focuses on the methods used by one group of practitioners, those in mental health, to maintain professional vitality. Hopefully the ideas presented here can be of use to a wide variety of practitioners across the rainbow of the high-touch fields.

Mental health practitioners encounter stressors that originate from both internal and external sources (Baker, 2003; Freudenberger, 1990; Norcross & Guy, 2007). Both have a direct effect on the practitioner. Burnout is especially prevalent in this group of helping professionals. Practitioners are expected to engage in an ongoing series of professional attachments and separations, as discussed in Chapter 3. The stress of attachment and separation is often intensified by a lack of client success, nonreciprocated giving within the counseling relationship, overwork, difficult client behaviors, discouragement as a result of the slow and uneven pace of the counseling process, the practitioner's existing personal issues that emerge in response to involvement in the counseling process, isolation, and administrative demands from agency and managed care organizations (Dupree & Day, 1995; Farber, 1990;

---

*This chapter is based on the work of Mullenbach, M. A. (2000). Expert therapists: A study of professional resiliency and emotional wellness. Unpublished doctoral dissertation, University of Minnesota, Minneapolis. Thomas Skovholt was the dissertation advisor.

Figley, 2002; Kassam-Adams, 1995). Burnout occurs when the practitioner is continuously depleted from this intense process of engagement.

The debilitating effects of the counseling role on the practitioner have long been recognized as an occupational hazard with far-reaching effects (Freudenberger & Robbins, 1979; Smith & Moss, 2009).

Based on his research, Farber (1983) concluded that counseling work can have a substantial negative impact on practitioners' self-identity, behavior, and attitudes both within and outside of the work setting. Historically, studies in this area have primarily focused on identifying work-related stressors.

In 1996, a research program was started with 10 peer-nominated mental health practitioners. The purpose of the initial study was to identify the components of mastery among this group of expert practitioners. Since that time, the research program has been expanded. The current study identified components relevant to wellness and professional resiliency in this group of practitioners. In this study, a qualitative design was utilized as a means of drawing a store of rich information from the sample group. Data were collected through the use of a semistructured interview format, with questions cultivated from existing research focused on stressors among mental health practitioners. The questions were designed to identify stressors and to access information pertaining to the emotional wellness and professional resiliency of these practitioners. The data analysis relied on an inductive approach that allowed for an in-depth exploration. Two interviews were completed with each of the participants. An analysis of a second data source obtained from a previous study with this same group of participants was used to supplement the findings. The selected findings presented in this chapter focus on high-level stressors and self-care strategies identified within this group of practitioners.

This chapter presents 20 themes within five categories that originated from the data analysis. The five categories are (1) professional stressors, (2) emergence of the expert practitioner, (3) creating a positive work structure, (4) protective factors, and (5) nurturing self through solitude and relationships. A summary of the information is in Table 11.1.

Category A: Professional Stressors

Category A contains four themes that identify stressor areas that are confronted by the participants in their work.

| TABLE 11.1 |
| Categories and Themes |

Category A: Professional Stressors
Participants are stressed by issues that challenge their competency.
A frozen therapy process is highly stressful for participants.
Breaches in peer relationships are stressful.
Intrapersonal crises negatively impact the professional role.

Category B: Emergence of the Expert Practitioner
Participants learned role limits and boundaries.
Over time, participants experienced less performance anxiety.
With experience, participants moved from theory to use of self.
Participants view attachment and separation as a natural process.
Participants understand human suffering at a profound level.

Category C: Creating a Positive Work Structure
Mentor and peer support was critical at the novice phase.
Participants have ongoing and enriching peer relationships.
Multiple roles are a protective factor.
Participants create health-promoting work environments.

Category D: Protective Factors
Participants directly engage highly stressful professional dilemmas.
Participants confront and resolve personal issues.
Highly engaged learning is a powerful source of renewal.

Category E: Nurturing Self through Solitude and Relationships
Participants foster professional stability by nurturing a personal life.
Participants invest in a broad array of restorative activities.
Participants construct fortifying personal relationships.
Participants value an internal focus.

Theme 1: Participants Are Stressed by Issues That Challenge Their Competency

Participants reported an array of issues and events that challenge their sense of wellness. Sometimes, as in the case of a suicidal client, these experiences represented unpredicted critical incidents for the practitioners. Other, less intense events and issues were chronic in nature and occurred on an ongoing basis. Regardless of the specific experience, a commonality that ran through was the participants' experience of feeling "tapped out" in regard to their level of competency or comfort. One participant discussed the emotional impact of a client who committed suicide during a hospitalization.*

> I know that she ended up in the hospital; I arranged it. ... So I took care of her safety, I felt. And I don't know what the heck they did; she was suicidal, and they weren't watching her, and she hung herself. And it was really hard; I just felt heartbroken, and I was so pissed at the psychiatrist.

One participant discussed the ongoing stressors that are related to working with chronically ill clients who don't progress:

> ... depression that doesn't lift. All kinds of interventions; I mean, some people have had therapy for years before they get to me. Some of them have had shock treatment, some of them have had medication, and nothing seems to be helpful. You know, people who have been searching for a long while, and maybe you can help them make some inroads, but there are some people for whom it just feels like we don't have what's needed yet.

Other participants discussed their sense of feeling lost or depleted when working with specific client behaviors:

> And I'm realizing that, for example, I don't work well with addictives, people who are addictive. I find I get sucked into their dynamics, and I can't keep track that these people are also con people because they need to be.
>
> I've had a few men who have been very abusive ... they're coming to me, and the allegation of physical or sexual abuse may be in the air, but they haven't dealt with it at all, or maybe it hasn't been in the air at all. But I find myself angry at the end of those sessions. Those are the people that I find myself, I feel used up rather than giving 100%; I feel like I've been stolen from; I feel like I've been taken from. It's totally unrewarding, like they don't give anything back.

Sometimes this sense of being tapped out resulted from the level of distress expressed by the client:

> I think it has more to do with when there's been a lot. So, for example, there are some weeks where it feels like you always thought you heard the worst that you could possibly hear and then someone comes in with

---

*Quotations have been edited with small changes that increase the clarity of the writing.

something worse about what people are able to do to people that causes pain and distress. ... And sometimes it's just in waves.

Theme 2: A Frozen Therapy Process Is Highly Stressful for Participants

Participants reported that they experienced a sense of boredom related to clients who were unmotivated or resistant to treatment. This experience of feeling bored within the therapeutic relationship was reported as a significant stressor. Participants stated:

> For me the issues would be probably somebody is just really without any willingness whatsoever to reflect. It is always something outside of themselves, continuously so ... mostly I think I lose interest.
>
> I think what's challenging, frankly, are the boring clients, you know, where it's time after time and very little is happening.

In reflecting on his work with clients who were resistant, one participant spoke about the need to deal with his own defensive response:

> Well, I find I don't mind their resistance; it's when I start getting resistant in the face of their resistance. I mean, they have the right; I expect them to get resistant. But then when they do their resistance in a way that engenders my resistance, then I don't like that.

Theme 3: Breaches in Peer Relationships Are Stressful

Participants consistently reported that they derived a beneficial sense of support from their peer relationships, both within the work environment and in the broader professional community. Not surprisingly, breaches in these relationships are especially stressful. One participant stated:

> Some of the most stressful times have been when I've accidentally ended up working with colleagues that I didn't feel compatible with, to come to work every morning and greet a face that you're not happy to see. Someone you don't trust or respect who doesn't seem to trust or respect me, that's very hard, but it's not my situation now.

Another participant discussed his struggle to stay engaged with peers in the broader professional community when discussing issues relevant to professional practice and integrity:

> [Stressful for me are] my own relationships and associations with colleagues where we hit points of important divergence. And my willingness

to stay present to those, to stay in a relationship with those colleagues and to stay present to the divergence without favoring a tendency to want to split off or isolate or withdraw.

In a similar way, a participant spoke about her negative response to conflicts between separate divisions in the psychological community:

They're both really good groups, and I think it's good for our practices and the community and everything else, but there are elements of competition and resentment and politics, I guess is what you'd call it, but I really dislike it, and when I'm caught in the middle of one of those frays, I'm very unhappy.

Theme 4: Intrapersonal Crises Have a Negative Impact on the Professional Role

Participants reported that personal life crises and related problems presented challenging situations in their professional role. Although the participants had developed proactive methods for coping with these issues, they reported a strong sense of discomfort when initially faced with this type of challenge. One participant described the unease that he felt when personal issues created a sense of incongruence in his perception of self:

When I was experiencing a lot of tearing in relation to my own family, which I did some years ago, a long time ago. That was pretty difficult, and I think the difficulty was having to redo my conception of myself while I was continuing to practice. And you really can't take yourself off line and decide to redo your conception of yourself and come back because that's always so closely integrated to whatever you're doing every place else.

Another participant described the hardship that she encounters when she is in the process of resolving her own crises:

So then I feel very split in terms of what I need to attend to with clients, and yet knowing this other thing is playing in my own life that is not going to resolve today in a phone call and is not going to resolve in a week, and it's going to be with me for whatever period of time. And so those, frankly, are torture chambers for me. ... When I'm sitting with clients and they're talking about anything that remotely is similar or identifies with or touches on, the anxiety just shoots up. ... How do I manage that level of anxiety and at the same time try to be here for my clients?

Category B: Emergence of the Expert Practitioner

Category B contains five themes that highlight aspects of the participants' approaches to professional practice. These themes reflect attitudes and techniques that promote wellness and preserve professional vitality.

Theme 1: Participants Learned Role Limits and Boundaries

Over time, participants learned the value of establishing clear boundaries and limits in areas that included their role as a helper, the level of responsibility that they assumed, the structure of their practice, the makeup of their caseloads, and their relationships with clients. The establishment of these boundaries and limits enabled the practitioners to maintain a sense of wellness and vitality, to cope more effectively with difficult client behaviors, and to manage their own continuous exposure to suffering. In discussing her evolving role, one participant stated:

> I'm far more wise about all the things that I don't need to know about and don't need to fix, and I think when I started out, like most of us when we start out, feeling a need to have all the answers. My job was to fix this, be helpful. I think with experience and time in the field, you learn that our job is really to relax more and sit back and listen and hear better what it is that the person is trying to sort through.

One participant discussed the establishment of limits and boundaries as a necessary ingredient in both practicing with integrity and fostering a sense of wellness and vitality:

> It is up to me to do everything I can to maintain my own emotional health so that I can actually be available to my patients without needing them. I think one of the ways therapy goes awry is that the therapist starts to use the patient for their own emotional sustenance, regulation of the therapist's self-esteem, all those sorts of things. I think that to be a good therapist, you must be well fed and well loved. Basically, have a life out there that is working.

Participants noted that limits and boundaries played a key role in structuring their actual workday. In discussing the framework of her schedule, one participant stated:

> It's important for me to keep track of the hours I'm putting in because it's very easy to start going over a 40-hour week. And I start to know that

something's wrong when I wake up in the morning and I'm not rested or when I'm dreading the day, or I'll find myself sleepy or bored, and this is not boring work, and I start to make mistakes, double schedule people, or there are just certain signs I recognize as that I'm working too hard.

Regarding his ability to implement limits on client behaviors, one participant stated:

I'm more sure of myself. … I can set limits with, you know, the authority of a Dutch uncle, and it can have the subtleties of both nurturance and a stop sign.

Another participant noted the importance of understanding her limitations as a practitioner:

Part of it has been to really advocate for clients where it feels like it's really important; part of it has been to make alternatives available, like sliding fees for people; some of it is just coming to grips with that there are certain agencies that can provide certain things, and that we can't provide everything for everybody. So part of it is accepting limitations.

Theme 2: Over Time, Participants Experienced Less Performance Anxiety

With time, participants became more comfortable in their professional role. With this change, they experienced a decrease in stress and an increase in confidence and ability to handle a variety of difficult therapeutic issues and client behaviors. This shift allowed them to be more open and genuine in their role as a helper. Three practitioners commented:

There's less of a need to prove yourself, and so you can be more open because you don't feel as much that you need to defend anything or protect anything. I think when you first start out sometimes, it feels like you're on the line, you know; no one knows who you are, how you're doing, and so I think there's much more a sense of protection around yourself; seems like as you grow older and more experienced, there's more of a sense of "We all don't know, and we're all learning," so you can be pretty open about hearing feedback, getting information.

I laugh a lot more, a lot more. I am old. That is one thing that helps. And … I am not forever wondering if I am good enough.

Comfort with coming to work each day and assuming that it would be okay. You know, I'd do all right somehow, or I'd be able to deal with whatever happened that day; I'm just guessing, but I'm thinking maybe 10 years into my practice, I started to have that kind of sense of equilibrium about it.

Theme 3: With Experience, Participants
Moved From Theory to Use of Self

Participants noted that, as they accumulated experience, they moved from a reliance on specific techniques and approaches to being more open and genuine. This change occurred as they became increasingly aware of the therapeutic process and how to best use their own self within the relationship. For these participants, the shift from a reliance on specific approaches to the use of self required an element of risk and openness. Once achieved, it felt more like a comfortable professional "fit" that was conducive in creating intimate and intense interactions with clients that enhanced their work. When focusing on the intense and intimate nature of the therapeutic relationship with clients, participants stated:

> In a sense it's a joy. … It's the fact of working with people and watching them grow and feeling that you have a part in that growth. It's fun.
>
> Well, I get off on it. I mean, honest to God, contact is very exciting. I mean, when two boundaries meet, that's where the energy is.
>
> Well, I think the one thing that has prevented me from burning out … is the fact that no two people look alike to me. The people who burn out begin to see everybody as alike; they see people as problems, and they see problems as the things they are working with.

Theme 4: Participants View Attachment and
Separation as a Natural Process

Participants discussed their belief that attachments and separations in the therapeutic relationship followed a natural course, similar to those experienced in other relationships. This belief appears to fortify the participants through years of fostering attachments and facilitating separations with a multitude of clients. They are committed to engaging in that process, even through times of difficulty, and hold the belief that it is a mutually beneficial process. One participant discussed her belief that the therapeutic process of attachment and separation mimics life:

> But it seems to me that all of life is about attachment and separation. You know, even with marriage, there are times when attachment is really important, but there's also times when separation is really important. Where you're individuals and you have different needs and different abilities to be present. So I think that's how I help myself with it, is that

it feels part and parcel with just what's true in life … I think it's totally important that people are able to attach in order to work through some of what might not have happened for them. But I also think it's important to be able to separate and let go.

Participants also discussed their experience that relationships continue beyond the separation. This continuation may exist on an internal level or, in other cases, actually involves the client returning to therapy. In some cases, work that began with a client eventually extended to the client's children. This belief regarding the ongoing nature of relationships appeared to insulate the participants from the potential distress of repeated attachments and separations:

And then a number of people come back over the years, so I have more and more confidence, sort of like an object constancy, in me at least, that these people remain alive in my psyche. They're out there in the world, and I feel connected to them and believe that they'd return if the situation arose.

I think in a core way, attachment is an internal phenomena rather than external. You can see people for years every day and probably not have that much attachment. So if you stop seeing people, there is some loss, but it doesn't mean that, therefore, something got yanked out.

I feel like I really do give people something, part of myself, and when they leave, I really have an investment. But these days, I almost never say a permanent goodbye to anybody. I'm always having old clients come back; I'm even having the children who were playing on the floor coming in with their spouses at this point.

Theme 5: Participants Understand Human Suffering at a Profound Level

Through their work, participants developed a profound understanding of suffering. This includes an awareness of the painful elements and the potential for growth. The participants' comments reflected a profound awareness of suffering and the healing process that is part of their role as a helper. Their hopeful outlook toward how suffering can be transformed also seemed to enhance their own lives. One participant talked about how his perspective has been altered through continual exposure to suffering:

I think all in all, it leaves me with a certain kind of enthusiasm because I see people go through extraordinary pain and come out the other side. And so it makes me patient.

Another participant differentiated between the short-term stressors and the long-term benefits continually confronting client suffering:

> In visiting the intensity of the private world of several people who are your clients, empathizing with the misery, and it can feel like, at the end of the day, lonely to have been so intensely in all of those places, and nobody had been in all of those places with me. And I couldn't tell anybody where I'd been. ... The loneliness of that is a big part of the burden, I think. But that's more like the immediate at the end of the day kind of thing. What I think I'm left with is more a sense of the humanity. ... And I think I'm a lot more comfortable with the topics of grief and sex and life crises. I just think that I just have that settled sense of the humanity of it.

Category C: Creating a Positive Work Structure

Category C contains four themes that focus on how, over time, the participants created important support that enhanced their sense of wellness in the work environment.

Theme 1: Mentor and Peer Support Was Critical at the Novice Phase

Participants reported that positive mentor and peer relationships had a great impact on the novice phase of their careers. These relationships often developed during long-term first placements that were frequently described as challenging but not overwhelming. The novice setting provided enriching work environments full of learning opportunities and encouragement for responsible autonomy and risk taking. While at these sites, a foundation was built for the participants' future practices. In reflecting on his first placement, one participant stated:

> I remember those as good years. I'm sure they were stressful because a lot was new, but I felt very supported. I had resources about me, and I was valued and also I had a tremendous amount of independence.

Another participant stated:

> [It was] a time of working intensely with colleagues in relation to having lots of feedback, lots of inspection of one's practice. All of that, by and large, was very good. I certainly wouldn't trade those years.

While discussing a supervisor at her first placement following graduate training, one participant stated:

> At my first job, I was fortunate enough to have a really fine supervisor who literally I credit with the major amount of training and experience that I have. And that was totally geared to emotional self-awareness and use of self in ways in which I grew a hell of a lot, but I also learned never to ignore that part. ... It opened all the doors for me, and it also made what I was doing very vital and real, and I feel real grateful for that.

Another participant discussed her decision to join a group of seasoned clinicians who then became important mentors and teachers:

> I think that I had either the good fortune or the good judgment to join a group of senior clinicians, all people 20 years older than I, very experienced, and I brought them something they needed which was the M.D. I could prescribe medications for their patients, and I could hospitalize their patients, which was fine. But they gave me the depth and breadth of clinical experience and an understanding of how the practice works, and it was very important to me.

Although the need for strong mentor relationships gradually diminished over time for many of the participants, the salience of these early relationships was highlighted in the reflections of one participant:

> It's more in retrospect than I was aware at the time, that there were people along the way who believed in me and kind of engaged with me because they believed in me. And I really thrived on that, more than I knew, in the moment. I got so much from that in a way that if I hadn't gotten that, my life ... would have taken a different path.

Theme 2: Participants Have Ongoing and Enriching Peer Relationships

Participants reported that they initiated and sustained relationships with a variety of peers and coworkers beyond the novice phase. These relationships served a critical role in supporting the participants. One participant described the value of combining ongoing experience with peer relationships in this way:

> I don't think years of experience by itself does it, because ... I might have the same year of experience 20 times, and so I need to put that together with good consultation and a good collegial system around you; that is a part of the therapist's well-being.

When discussing peer relationships specific to the work environment, one participant stated:

> I think that it is actually kind of a unique and rare environment that offers a therapist that kind of support for continuing growth. One that says even if you've been in this business for a number of years, you are still allowed to not know, you're still allowed to be afraid of what's happening, you're still allowed to feel like a failure, or whatever the issue is.

Both formal and informal interactions were emphasized as being important components of peer relationships in the work environment. One participant described how she and her coworkers had strategically created a work environment that provided a variety of interactions:

> We've made a coffee room so that we run into each other on purpose, and we meet once a week for lunch, and that's very helpful both for relaxation and socializing and for consulting. There's always somebody I can say, "Listen to this situation, tell me what you think," and without naming names, I can describe the problem and get feedback from somebody that I respect.

In reflecting on his peer relationships, one participant highlighted the value of friendship and of sharing life events along with professional concerns:

> We sit down for our staff meeting, and before we do anything else, we just sit at the table, take a few minutes, and talk about our lives. It's sort of this is what's happening with my kids; this is what I did last weekend; by the way, I saw a great movie; and just that personal level, before we get into talking about [clients].

Oftentimes, the intimate quality of peer and coworker relationships was an enriching factor in the participants' ability to deepen their level of self-awareness and, in turn, to invest more intensely in the therapeutic process with clients. Two participants described the importance of sustained, close relationships in the actual work environment:

> Here, for example, we have a group of six, and some of us have been together for about 14 years, so you really have a chance to deepen the experience with one another and, therefore, I think also be able to deepen your work with clients, because you're better able to know about yourself in relationship to the work, and other people know you well enough to say, "Hey, look at this."
>
> … we've been present here in this practice for going on 18 years, and we've always done weekly consultations and the kind that really gets at

what might be stopping us, what might be blocking us, what we might be struggling with.

Diverse peer relationships in the broader professional community were also highlighted as vital sources of support. Participants tended to be actively involved in numerous professional activities, organizations, and community groups. One participant discussed the value of serving on a committee with a cross-section of helping professionals:

> To have all these people giving time and energy to thinking about what will make our work improve. It's just inspiring, and for me it's invigorating and energizing. Just helpful in that way.

Similarly, another participant stated:

> I have a group of colleagues that are very important to me, have been for 10 years now, and we meet in the West Coast every year; we spend a week together; we rent a room together for a week. They're all existentialists, and they're my closest colleagues in terms of tradition, and I see them maybe two, three times a year in groups or individually. ... And that has been very, very helpful over the years.

Theme 3: Multiple Roles Are a Protective Factor

Participants reported that they structured their practices to include multiple tasks and professional involvements. They also exhibit a measure of freedom in choosing the type of clients they work with and how they do their billing. The ability to control the nature of their practice provided the participants with a stimulating balance of professional responsibilities while limiting the stressors that they encounter. In discussing her need for task diversity versus doing only clinical work, one participant stated:

> If I did only this work, I would be bored out of my mind. ... It has nothing to do with the people I see; it's about having to empty yourself out so constantly and regularly to do that work. And that wouldn't be healthy; it just wouldn't be healthy.

Another participant discussed how involvement in diverse activities improved her professional and clinical work:

> I think there is something really enriching about supervising and teaching. It keeps me interested in my work and feeling alive and motivated to read and to think from some point of view other than just inside my head.

Participants reported that freedom to design one's caseload and control the billing also contributed positively to the professional experience. On client-related stressors, one participant stated:

> I don't think of my clients as impacting me in ways that I would consider stressors; ... there's been stuff obviously over the years ... we'll be dealing with suicide or we'll be dealing with this or that. ... I haven't had much of that for a long time, and it's partly this practice; I mean, it's set up in a way in which I'm not dealing with crisis. I mean I'm dealing with ... wellness perspectives. So I'm also not in situations at this point that would push that.

One participant discussed the way that she structured her caseload and completed billing:

> I've been very fortunate in two ways. One is that I'm an old-timer, so I've developed my own reputation and my own referral. Most of my patients come referred by other patients. And many pay out of pocket, and I'm willing to make some adjustments; I'd rather give them the money than the insurance company actually in terms of discount.

Theme 4: Participants Create Health-Promoting Work Environments

Participants said that their work environments were suited to meet specific needs of space, aesthetics, and personal comfort. Equally important, these environments were conducive to facilitating successful therapeutic relationships. One participant outlined the benefits of her work area:

> I really like it here. I like my space. I like being here. I love being here when it's raining or snowing, and it's kind of a cocoon kind of feel to it. I think about the holding environment that helps therapy to work. That is part of what's here, and I like it, and I've heard clients talk about that it's nice to be here.

Other participants also discussed the need to create a comfortable, therapeutic work area:

> Space that allows for both enough distance to accommodate mine but also the other person's personal space requirements. And with clients, that varies actually. So I think sometimes I move forward or backward, depending on what I'm sensing, but also not so big that it feels like you're talking into a room rather than connect to people. I think

something that feels, that gives the sense of privacy and safety. I think it has the sense of being protected but not trapped.

You know, I'm really into friendly textures and colors, and the light is important; the quiet is important. We went to great lengths to sound-proof all these offices. The building would think that it was adequately soundproof, but I could still hear what was going on next door. We just kept putting insulation in the walls until it was soundproof. I guess I have to feel generally safe. I know people who work in clinics and kind of dangerous parts of town, and I think that's not conducive to the comfort of therapist or patient.

Category D: Protective Factors

Category D contains three themes identifying proactive strategies that participants employ to master stressors.

Theme 1: Participants Directly Engage Highly Stressful Professional Dilemmas

Participants are skilled in their ability to handle ongoing difficult situations and to manage crises in a proactive manner that serves to prevent future incidents. Their strategies reflect an ability to adapt to change, and to bounce about unexpected or shifting events and issues. Participants tended to identify and frame challenges and issues in a hopeful light and to access appropriate resources. In confronting challenges and issues, participants discussed their need to remain receptive to possibilities and approaches on both internal and external levels:

> And then I have to engage [the stressful issue] in myself because there's always the possibility that there's some piece of me working here that would rather not see this, would rather not own the power that I have; I'd rather see that I wasn't that important, diminish my own responsibility in that way, or minimize my responsibility to be a better attender to somebody else's experience.
>
> One of my most profound learning experiences was stimulated by, first of all, working with a couple of therapists who turned out to be highly unethical and abusing their patients, and I had a dear friend of mine exploited by a therapist, and I'm thinking, "I've got to understand this; something really went wrong here." I find myself somewhat of an expert on boundaries and boundary violations because it really challenged my whole self-concept as a therapist or challenged the whole idea of therapy as a healing process. So I wanted to go after that problem.

An appropriate reliance on peer consultation was a critical resource that participants used in their process of exploring important issues and incidents:

> I get lots of consultation, so I'm not by myself with the really hard cases. That's primary for me. If there's anything that feels really important, it's not to be by myself in really hard situations, that I have colleagues with me. So that I feel that kind of a sense that I'm not all alone in this. It's really important to me that I'm seeing things clearly, and I think it's hard sometimes when you're all by yourself. And to have other eyes and ears looking at something with you. So that's one major way [to protect myself].

A key characteristic of the participants' reports was their willingness to remain open and to adapt. In discussing these traits, one participant stated:

> I think sometimes it's caused me not to feel like I know what I know at times, but on the other hand, it also keeps me kind of fresh and open. I'm willing to entertain almost anything, and I'm willing to look at where I could be off base about almost anything.

Another participant described her daily clinical work and provided an example of her ability to adapt from one client to another:

> I think I'm emotionally resilient in the sense of I can be with someone in their pain. ... but then I can in the next session be laughing with somebody about something or celebratory with somebody. So it feels like that's a way that I can move.

Theme 2: Participants Confront and Resolve Personal Issues

Participants reported that their own personal life crises and problems were a challenging area for them. They also believed that direct acknowledgment and resolution of these issues allowed for congruence between the personal self and the professional self. One participant explained how her experience in dealing with the unexpected death of a family member challenged her at a profoundly personal level yet allowed her to be more attuned to clients:

> Well, I think the suicide [in the family] made the work very challenging. And yet at the same time, I was fortunate in that I had a very fine therapist. And because I had that therapist, while the work was difficult, I constantly felt like I was being so tended to emotionally ... I found myself taking from that experience and just automatically moving it into what I was doing with clients. So it's like as the therapist was willing to go with me where I needed to go and that opened up areas

or that developed areas inside of me that I didn't even know were there. Then, automatically, I would hear those areas in clients. I would ask the questions because they were coming from where I'd been taken to.

Theme 3: Highly Engaged Learning Is a Powerful Source of Renewal

Participants reported that they had histories of being open to new experiences, seeking out diverse avenues of learning, and synthesizing information from multiple sources. Their lives were marked by an insatiable curiosity, a deep comfort with ambiguity, and constant consumption of knowledge. This ongoing learning process helped them to maintain an energy level necessary to continually engage in the helper role. In discussing a draw toward learning and its effect on her, one participant stated:

> Well, it provides constant energy for one thing, and I think what happens in our field is that we can get tired and exhausted, but I think that's one of the things that keeps me feeling high energy and a lot of interest and love for what we do, and it's exciting.

Some participants described why a tolerance for ambiguity and an openness for learning were critical ingredients in their work:

> I mean, we don't throw away what we know in favor of mystery, but to favor mystery is to prefer it above what we know.
>
> If nothing else, you want to work with these people from all walks of life with various occupations and various interests, and if you don't sustain at least some awareness or at least openness to learn from your patients about their work, then how can you be of any use to them if you stay on the outside? So one has to have the interest and curiosity and some fondness, I think, for the client. If you're not interested in joining them, then why would they trust you to come and open themselves up.
>
> If you can't work with the unknown and the uncertain, you can't last in this business.

Another participant discussed her efforts to bring new information into her work:

> When I read, I always know what I define as active learning, which is trying to take the new information and see how I can incorporate it into what's already there, which means that I'm always modifying existing information too. And adapting it to my needs and integrating what I already know. It can be a negative thing if you go with the approach that

everything has to fit to some rigid fixed scheme set already in existence. But I don't think I do that. I think I really constantly modify my schemes by incorporating the new stuff, but it's probably the integration and incorporation that are really important.

One participant discussed how she utilized peers to facilitate her own learning process:

I think being in a group practice has helped because it keeps you kind of interested and hungry for what's available and keeps you open, I think. I've done groups with co-therapists for years upon years. I've done co-therapy, marriage therapy. I think that also helps to stay open because you're constantly getting new information, getting new ways of thinking when working with someone. Getting input about your ways of working, so I think that also helps.

Category E: Nurturing Self Through Solitude and Relationships

Participants clearly identified their need to maintain a strong sense of self. Category E contains four themes that focus on components important to the participants for this need. The themes reflect multiple approaches and a network of internal and external involvements that enable the participants to maintain a personal and professional congruency.

Theme 1: Participants Foster Professional
Stability by Nurturing a Personal Life

Participants were aware of the importance of maintaining a balance between their personal and professional lives. They believe that their role as a helper is facilitated by a lifestyle that includes multiple involvements and connections apart from their professional life. One participant verbalized this sentiment when he stated:

What helps me do it well is to give a damn about what I'm doing, but … I've got to have a life out of here. This can't be everything. I can't be over-invested in it. There's an appropriate kind of investment in which I care very much about what happens here, and I'm willing to invest myself as fully as I can, and part of what helps me do that is the fact that I've got a very real existence in a lot of ways, not just this.

Another participant succinctly stated:

> There's [need for] some kind of larger balance. I don't think anybody could do this work just and not tip over in some way. The tendency to get off center is too great.

One participant reported a very similar point of view and then elaborated on the hazards of not maintaining a life outside of her professional role:

> It is up to me to do everything I can to maintain my own emotional health so that I can actually be available to my patients without needing them. I think one of the ways therapy goes awry is that the therapist starts to use the patient for their own emotional sustenance, regulation of the therapist's self-esteem, all those sorts of things. I think to be a good therapist you must be well fed and well loved. Basically, have a life out there that is working.

Theme 2: Participants Invest in a Broad Array of Restorative Activities

Participants cultivate a collection of activities and leisure pursuits. Although the actual involvements are varied, a shared theme that runs through them is their function of providing a diversion from work-related stressors and an avenue for reconnecting with self and others. The function of these activities and pursuits was reflected in one participant's statement:

> [Helpful is] doing things personally like physical kinds of things. When we talked about secondary post-trauma, there are some days when I just feel like I need to go out and kick something and just kind of biking real hard or walking real fast; doing things like that can be really help-ful I think. I do a lot of going to plays, going to movies, getting together with friends, and just talking about plays we've seen, books we've read.

A similar draw toward multiple involvements was reflected when this par-ticipant stated:

> I love mystery stories and historical biography; that's where I learn my history, from historical novels. I like movies; I love sports; I'm an avid football fan; I knit; I do a lot of knitting and crocheting.

Other participants discussed the pull that they feel to nature and other creative activities:

> I think something happens for me spiritually when I'm doing stuff with flowers and plants. I've got plants all over the place in my home, and

it's kind of a ritualistic piece about tending those. I have gardens here and at a cabin up north, and there's, again, sort of a ritualistic peace with tending those. I think that takes me to a place that is real deeply nourishing, and I can get lost in it in a whole different way. I love the creative so the book that I wrote and stuff that I do for school and the papers, I really try to approach those as creative endeavors.

I find that music is a way for me to ground myself in the larger experience of my life and life itself. I suppose that's true for a lot of people … but that's certainly true for me, and always has been. And one of the ways, when I find myself feeling deprived of being able to cry, it'll come through that way.

One participant discussed the critical function of travel:

It's very helpful for perspective purposes. Very helpful. The trick is to be gone long enough … so you recognize fully your entire replaceability. That you are absolutely replaceable. And there, you talked about freedom and relief; there is real freedom and relief in that.

Theme 3: Participants Construct Fortifying Personal Relationships

Participants are highly skilled relationship builders. They establish nurturing and challenging connections with family, friends, and other social groups that are intimate and rich. Among other things, their relationships with others provide consistent, ongoing support and enable a realistic perspective of self. Although these relationships are important on a day-to-day basis, they are especially critical in times of crisis. Some of the participants discussed how a network of supportive relationships fortified their lives and acted as an emotional safety net:

If you have good friends in your life, if you have a good support system, folks will let you know that you're feeling worn out or depleted or whatever and then will support you getting some help.

A lot of close friends and my children are best friends. And they keep me very well balanced and keep my perspective, don't let me get a big head. They're very good, a very supportive bunch.

Having your own family connection solid is, at least for me, pretty important. I think I have a lot of reliance on other people in my life or friends or my wife, catching me in areas where I don't catch myself.

Some participants spoke about the encouragement and comfort they derived from a relationship with a spouse or life partner:

I married the right lady; my wife has a master's level degree in child development. And so we can talk, and she understood what I did. She never worked after we got married because she started having kids right away. But we could communicate and understand each other. And she was always a nice balance when my head started getting too big. She would pop it. ... And so that was very supportive, still is.

We met actually as classmates. And I'm sure that's probably the most important relationship personally, but also I think probably professionally in some ways. We do talk psychology with each other, have all these years. So I'm sure that's been very important.

One participant highlighted the essential function of children and family:

We do a lot with family celebrations. Socializing, having people over for dinner. My children, now they are out of the home, but when they were younger, I think we did some things that were really helpful. Taking time just to play some games together. Just do something completely separate from work.

Another participant also commented on the very significant role that her friends play:

What I would say is that there are a few close friends, and when I'm in trouble, when they're in trouble, the rules are we get access to each other whenever and however long we need it. And when the trouble's over, we go back to our lives. And those people are very in place, and I think I am for them too.

Participants also fostered an essential relationship with the world at large, and they usually spoke about this in terms of a spiritual awareness or seeking a greater sense of connection with others:

I have a sense of spirit. I have a sense of reverence. I have a sense of place in the universe even though I know it's just a speck; it's a place to participate. I believe that there's benevolence in all that. I believe that warm, gentle breezes blow my way besides the cold, bitter winds.

Theme 4: Participants Value an Internal Focus

Participants reported that they are aware of the significant role that their internal processes play in sustaining their own sense of wellness and in their ability to function effectively as practitioners. They are open to, and willingly engage in, their own personal therapy as a means of enhancing this process of introspection and self-examination. This commitment to understanding self represents an important self-care method that has a positive impact on their sense of resiliency and wellness in the helping role. Statements by the participants reflected the value of being continually self-aware. One said that it was important to attend to

> what's coming up in my world that needs me to understand what's going on or feel like I get it in terms of whatever's happening internally so that when I'm doing my work, I'm sort of cleared out, and it isn't that the stuff isn't in there, but I'm not obsessing about it; it's not taking me some other place than where I need to be in the room.

Another stated:

> To learn something about vulnerability yourself, I don't know that anybody can really do therapy well until they know vulnerability, unless they are aware of their woundedness. ... And be able to work from there.

One participant shared her belief that staying attuned to internal processes was, in part, an ethical responsibility:

> I think that's where we need to build this self-monitoring and be self-aware. If I become psychotic, then probably those around me would notice it, but outside of those extremes, if my work fluctuates on life events or whatever like physical health ... I think to what extent one is ethical in their conduct [relates to] the kind of posture of self-reflection and self-monitoring and judgment.

Other participants discussed their belief that personal therapy was an important vehicle in their quest for self-awareness. One participant stated:

> The other thing I would say is it's important for every therapist to know when it's time to go back for some therapy of your own; personal anxieties or problems are either getting stirred up by the work or are intruding from the outside world.

Conclusion

Several pertinent areas were highlighted in this chapter. Participants identified stressors connected to various therapeutic issues and client behaviors, breaches in peer relationships, and the impact of their own personal crises and life changes. The areas of stressors that were reflected in the participants' comments underscore the demanding nature of the helping role and reinforce the value of protective approaches and self-care strategies as a means of ensuring practitioner wellness and professional vitality.

The participants identified important protective factors. These factors ranged from internal coping strategies to variables within the external environment. A commonality that existed among this group of participants was their commitment to self-care and their high-level skill in accessing valuable resources.

This group of practitioners has acute awareness of the internal landscape and maintains a watchful focus on their emotional selves. Their strong commitment to self-observation was frequently combined with a proactive style in directly confronting stressors that emerged both from their work and in their personal lives. When combined, these approaches allowed the participants to maintain a sense of personal congruence and an energy level that are critical components in professional wellness and burnout prevention.

This group of participants was nurtured through multiple avenues and relationships. The role that peers played in providing the participants with a realistic perspective and ongoing professional support was emphasized. While peer support was vital throughout the participants' careers, it played an especially key role during the participants' novice phase of development and also during times of unexpected crisis. In a similar way, participants also noted the importance of immersing themselves in enriching relationships and activities apart from their work environments. It appears that these diverse involvements were essential components to self-care plans that maintained a healthy sense of balance.

Self-Reflection Exercises

1. What impresses you most about the methods used by experts to maintain professionally vitality?

_____

_____

_____

_____

_____

_____

_____

_____

_____

2. What can the experts teach you for your own resiliency development and self-care?

_____

_____

_____

_____

_____

_____

_____

_____

_____

_____

12

Epilogue

Helping others with significant concerns in their lives can be highly effective, satisfying, and meaningful. It can be great work. To do this well, however, we must constantly attach and separate successfully, over and over again, with person after person. We experience ambiguous professional loss, normative failure, secondary trauma, and vicarious traumatization. Yet, we must continually invest positively in others, and this means constant renewal of the self and an ongoing focus on the intricate balance between caring for others versus caring for self.

Our work can be so valuable and so pleasurable. A 68-year-old psychologist said in reflecting on her work at that age:

> With diminishing anxiety, I became less and less afraid of my clients and with that came an ease for me in using my own wide repertoire of skills and procedures. They became more available to me when I needed them. And during those moments it became remarkable to me that someone would have the willingness to share their private world with me and that my work with them would bring very positive results for them. This brought a sense of intense pleasure to me. (Skovholt & Rønnestad, 1995, p. 96)

Imagery Exercise

Let us suggest that you imagine a favorite tree in front of you. See its beauty, vibrance, vitality, and strength. Now imagine yourself as the tree—beautiful, vibrant, vital, and strong. As a tree, you take in carbon dioxide and give off oxygen to those you help. Taking in carbon dioxide and giving off oxygen is literally giving life to those you serve. To do so, however, the tree must work hard, and to work hard, it must be healthy. That means it must have ample sunlight, plenty of rain, rich soil, and freedom from dangerous pests like the insidious larvae of the emerald ash borer that kills trees by cutting off the water supply and nutrients. There are lots of tree pests, both overt and subtle. To grow, the tree must branch out and respond well to pruning. How then can you ensure that you, as a helping professional, will keep away those excessive professional losses, those dangerous pests that might cut off your nutrients and eat your leaves, and that you will have abundant soil, rain, and sunlight? And what for you comprises the sunlight, the rain, and the soil?

What ultimately is a better way to spend one's working days than giving off oxygen to those choking and gasping for air? What is more beautiful than a strong, healthy tree doing its work, or more tragic than a tree that is now dead and devoid of the capacity to give life? How will you remain as the healthy tree and never forget the constant need, over 30 to 40 years as a caring professional, to avoid pests and always have rain, soil, and sunlight?

We wish you well.

Self-Reflection Exercises

In the epilogue, we suggested that you think of a favorite tree and the way that a tree takes in carbon dioxide and gives off oxygen. Working with people, practitioners do the same thing. Apply this tree metaphor to your life as a helper of others.

1. What is your water, your sun, your soil? How adequate are they for you?

_____

_____

_____

_____

_____

_____

_____

_____

_____

2. What are the large pests that can potentially eat away at your vitality? What are the small, invisible, and stealthlike, but dangerous pests?

_____

_____

_____

_____

_____

_____

_____

_____

_____

3. What changes, if any, do you need to make to have a healthy tree that can serve others by taking in carbon dioxide and giving off oxygen?

_____

_____

_____

_____

_____

_____

_____

_____

_____

13

Self-Care Action Plan

The intent of the first 12 chapters in this book is to engage you, the reader, in topics that are central to your work as a practitioner. In this chapter on a self-care action plan, the focus is on doing more than reading. We urge you to employ this chapter in a practical way that can be directly applied to your life as a practitioner. This chapter on self-care asks you to respond in writing to ideas in the text and also to additional inventories and charts. Then you are asked to make a self-care action plan for yourself. The chapter has two parts:

Part 1—You are to assess your own other-care–self-care balance while finding out what activities other practitioners choose for self-care.

Part 2—You are to decide if any changes in your behavior, thinking patterns, or feelings are necessary to achieve a healthy other-care–self-care balance. Last, you are asked to make concrete but realistic plans for any change that seems needed.

Part 1: Assess Your Own Other-Care vs. Self-Care Balance

Step 1: Assessing the Stress Level of Your Work

A first step is to assess your job stress level. In stressful jobs, individuals often feel high demands and low control. For example, quadrant four (low

**FIGURE 13.1
Elements of Job Stress.**

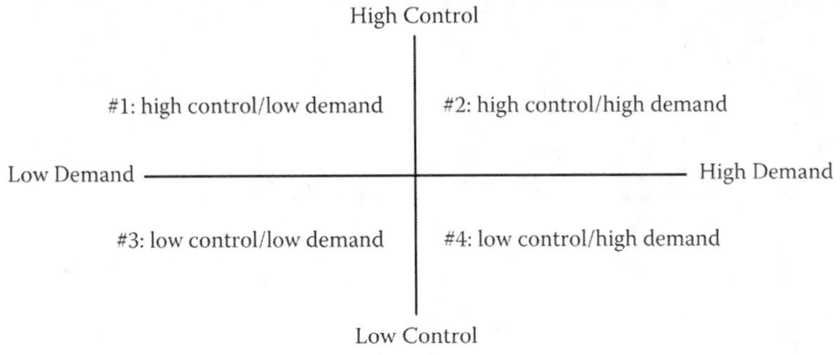

```
                          High Control
                              │
  #1: high control/low demand │ #2: high control/high demand
                              │
Low Demand ───────────────────┼─────────────────── High Demand
                              │
  #3: low control/low demand  │ #4: low control/high demand
                              │
                          Low Control
```

Source: Adapted from Karasek, R. & Theorell, T., *Healthy Work: Stress Productivity and the Restructuring of Working Life*, Basic Books, New York, 1992.

control–high demands) in Figure 13.1 is often thought of as much more stressful than quadrant one. How would you assess the stress level of your job? The results are helpful in calibrating the other-care versus self-care balance. Next, fill out the short questionnaire in Figure 13.2.

Using the four-quadrant chart and the inventory, describe the stress level of your job.

_____

_____

_____

_____

_____

_____

_____

_____

FIGURE 13.2
Questionnaire: How stressful is your job?

How stressful is your job?

This test can give you a rough indication of how much stress you're under at work. The test was adapted for us by researcher Robert Karasek, Ph.D., of the University of Massachusetts at Lowell, based on a longer questionnaire of his. Answer yes or no:

	Yes	No
Demand		
I have to work very hard		
I am not asked to do an excessive amount of work*		
I have enough time to get my work done*		
Control		
I have to do a lot of repetitive work*		
I have to be creative		
I have learn new things		
I have a lot of say about what happens		
I have very little freedom to decide how I do my work*		
Social support		
I work with helpful people		
I work with people who take personal interest in me		
My supervisor is helpful		
My supervisor is concerned about my welfare		

Scoring: Calculate a separate score for each of the three parts—demand, control, and social support. In each part, give yourself one point for every "yes" answer to the questions that don't have an asterisk(*). For those that do have an asterisk, give yourself one point if you answered "no." Jot down your three scores in the spaces below. Then write in the word that describes each of those scores.

Demand score: ☐
   My job demands are _____
   (Write "low" if your score was 0 or 1; "high" if your score was 2 or 3.)

Control score: ☐
   My control at work is _____
   (Write "low" if your scored 0 or 2; "high" if your scored 3 or 5.)

Social-support score: ☐
   My social support at work is _____
   (Write "low" if your score was 0 or 1; "moderate" if 2; "high" if 3 or 4.)

Interpretation: High demand, low control, and low social support all tend to increase job stress. The more of those factors that you face at work—and the more extreme your score on each factor—the greater your stress. Jobs where you experience all three tension-producing features are generally very stressful, while jobs with two such features generate moderately high stress. Those with only one stressful factor may be moderate or moderately high stress, depending on how much the other two scores offset that factor. The least stressful jobs combine high control and high social support with low demand.

Source: From Consumer Reports on Health, 1996. Used by permission of Robert Karasek.

FIGURE 13.3
Other-care–self-care balance.

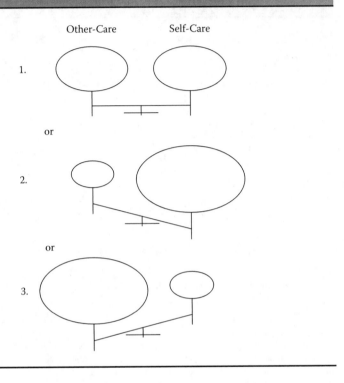

Step 2: Assessing Your Other-Care–Self-Care Balance

Another step is to assess your other-care–self-care balance. Choose your type in Figure 13.3, and indicate the other-care–self-care balance score. Is it 50–50, 10–90, 90–10, 70–30, or 30–70?

What is your other-care–self-care balance score? _____–_____

Often, other-care practitioners are more oriented to other-care than self-care. Some imbalance can be fine, but when is this direction excessive for you?

_____

_____

_____

_____

_____

_____

_____

_____

Step 3: Assessing Your Professional Self-Care

In Chapter 9, 16 factors are presented to sustain the professional self. For each factor, what are you doing to sustain your professional self? How well are you sustaining your professional self?

1. In the second column of the following table, list example activities that you are doing to sustain your professional self.
2. Assess how well you are sustaining your professional self regarding each factor, and indicate the assessment score of 0 to 6 in the third column.

0	1	2	3	4	5	6
Not at all				→		*Very well*

Factors	Example Activities (That You Do/Plan to Do in Your Life)	Assessment
Avoiding the grandiosity impulse		
Thinking long-term		
Creating and sustaining an active, individual development method		
Professional self-understanding		
Creating a professional greenhouse at work		
Leadership that promotes balance between caring for others and self		
Professional social support from peers		
Receiving support from mentors, supervisors, or bosses		
Being nurtured from your work as mentors, supervisors, or managers		
Learning how to be professional and playful		
Using professional venting to release distress emotions		
Being a "good enough practitioner"		
Understanding the reality of pervasive early professional anxiety		
Increasing excitement and decreasing boredom by reinventing yourself		
Minimizing ambiguous professional loss		
Learning to say no to unreasonable requests		

From the preceding assessment, list your three strongest professional self-care areas and your three areas for growth.

Strongest professional self-care areas:

1. _____
   _____

2. _____
   _____

3. _____
   _____

Areas for growth in professional self-care:

1. _____
   _____

2. _____
   _____

3. _____
   _____

Step 4: Assessing Your Personal Self-Care

In Chapter 10, parts of the personal self are presented. What are you doing to nurture each part of yourself? How well are you nurturing each part of your self?

1. In the second column of the following table, list specific activities to nurture each part of your self.
2. Assess how well you are nurturing each part of your self, and indicate the assessment score of 0 to 6 in the third column.

0	1	2	3	4	5	6
Not at all				⟶		Very well

Part of Your Self	Specific Activities to Nurture This Part of Your Self	Assessment
Emotional self		
Financial self		
Humorous self		

Continued

Part of Your Self	Specific Activities to Nurture This Part of Your Self	Assessment
Loving self		
Nutritious self		
Physical self		
Playful self		
Priority-setting self		
Recreational self		
Relaxation and stress-reduction self		
Solitary self		
Spiritual or religious self		

From the preceding assessment, list your three strongest personal self-care areas and your three areas for growth.

Strongest personal self-care areas:

1. _____

_____

2. _____

_____

3. _____

_____

Areas for growth in professional self-care:

1. _____

_____

2. _____

_____

3. _____

_____

Step 5: Review Positive Strategies

Review positive strategies used by psychologists and other practitioners in Tables 13.1 and 13.2 and the following Poor Self-Care Deadly Dozen.

TABLE 13.1
Three Studies of Therapists' Self-Care Activities

Study 1: Top 10 Helpful Activities[a]	Study 2: Top 10 Career-Sustaining Behaviors[b]	Study 3: 234 Well-Functioning Psychologists' Top 10 Activities Contributing to Well Functioning[c]
Utilize close friends, significant others, or family as a source of support	Spending time with partner/family	Self-awareness and self-monitoring
Seek solutions to difficulties	Maintaining balance between professional and personal lives	Personal values
Use humor	Maintaining a sense of humor	Preserving balance between personal and professional lives
Choose internship activities of interest	Maintaining self-awareness	Relationship with spouse, partner, or family
Maintain self-awareness of the impact my internship experiences has on me and my work	Maintaining professional identity	Personal therapy
Seek out pleasurable diversions outside of internship	Engaging in quiet leisure activities	Relationships with friends
Consult with my fellow interns	Maintaining a sense of control over work responsibilities	Vacations
Set realistic goals for myself regarding internship	Engaging in physical activities	Professional identity
Seek supervision from clinical supervisor	Taking regular vacations	Informal peer support
Work to create a comfortable work environment for myself	Perceiving clients' problems as interesting	Mentor

[a]*Source:* "Intern Self-Care: An Exploratory Study into Strategy Use and Effectiveness," by J. A. Turner, L. M. Edwards, I. M. Eicken, K. Yokoyama, J. R. Castro, A. N. Tran, and K. L. Haggins, 2005, *Professional Psychology: Research and Practice, 36*, pp. 674–680.

[b]*Source:* "Career-Sustaining Behaviors, Satisfactions, and Stresses of Professional Psychologists," by P. Stevanovic and P. A. Rupert, 2004, *Psychotherapy: Theory, Research, Practice, Training, 41*, pp. 301–309.

[c]*Source:* "Well-Functioning in Professional Psychologists," J. J. Coster and M. Schwebel, 1997, *Professional Psychology: Research and Practice, 28*, pp. 5–13.

TABLE 13.2
Self-Care Methods of Practitioners

Trauma Therapists' Top 10 Helpful Activities[a]	Counselors', Teachers', and Health Professionals' 10 Commonly Described Activities[b]
Discussing cases with colleagues	Being with family
Attending workshops	Education for job skills
Spending time with family or friends	Fun hobby
Travel, vacations, hobbies, movies	Physical activity
Talking with colleagues between sessions	Reading
Socializing	Receiving consultation or supervision
Exercising	Social activity
Limiting case load	Time alone
Developing spiritual life	Time with friends, partner, spouse
Receiving general supervision	Vacation

[a]*Source:* "Vicarious Traumatization: An Empirical Study of the Effects of Trauma Work on Trauma Therapists," by L. A. Pearlman, and P. J. Maclan, 1995, *Professional Psychology: Research and Practice, 26,* pp. 558–565.
[b]In alphabetical order. Data from workshops by T. M. Skovholt in 1996.

The Poor Self-Care Deadly Dozen

1. Toxic supervisor and colleague support
2. Little fun (e.g., playfulness, humor, laughing) in life or work
3. Only a fuzzy and unarticulated understanding of one's own needs
4. No professional development process that turns experience into more competence and less anxiety
5. No energy-giving personal life
6. An inability to say no to unreasonable requests
7. Vicarious traumatization that takes an accumulated toll
8. Personal relationships that are predominantly one-way caring relationships with self as giver
9. Constant perfectionism in work tasks
10. Continual unresolved ambiguous professional losses
11. A strong need to be needed
12. Professional success defined solely by client, student, or patient positive change or appreciation

Step 6: Assessing Self-Care Strengths and Weaknesses

Using information gathered from Steps 1 to 5, write an assessment of your self-care strengths and areas of growth. As has been noted throughout the preceding chapters, there are joys in the work but also hazards—plenty of them. The constant giving of the self, a necessity in optimal work by counselors, therapists, teachers, and health professionals means that practitioners must assertively nurture the wellness of the professional and personal selves. How are you doing with nurturing your own wellness?

_____
_____
_____
_____
_____
_____
_____
_____
_____
_____

Part 2: Action Plan for Change

Step 7: Action Plan

Now, develop an action plan to work on one or two self-care growth areas. Remember that slower behavioral change usually works best. We suggest that you be modest in your goals and build on attainable change with reinforcement to maintain the change.

Your general action plan:

_____
_____
_____
_____
_____
_____
_____
_____

Specific Goal 1:

_____

_____

_____

_____

_____

_____

_____

_____

Method for achieving Goal 1:

_____

_____

_____

_____

_____

_____

_____

Reinforcement to maintain new behavior:

_____

_____

_____

_____

_____

_____

Specific Goal 2:

_____

_____

_____

_____

_____

_____

Method for achieving Goal 2:

_____

_____

_____

_____

_____

_____

_____

_____

Reinforcement to maintain new behavior:

_____

_____

_____

_____

_____

_____

_____

References

Ackerley, G. D., Burnell, J., Holder, D. C., & Kurdek, L. A. (1988). Burnout among licensed psychologists. *Professional Psychology: Research and Practice, 19,* 624–631.

Ackerman, D. (1999). *Deep play.* New York: Random House.

Adams, H. (1918). *The education of Henry Adams.* New York: Houghton Mifflin.

Adolson, M. J. (1995). Clinical supervision of therapists with difficult-to-treat patients. *Bulletin of the Menninger Clinic, 59,* 32–52.

Ambrose, S. E. (1996). *Undaunted courage.* New York: Touchstone.

Anonymous (Ed.). (1982). *Each day a new beginning.* San Francisco, CA: HarperCollins.

Association of Psychology Postdoctoral and Internship Centers. (2006, May). *APPIC Membership Criteria: Doctoral Psychology Internship Programs.* Retrieved May 12, 2010, from http://www.appic.org/about/231 about policies and procedure internship.html

Ayers, W. (1993). *To teach: The journey of a teacher.* New York: Teachers College Press.

Bachelor, A., & Horvath, A. (1999). The therapeutic relationship. In M. A. Hubble, B. L. Duncan, & S. D. Miller (Eds.), *The heart and soul of change: What works in therapy* (pp. 133–178). Washington, DC: American Psychological Association.

Baker, E. (2003). *Caring for ourselves: A therapist's guide to personal and professional well-being.* Washington, DC: American Psychological Association.

Balch, J. F., & Balch, P. A. (1997). *Prescription for nutritional healing.* Garden City Park, NY: Avery Publishing Group.

Baltes, P. B., & Smith, J. (1990). Toward a psychology of wisdom and its ontogenesis. In R. E. Sternberg (Ed.), *Wisdom: Its origins and development.* Cambridge: Cambridge University Press.

Bandhauer, B. (1997). Waiting for wisdom to arrive. In J. Kottler (Ed.), *Finding your way as a counselor* (pp. 7–9). Alexandria, VA: American Counseling Association.

Barnett, J. E., Baker, E. K., Elman, N. S., & Schoener, G. R. (2007). In pursuit of wellness: The self-care imperative. *Professional Psychology: Research and Practice, 38*(6), 603–612.

Barnett, J. E., Johnston, L. C., & Hillard, D. (2006). Psychologist wellness as an ethical imperative. In L. VandeCreek & J. B. Allen (Eds.), *Innovations in clinical practice: Focus on health and wellness* (pp. 257–271). Sarasota, FL: Professional Resources Press.

Beck, H. (2009, December 20). Bowing to body clocks, N.B.A. teams are sleeping in. *New York Times,* pp. SP1, SP3.

Becker, E. (1973). *The denial of death.* New York: Free Press.

Beckett, S. (1997). *Waiting for Godot.* New York: Grove Press.

Belenky, M., Chinchy, B., Goldberger, N. & Tarule, J. (1986). *Women's ways of knowing.* New York: Basic Books.

Benner, P., & Wrubel, J. (1982). Skilled clinical knowledge: The value of perceptual awareness, part 2. *Journal of Nursing Administration, 12,* 28–33.

Bennet, J. (1997, January 19). I see 'em! We'll fight 'em! Profiles in courage beyond the call. *New York Times,* p. E7.

Benson, H. (1975). *The relaxation response.* New York: Morrow.

Benson, H. (1999, August). *Power and biology of belief.* Presented at the annual convention of the American Psychological Association, Boston.

Benson-Henry Institute for Mind Body Medicine. (2010). *Eliciting the relaxation response.* Retrieved May 18, 2010, from http://www.massgeneral.org/bhi/basics/eliciting_rr.aspx

Bergin, A. E., & Garfield, S. L. (1994). Overview, trends, and future issues. In A. E. Bergin & S. L. Garfield (Eds.), *Handbook of psychotherapy and behavior change* (pp. 821–830). New York: John Wiley & Sons.

Bernard, J. M., & Goodyear, R. K. (2008). *Fundamentals of clinical supervision* (4th ed.). Boston: Allyn & Bacon.

Blatt, S. (2008). *A dialectical psychology: Implications for research and practice.* Washington, DC: American Psychological Association.

Bohart, A. C., Elliot, R., Greenberg, L. S., & Watson, J. C. (2002). Empathy. In J. C. Norcross (Ed.), *Psychotherapy relationships that work: Therapist contributions and responsiveness to patients* (pp. 89–108). London: Oxford University Press.

Borders, L. D. (1992). Learning to think like a supervisor. *Clinical Supervisor, 10,* 135–148.

Borders, L. D., & Brown, L. L. (2005). *The new handbook of counseling supervision* (5th ed.). Mahwah, NJ: Lawrence Erlbaum Associates.

Boss, P. (1999). *Ambiguous loss: Learning to live with unresolved grief.* Cambridge, MA: Harvard University Press.

Boss, P. (2006). *Loss, trauma, and resilience: Therapeutic work with ambiguous loss.* New York: W. W. Norton.

Boss, P., Caron, W., Horbal, J., & Mortimer, J. (1990). Predictors of depression in care-givers of dementia patients: Boundary ambiguity and mastery. *Family Process, 29,* 245–254.

Bowlby, J. (1969). *Attachment.* New York: Basic Books.

Bowlby, J. (1973). *Separation: Anxiety and anger.* New York: Basic Books.

Bowlby, J. (1980). *Loss: Sadness and depression.* New York: Basic Books.

Bowlby, J. (1988). *A secure base: Parent–child attachment and healthy human development.* New York: Basic Books.

Brinson, J. (1997). Reach out and touch someone. In J. Kottler (Ed.), *Finding your way as a counselor* (pp. 165–167). Alexandria, VA: American Counseling Association.

Buber, M. (1970). *I and thou.* New York: Touchstone.

By a general practitioner. (1985). Hope is the key. In V. Rippere & R. Williams (Eds.), *Wounded healers: Mental health workers' experiences of depression.* Chichester, UK: John Wiley & Sons.

Canfield, J. (2005). Secondary traumatization, burnout, and vicarious traumatization: A review of the literature as it relates to therapists who treat trauma. *Smith College Studies in Social Work, 75*(2), 81–101.

Carey, B., Cave, D., & Alvarez, L. (2009, November 8). A military therapist's world: Long hours, filled with pain. *New York Times,* p. 1.

Carkhuff, R. (1969). *Helping and human relations.* New York: Holt, Rinehart and Winston.

Cassidy, J. (1999). No satisfaction: The trial of a shopping nation. *The New Yorker, 129*(43), 88–92.

Castonguay, L. G., Constantino, M. J., & Grosse Holtforth, M. (2006). The working alliance: Where are we and where should we go? *Psychotherapy: Theory, Research, Practice, Training, 43*(3), 271–279.

Cedoline, A. J. (1982). *Job burnout in public education.* New York: Teachers College Press.

Chang, V. Y., Palesh, O., Caldwell, R., Glasgow, N., Abramson, M., & Luskin, F. (2004). The effects of a mindfulness-based stress reduction program on stress, mindfulness self-efficacy, and positive states of mind. *Stress and Health: Journal of the International Society for the Investigation of Stress, 20*(3), 141–147.

Cherniss, C. (1980). *Staff burnout: Job stress in the human services.* Thousand Oaks, CA: Sage.

Cherniss, C. (1995). *Beyond burnout.* New York: Routledge.

Chi, M. T. H., Glaser, R., & Farr, M. J. (Eds.). (1988). *The nature of expertise.* Hillsdale, NJ: Erlbaum.

Chodorow, N. (1978). *The reproduction of mothering.* Berkeley: University of California Press.

Christopher, J. C. (2010). Mindfulness and my search for meaning. In M. Trotter-Mathison, J. M. Koch, S. Sanger, and T. M. Skovholt (Eds.), *Voices from the field: Defining moments in counselor and therapist development* (pp. 37–40), New York: Routledge.

Corey, M. S., & Corey, G. (1989). *Becoming a helper.* Pacific Grove, CA: Brooks/Cole.

Corsini, R. J., & Wedding, D. (2010). *Current psychotherapies* (9th ed). Belmont, CA: Brooks/Cole.

Cousins, N. (1979). *Anatomy of an illness as perceived by the patient.* New York: Norton.

Danby, H. (Trans.). (1933). *The Mishnah, Talmud.* London: Oxford University Press.

Davis, D. D. (2008). *Terminating therapy.* New York: Wiley.

Davis, M., Eshelman, E. R., & McKay, M. (1995). *The relaxation and stress reduction workbook* (6th ed.). Oakland, CA: New Harbinger Publications.

Diener, E., Suh, E. M., Lucus, R. E., & Smith, H. L. (1999). Subjective well-being: Three decades of progress. *Psychological Bulletin, 125,* 276–302.

Dodge, K. A., & Feldman, E. (1990). Issues in social cognition and sociometric status. In S. R. Asher & J. D. Coie (Eds.), *Peer rejection in childhood* (pp. 119–155). New York: Cambridge.

Doehrman, M. J. (1976). Parallel processes in supervision and psychotherapy. *Bulletin of the Menninger Clinic, 40,* 1–104.

Dominguez, J., & Robin, V. (1992). *Your money or your life.* New York: Penguin Books.

Donne, J. (1975). *Devotions: Upon emergent occasions* (A. Raspa, Ed.). Montreal: McGill-Queen's University Press.

Dreyfus, H. L., & Dreyfus, S. E. (1986). *Mind over machine: The power of human intuition and expertise in the era of the computer.* New York: Free Press.

Duncan, B. L., & Miller, S. D. (2000). *The heroic client: Doing client-centered, outcome-informed therapy.* San Francisco, CA: Jossey-Bass.

Dupree, P. I., & Day, H. D. (1995). Psychotherapists' job satisfaction and job burn-out as a function of work setting and percentage of managed care clients. *Psychotherapy in Private Practice, 14*(2), 77–93.

Eison, J. A. (1985, August). *Coming of age in academe: From teaching assistant to faculty member.* Presented at the annual convention of the American Psychological Association, Los Angeles.

Ellwein, M. C., Grace, M. E., & Comfort, R. E. (1990). Talking about instruction: Student teachers' reflections on success and failure in the classroom. *Journal of Teacher Education, 41*(4), 3–14.

Emmons, H., & Kranz, R. (2006). *The chemistry of joy: A three-step program for overcoming depression through western science and eastern wisdom.* New York: Fireside.

Ericsson, K. A. (2007). An expert-performance perspective of research on medical expertise: The study of clinical performance. *Medical Education, 41,* 1124–1130.

Ericcson, K. A., Charness, N., Feltovich, P. J., & Hoffman, R. R. (2006). *The Cambridge handbook of expertise and expert performance.* New York: Cambridge University Press.

Ericsson, K. A., Prietula, M. J., and Cokely, E. T. (2007). The making of an expert. *Harvard Business Review, 85*(7–8), 114–121.

Erikson, E. (1950). *Childhood and society.* New York: W. W. Norton & Co.

Erikson, E. (1968). *Identity, youth and crisis.* New York: Norton.

Etringer, B. D., Hillerbrand, E., & Claiborn, C. D. (1995). The transition from novice to expert counselor. *Counselor Education and Supervision, 35,* 4–17.

Farber, B. (1983). The effects of psychotherapeutic practice upon the psychotherapists. *Psychotherapy: Theory, Research, and Practice, 20*(2), 174–182.

Farber, B. (1990). Burnout in psychotherapists: Incidence, types, and trends. *Psychology in Private Practice, 8*(1), 35–44.

Farber, B. A., & Heifetz, L. J. (1981). The satisfactions and stresses of psychotherapeutic work: A factor analytic study. *Professional Psychology: Research and Practice, 12,* 621–630.

Figley, C. R. (1995). Compassion fatigue: Toward a new understanding of the costs of caring. In B H. Stamm (Ed.), *Secondary traumatic stress: Self-care issues for clinicians, researchers and educators* (pp. 3–28). Baltimore: Sidran Press.

Figley, C. (2002). Compassion fatigue: Psychotherapists' chronic lack of self-care. *Journal of Clinical Psychology, 58,* 1433–1441.

Firestone, R. W., & Catlett, J. (1999). *Fear of intimacy.* Washington, DC: American Psychological Association.

Foa, V. G. (1971). Interpersonal and economic resources. *Science, 171,* 345–351.

Frank, J. D., & Frank, J. B. (1991). *Persuasion and healing* (3rd ed.). Baltimore: Johns Hopkins University Press.

Frankl, V. (1959). *Man's search for meaning.* Boston: Beacon Press. (Original work published 1946)

Frattaroli, J. (2006). Experimental disclosure and its moderators: A meta-analysis. *Psychological Bulletin, 132,* 823–865.

Freshwater, D., & Johns, C. (2005). *Transforming nursing through reflective practice* (2nd ed.). Oxford, UK: Blackwell.

Freudenberger, H. (1974). Staff burnout. *Journal of Social Work, 30,* 159–165.

Freudenberger, H. J. (1990). Hazards of psychotherapeutic practice. *Psychotherapy in Private Practice, 8*(1), 31–34.

Freudenberger, H. J., & Robbins, A. (1979). The hazards of being a psychoanalyst. *The Psychoanalytic Review, 66*(2), 275–295.

Galluzzo, G. R., & Kacer, B. A. (1991). *The best and worst of high school student teaching.* Paper presented at the annual meeting of the American Educational Research Association, Chicago.

Garfield, C. (1995). *Sometimes my heart goes numb.* San Francisco, CA: Jossey-Bass.

Garfunkel, G. (1995). Lifeline. In M. R. Sussman (Ed.), *A perilous calling: The hazards of psychotherapy practice* (pp. 148–159). New York: John Wiley & Sons.

Geller, J. D., Norcross, J. C., & Orlinsky, D. E. (Eds.). (2005). *The psychotherapist's own psychotherapy: Patient and clinician perspectives.* New York: Oxford University Press.

Gilligan, C. (1982). *In a different voice.* Cambridge, MA: Harvard University Press.

Gladwell, M. (2008). *Outliers: The story of success.* New York: Little Brown and Co.

Glaser, R., & Chi, M. T. H. (1988). Overview. In M. T. H. Chi, R. Glaser, & M. J. Farr (Eds.), *The nature of expertise.* Hillsdale, NJ: Erlbaum.

Goffman, E. (1967). *Interaction ritual.* Garden City, NY: Doubleday Anchor.

Golden, A. (1997). *Memoirs of a geisha.* New York: Vintage.

Goldfried, M. R. (1980). Toward the delineation of therapeutic change principles. *American Psychologist, 35,* 991–999.

Goodyear, R. (1981). Termination as a loss experience for the counselor. *Personnel and Guidance Journal, 59,* 347–350.

Gray, L. A., Ladany, N., Walker, J. A., & Ancis, J. R. (2001). Psychotherapy trainees' experience of counterproductive events in supervision. *Journal of Counseling Psychology, 48,* 371–383.

Grosch, W. N., & Olsen, D. C. (1994). *When helping starts to hurt: A new look at burnout among psychotherapists.* New York: Norton.

Grotevant, H., & Cooper, C. (1986). Individuation in family relationships: A perspective on individual differences in the development of identity and role-taking skill in adolescence. *Human Development, 29,* 82–100.

Guy, J. (1987). *The personal life of the psychotherapist.* New York: John Wiley & Sons.

Guy, J., Brown, K., & Poelstra, P. (1990). Who gets attacked? A national survey of patient violence directed at psychologists in clinical practice. *Professional Psychology: Research and Practice, 21,* 493–495.

Guy, J., Brown, K., & Poelstra, P. (1992). Safety concerns and protective measures used by psychotherapists. *Professional Psychology: Research and Practice, 23,* 421–423.

Gysbers, N. C., & Henderson, P. (2005). *Developing & managing your school guidance and counseling program* (4th ed.). Alexandria, VA: American Counseling Association.

Gysbers, N. C., & Rønnestad, M. H. (1974). Practicum supervision: Learning theory. In G. F. Farwell, N. R. Gamsky, & P. Mathieu-Coghlan (Eds.), *The counselor's handbook: Essays on preparation* (pp. 133–140). New York: Intext Educational Publishers.

Hage, S. (2010). Caring and letting go: Balancing both sides of the turtle. In M. Trotter-Mathison, J. M. Koch, S. Sanger, & T. M. Skovholt (Eds.), *Voices from the field: Defining moments in counselor and therapist development* (pp. 182–185). New York: Routledge.

Hagstrom, S. J., Skovholt, T. M., & Rivers, D. A. (1997). The advanced undecided college student: A qualitative study. *NACADA Journal, 17*(2), 23–30.

Hampl, P. (1995). *Burning bright: An anthology of sacred poetry.* New York: Ballantine Books.

Harmon, C., Hawkins, E. J., Lambert, M. J., Slade, K., & Whipple, J. (2005). Improving outcomes for poorly responding clients: The use of clinical supports tools and feedback to clients. *Journal of Clinical Psychology, 61*(2), 175–185.

Hartmann, P. S. (2001). Women developing wisdom: Antecedents and correlates in a longitudinal sample. *Dissertation Abstracts International, 62*(01), 501B.

Hays, K. F. (1999a, August). Nutrition and exercise: Key components of taking care of yourself. In L. T. Pantano (Chair), *Taking care of yourself: The continuing quest.* Symposium conducted at the annual convention of the American Psychological Association, Boston.

Hays, K. F. (1999b). *Working it out: Using exercise in psychotherapy.* Washington, DC: American Psychological Association.

Help for helpers: Daily meditations for counselors. (1989). Center City, MN: Hazelden Foundation.

Henry, W. E. (1966). Some observations on the lives of healers. *Human Development, 9,* 47–56.

Heppner, P. P. (1989). Chance and choices in becoming a therapist. In W. Dryden & L. Spurling (Eds.), *On becoming a therapist* (pp. 69–86). New York: Routledge.

Hill, L. (1988). From chaos to organization. *Journal of Counseling and Development, 67,* 105.

Johnson, T. H., & Ward, T. (Eds.). (1958). *The letters of Emily Dickinson* (Vol. 2). Cambridge, MA: Belknop Press of Harvard University.

Kabat-Zinn, J. (2003). Mindfulness-based interventions in context: Past, present, and future. *Clinical Psychology: Science and Practice, 10*(2), 144–156.

Kabat-Zinn, J., Lipworth, L., & Burney, R. (1985). The clinical use of mindfulness meditation for the self-regulation of chronic pain. *Journal of Behavioral Medicine, 8,* 163–190.

Karasek, R., & Theorell, T. (1992). *Healthy work: Stress, productivity and the restructuring of working life.* New York: Basic Books.

Kassam-Adams, N. (1995). The risks of treating sexual trauma: Stress and secondary trauma in psychotherapists. In B. H. Stamm (Ed.), *Secondary traumatic stress: Self-care issues for clinicians, researchers, and educators* (pp. 37–48). Lutherville, MD: Sidran Press.

Kendrick, R., Chandler, J., & Hatcher, W. (1994). Job demands, stressors and the school counselor. *The School Counselor, 41,* 365–369.

Kinnetz, P. L. (1988). Saving myself vs. serving clients. *Journal of Counseling and Development, 67,* 87.

Klem, A. M., & Connell, J. P. (2004). Relationships matter: Linking teacher support to student engagement and achievement. *Journal of School Health, 74*(7), 262–273.

Kohlberg, L. (1979). *Measuring moral judgment.* Worcester, MA: Clark University Press.

Kram, K. (1985). *Mentoring at work: Developmental relationships in organizational life.* Glenville, IL: Scott, Foresman.

Kramer, K. P. (2004). *Martin Buber's I and thou: Practicing living dialogue.* Mahwah, NJ: Paulist Press.

Kristof, N. D. (2009, February 16). Week in review: Our greatest national shame. *New York Times,* p. 11.

Kushner, H. S. (1996). *How good do we have to be? A new understanding of guilt and forgiveness.* Boston: Little, Brown & Co.

Ladany, N., Hill, C. E., Corbett, M. M., & Nutt, E. A. (1996). Nature, extent, and importance of what psychotherapy trainees do not disclose to their supervisors. *Journal of Counseling Psychology, 43*(1), 10–24.

Lambert, M. J., Garfield, S. L., & Bergin, A. E. (2004). Overview, trends, and future issues. In M. J. Lambert (Eds.), *Handbook of psychotherapy and behavior change* (pp. 805–821). New York: John Wiley & Sons.

Lange, S. (1988). Critical incidents aren't accidents. *Journal of Counseling and Development, 67,* 109.

Larson, D. G. (1993). *The helper's journey.* Champaign, IL: Research Press.

Leiter, M. P., & Maslach, C. (2005). *Banishing burnout: Six strategies for improving your relationship with work.* San Francisco, CA: Jossey-Bass.

Levinson, D., Darrow, D., Klein, E., Levinson, M., & McKee, R. (1978). *The seasons of a man's life.* New York: Ballantine Books.

Lieberman, M. A., Yalom, I. D., & Miles, M. B. (1973). *Encounter groups: First facts.* New York: Basic Books.

Lief, H. I., & Fox, R. C. (1963). Training for "detached concern" in medical students. In H. I. Leif, V. I. Lief, & N. R. Leif (Eds.), *The psychological basis of medical practice* (pp. 12–35). New York: Harper & Row.

Lindbergh, A. M. (1975). *Gift from the sea.* New York: Pantheon Books.

Linley, A., & Joseph, S. (2007). Therapy work and therapists' positive and negative well-being. *Journal of Social and Clinical Psychology, 26*(3), 385–403.

Linville, M. (1988). The long afternoon. *Journal of Counseling and Development, 67,* 101.

Lisle, L. (1987). *Portrait of an artist: A biography of Georgia O'Keeffe.* Albuquerque: University of New Mexico Press.

Maclay, E. (1977). *Green winter: Celebrations of later life.* New York: Readers Digest Press.

Maggio, R. (1997). *Quotations from women on life.* Paramus, NJ: Prentice-Hall.

Mahoney, M. J. (1997). Psychotherapists' personal problems and self-care patterns. *Professional Psychology: Research and Practice, 28*(1), 14–16.

Majeski, T. (1996, August 6). Hospital turns a corner. *St. Paul Pioneer Press,* pp. 1A, 5A.

Mallinckrodt, B., & Bennett, J. (1992). Social support and the impact of job loss in dislocated blue-collar workers. *Journal of Counseling Psychology, 39,* 482–489.

Mallinckrodt, B., & Wei, M. (2005). Attachment, social competencies, social support, and psychological distress. *Journal of Counseling Psychology, 52,* 358–367.

Mann, K., Gordon, J., & MacLeod, A. (2009). Reflection and reflective practice in health professions education: A systematic review. *Advances in Health Sciences Education, 14*(4), 595–621.

Mann, T., Tomiyama, A. J., Westling, E., Lew, A., Samuels, B., & Chatman, J. (2007). Diets are not the answer. *American Psychologist, 62(3),* 220–233.

Martin, J., Slemon, A. G., Hiebert, B., Halberg, E. T., & Cummings, A. L. (1989). Conceptualizations of novice and experienced counselors. *Journal of Counseling Psychology, 36,* 395–400.

Maslach, C. (1982). *Burnout: The cost of caring.* Englewood Cliffs, NJ: Prentice-Hall.

Maslach, C. (2003). *Burnout: The cost of caring.* Cambridge, MA: Malor Books.

Maslach, C., & Jackson, S. E. (1981). *The Maslach Burnout Inventory.* Palo Alto, CA: Consulting Psychologists Press.

Maslach, C., & Leiter, M. P. (1997). *The truth about burnout.* San Francisco, CA: Jossey-Bass.

Maslach, C. & Leiter, M. P. (2008). Early predictors of job burnout and engagement. *Journal of Applied Psychology, 93,* 3, 498–512.

Maslow, A. H. (1968). *Toward a psychology of being.* New York: Van Nostrand Reinhold.

May, R. (1969). *Love and will.* New York: Norton.

Mayeroff, M. (1990). *On caring.* New York: Harper Perennial.

McConnell, E. A. (Ed.). (1982). *Burnout in the nursing profession.* St. Louis, MO: Mosby.

Milbouer, S. (1999, August 21). Social worker slain outside client's home. *Boston Globe,* pp. B1–B2.

Miller, W. R. (1983). Motivational interviewing with problem drinkers. *Behavioural Psychotherapy, 1,* 147–172.

Miller, W. R., & Rollnick, S. (2002). *Motivational interviewing: Preparing people for change* (2nd ed.). New York: Guilford.

Mitchell, K. R., & Anderson, H. (1983). *All our losses, all our griefs: Resources for pastoral care.* Louisville, KY: Westminster, John Knox.

Molassiotis, A., & Haberman, M. (1996). Evaluation of burnout and job satisfaction in marrow and transplant nurses. *Cancer Nursing, 19,* 360–367.

Moleski, S. M., & Kiselica, M. S. (2005). Dual relationships: A continuum ranging from the destructive to the therapeutic. *Journal of Counseling & Development, 83,* 3–11.

Montagu, A. (1974). *The natural superiority of women.* New York: Collier Books.

Moreland, L. (1993). Learning cycle. *Family Therapy Networker,* May/June, 13.

Morton, L. L., Vesco, R., Williams, N. H., & Awender, M. A. (1997). Student teacher anxieties related to class management, pedagogy, evaluation and staff relations. *British Journal of Educational Psychology, 67,* 69–89.

Moskowitz, S. A., & Rupert, P. A. (1983). Conflict resolution within the supervisory relationship. *Professional Psychology: Research and Practice, 14,* 632–641.

National Sleep Foundation. (2006). *Sleep-wake cycle: Its physiology and impact on health.* Retrieved May 21, 2010, from http://www.sleepfoundation.org

Neff, K. D. (2003). Development and validation of a scale to measure self-compassion. *Self and Identity, 2,* 223–250.

Neff, K. D., Kirkpatrick, K. L., & Rude, S. S. (2007). Self-compassion and adaptive psychological functioning. *Journal of Research in Personality, 41,* 139–154.

Neufeldt, S. A. (1999). *Supervision strategies for the first practicum* (2nd ed.). Alexandria, VA: American Counseling Association.

Neufeldt, S. A., Karno, M. P., & Nelson, M. L. (1996). A qualitative study of experts' conceptualization of supervisee reflectivity. *Journal of Counseling Psychology, 43*(1), 3–9.

Neusner, J. (Trans.). (1984). *Torah from our sages.* Dallas: Rossel Books. (Original work approximately 900 A.D.)

Norcross, J. C. (2010). The therapeutic relationship. In B. L. Duncan, S. D. Miller, B. E. Wampold, M. A. Hubble (Eds.). *The heart and soul of change: Delivering what works in therapy.* Washington DC: American Psychological Association.

Norcross. J. C., & Guy, J. D. (2007). *Learning to leave it at the office: A guide to psychotherapist self-care.* New York: Guilford.

Okun, B. F., & Kantrowitz, R. E. (2008). *Effective helping: Interviewing and counseling techniques* (7th ed.) Belmont, CA: Brooks/Cole.

Oliner, S. P. (2003). *Do unto others: Extraordinary acts of ordinary people*. Boulder, CO: Westview Press.

Olson, S. (1997). *The singing wilderness*. Minneapolis: University of Minnesota Press.

Olson, D. H. (2000). Circumplex model of marital and family functioning. *Journal of Family Therapy, 22*(2), 144–167.

Orlinsky, D. E., Botermans, J.-F., & Rønnestad, M. H. (2001). Toward an empirically grounded model of psychotherapy training: 5000 therapists rate influences on their development. *Australian Psychologist, 36,* 139–148.

Orlinsky, D. E., & Rønnestad, M. H. (2005). *How psychotherapists develop: A study of therapeutic work and professional growth*. Washington, DC: American Psychological Association.

Orlinsky, D. E., Rønnestad, M. H., Ambuhl, H., Willutzki, U., Botermans, J.-F., Cierpka, M., Davis, J., & Davis, M. (1999). Psychotherapists' assessment of their development of their development at different career levels. *Psychotherapy, 35,* 203–215.

Orlinsky, D. E., Rønnestad, M. H., Willutzki, U., Wiseman, H., Botermans, J.-F., & Collaborative Research Network (CRN). (2005). The prevalence and parameters of personal therapy in Europe and elsewhere. In J. D. Geller, J. C. Norcross, & D. E. Orlinsky (Eds.), *The psychotherapist's own psychotherapy: Patient and clinician perspectives* (pp. 177–191). New York: Oxford University Press.

Osachuk, T. A. G. (2010). The transforming moment with David. In M. Trotter-Mathison, J. M., Koch, S. Sanger, & T. M. Skovholt (Eds.), *Voices from the field: Defining moments in counselor and therapist development* (pp. 64–66), New York: Routledge.

Otto, R. K., & Schmidt, W. C. (1991). Malpractice in verbal psychotherapy: Problems and potential solutions. *Forensic Reports, 4,* 309–339.

Oxford dictionary of quotation. (1979). Oxford, UK: Oxford University Press.

Palmer, P. J. (1998). *The courage to teach: Exploring the inner landscape of a teacher's life*. San Francisco, CA: Jossey-Bass.

Palmer, P. J. (2004). *A hidden wholeness: The journey toward an undivided life*. San Francisco, CA: John Wiley & Sons.

Papastylianou, A., Kaila, M., & Polychronopoulos, M. (2009). Teachers' burnout, depression, role ambiguity and conflict. *Social Psychology of Education, 12*(3), 295–314.

Pearlman, L. A. (1995). Self-care for trauma therapists: Ameliorating vicarious traumatization. In B. H. Stamm (Ed.), *Secondary traumatic stress: Self-care issues for clinicians, researchers, and educators* (pp. 51–64). Lutherville, MD: Sidran Press.

Pearlman, L. A., & MacIan, P. S. (1995). Vicarious traumatization: An empirical study of the effects of trauma work on trauma therapists. *Professional Psychology: Research and Practice, 26,* 558–565.

Peck, M. S. (1978). *The road less traveled: A new psychology of love, traditional values and spiritual growth*. New York: Simon & Schuster.

Penedo, F. J., & Dahn, J. R. (2005). Exercise and well-being: A review of mental and physical health benefits associated with physical activity. *Current Opinion in Psychiatry, 18,* 189–193.

Perry, W. G. (1981). Cognitive and ethical growth: The making of meaning. In W. Chickering & Associates. (Eds.). *The modern American college* (pp. 76–116). San Francisco: Jossey-Boss.

Piaget, J. (1972). Intellectual evolution from adolescence to adulthood. *Human Development, 15,* 1–12.

Pica, M. (1998). The ambiguous nature of clinical training and its impact on the development of student clinicians. *Psychotherapy, 35,* 361–365.

Pilpay. (1872). *The fables of Pilpay.* New York: Hurd and Houghton.

Pincus, S. (1997). Recognizing your emotional vulnerabilities. In J. Kottler (Ed.), *Finding your way as a counselor* (pp. 59–61). Alexandria, VA: American Counseling Association.

Pistole, M. C. (2003). Linking work, love, individual, and family issues in counseling: An attachment theory perspective. In P. Erdman & T. Caffery (Eds.), *Attachment and family systems: Conceptual, empirical, and therapeutic relatedness.* New York: Brunner-Routledge.

Pistole, M. C., & Fitch, J. C. (2008). Attachment theory in supervision: A critical incident experience. *Counselor Education and Supervision, 47,* 193–205.

Plante, T. G. (1993). Aerobic exercise in prevention and treatment of psychopathology. In P. Seraganian (Ed.), *Exercise psychology: The influence of physical exercise on psychological processes* (pp. 358–379). New York: John Wiley & Sons.

Pollack, S. K. (1988). Grieving and growing. *Journal of Counseling and Development, 67,* 117.

Pope, K. S., & Tabachnick, B. G. (1994). Therapists as patients: A national survey of psychologists' experiences, problems and beliefs. *Professional Psychology: Research and Practice, 25,* 247–258.

Pope, K., & Vasquez, M. (1991). *Ethics in psychotherapy and counseling.* San Francisco, CA: Jossey-Bass.

Prochaska, J. O. (1999). How do people change, and how can we change to help more people? In M. A. Hubble, B. A. Duncan, & S. M. Miller (Eds.), *The heart and soul of change: What works in therapy* (pp. 227–255). Washington, DC: American Psychological Association.

Prochaska, J. O., DiClemente, C. C., & Norcross, J. C. (1992). In search of how people change: Applications to addictive behavior. *American Psychologist, 47*(9), 1102–1114.

Prochaska, J. O., & Norcross, J. C. (2001). Stages of change. *Psychotherapy, 38*(4), 443–448.

Radeke, J. T., & Mahoney, M. J. (2000). Comparing the personal lives of psychotherapists and research psychologists. *Professional Psychology: Research and Practice, 31,* 82–84.

Raimy, V. C. (Ed.). (1950). *Training in clinical psychology.* Upper Saddle River, NJ: Prentice Hall.

Readings book. (n.d.). Minneapolis: Voyageur Outward Bound School (P.O. Box 450, Ely, MN 55731).

Reibel, D. K., Greeson, J. M., Brainard, G. C., & Rosenzweig, S. (2001). Mindfulness-based stress reduction and health-related quality of life in a heterogeneous patient population. *General Hospital Psychiatry, 23*(4), 183–192.

Reissman, F. (1965). The "helper" therapy principle. *Social Work, 10,* 27–32.

Roberts, C. A. (1986). Burnout: Psychobabble, or a valuable concept? *British Journal of Hospital Medicine, 36,* 194–197.

Robiner, W. N., Fuhrman, M., & Ristvedt, S. (1993). Evaluation difficulties in supervising psychology interns. *Clinical Psychologist, 46,* 3–13.

Robinson, B. E. (1992). *Overdoing it: How to slow down and take care of yourself.* Deerfield Beach, FL: Health Communications.

Rodolfa, E. R., Kraft, W. A., & Reilley, R. R. (1988). Stressors of professionals and trainees at APA-approved counseling and VA Medical Center internship sites. *Professional Psychology: Research and Practice, 19,* 43–49.

Rogers, C. R. (1957). The necessary and sufficient conditions of therapeutic personality change. *Journal of Consulting Psychology, 21*(2), 95–103.

Rogers, C. R. (1961). *On becoming a person.* Boston: Houghton Mifflin.

Rogers, C. R. (1995). *A way of being.* Boston: Houghton Mifflin.

Rønnestad, M. H. (1977). The effect of modeling, feedback, and experiential methods on counselor empathy. *Counselor Education and Supervision, 17,* 194–201.

Rønnestad, M. H. (2008). Profesjonell utvikling [Professional development]. In A. Molander & L. I. Terum (Eds.), *Profesjonsstudier [Professional studies].* Oslo: Universitetsforlaget.

Rønnestad, M. H., & Lippe, A. L. von der. (2002). *Det kliniske intervjuet [The clinical interview].* Oslo: Gyldendal Akademisk.

Rønnestad, M. H., & Skovholt, T. M. (1993). Supervision of beginning and advanced graduate students in counseling and psychotherapy. *Journal of Counseling and Development, 71,* 396–405.

Rønnestad, M. H., & Skovholt, T. M. (2001). Learning arenas for professional development: Retrospective accounts of senior psychotherapists. *Professional Psychology: Research and Practice, 32,* 181–187.

Rønnestad, M. H., & Skovholt, T. M. (2003). The journey of the counselor and therapist: Research findings and perspectives development. *Journal of Career Development, 30*(1), 5–44.

Rothschild, B., with M. Rand (2006). *Help for the helper: The psychophysiology of compassion fatigue and vicarious trauma.* New York: W. W. Norton & Co.

Ruddick, S. (1989). *Maternal thinking: Toward a politics of peace.* Boston: Beacon Press.

Rupert, P. A., Stevanovic, P., & Hunley, H. A. (2009). Work-family conflict and burnout among practicing psychologists. *Professional Psychology: Research and Practice, 40*(1), 54–61.

Rupp, J. (1994). *Little pieces of light.* Mahwah, NJ: Paulist Press.

Sabin-Farrell, R., & Turpin, G. (2003). Vicarious traumatization: Implications for mental health of health workers? *Clinical Psychology Review, 23,* 449–480.

Samples, P. (1991). *Self-care for caregivers.* Center City, MN: Hazelden Foundation.

Sanger, S. (2010). How to fail. In M. Trotter-Mathison, J. M. Koch, S. Sanger, & T. M. Skovholt (Eds.), *Voices from the field: Defining moments in counselor and therapist development* (pp. 72–75), New York: Routledge.

Schafer, W. (1996). *Stress management for wellness.* Fort Worth, TX: Harcourt Brace.

Schaufeli, W. B., Leiter, M. P., & Maslach, C. (2009). Burnout: 35 years of research and practice. *Career Development International, 14*(3), 204–220.

Schelske, M. T., & Romano, J. L. (1994). Coping skills and classroom management training for student teachers. *The Teacher Educator, 29,* 21–33.

Schoefield, W. (1974). *Psychotherapy: The purchase of friendship.* Englewood Cliffs, NJ: Prentice-Hall.

Schor, J. (1998). *The overspent American.* New York: Basic Books.

Schorr, M. (1997). On being a wounded healer. In J. Kottler (Ed.), *Finding your way as a counselor* (pp. 55–58). Alexandria, VA: American Counseling Association.

Schweitzer, A. (1975). In *The Reader's Digest Treasury of Modern Quotations*. New York: Readers Digest Press.

Selye, H. (1974). *Stress without distress*. New York: Signet.

Sexton, T. L., & Whiston, S. C. (1994). The status of the counseling relationship: An empirical review, theoretical implications, and research directions. *The Counseling Psychologist, 22*(1), 6–78.

Shirom, A., Oliver, A., & Stein, E. (2009). Teachers' stressors and strains: A longitudinal study of their relationships. *International Journal of Stress Management, 16*(4), 312–332.

Skinner, B. F. (1953). *Science and human behavior*. New York: Macmillan.

Skovholt, T. M. (1974). The client as helper: A means to promote personal growth. *The Counseling Psychologist, 4*(3), 56–64.

Skovholt, T. M. (1986, Spring). Learning to teach. In *Focus: On teaching and learning*, (p. 8), Minneapolis, MN: Office of Educational Development, University of Minnesota.

Skovholt, T. M. (1988). Searching for reality. *The Counseling Psychologist, 16,* 282–287.

Skovholt, T. M. (2001). *The resilient practitioner: Burnout prevention and self-care strategies for counselors, therapists, teaches and health professionals*. Needham Heights, MA: Allyn & Bacon.

Skovholt, T. M. (2008). Two versions of erosion in the helping professions: Caring burnout and meaning burnout. *New Therapist, 52,* 28–29.

Skovholt, T. M., & D'Rozario, V. (2000). Portraits of outstanding and inadequate teachers in Singapore: The impact of emotional intelligence. *Teaching & Learning, 40*(1), 9–17.

Skovholt, T. M. & Jennings, L. (2004). *Master Therapists: Exploring expertise in therapy and counseling*. Boston: Allyn & Bacon.

Skovholt, T. M., & McCarthy, P. R. (Eds.). (1988). Critical incidents in counselor development [special issue]. *Journal of Counseling and Development, 67,* 69–135.

Skovholt, T. M., Morgan, J., & Cunningham, H. N. (1989). Mental imagery in career counseling and life planning: A review of research and intervention methods. *Journal of Counseling and Development, 67,* 287–291.

Skovholt, T. M., & Rønnestad, M. H. (1995). *The evolving professional self: Stages and themes in therapist and counselor development*. New York: John Wiley & Sons.

Skovholt, T. M., Rønnestad, M. H., & Jennings, L. (1997). Searching for expertise in counseling, psychotherapy, and professional psychology. *Educational Psychology Review, 9*(4), 361–369.

Skovholt, T. M., & Starkey, M. (in press). The three legs of the practitioner's learning stool: Practice, research/theory and personal life. In T. M. Skovholt, *Becoming a therapist: Reflections and exercises on the path to mastery*. New York: Wiley.

Smetanka, M. J. (1992, November 6). Burnout vaccine: Institute gives teachers a shot of enthusiasm. *Minneapolis Star Tribune*, p. 1B.

Smiley, J. (1991). *A thousand acres*. New York: Ivy Books.

Smith P. L., & Moss, S. B. (2009). Psychologist impairment: What is it, how can it be prevented and what can be done to address it? *Clinical Psychology: Science and Practice, 16,* 1–15.

Smith, T., & Hawks, S. R. (2006). Intuitive easting, diet composition, and the meaning of food in healthy weight promotion. *American Journal of Health Education, 37*(3), 130–136.

Söderfeldt, M., Söderfeldt, B., & Warg, L. E. (1995). Burnout in social work. *Social Work, 40*, 638–646.

Stamm, B. H. (1995). Preface. In B. H. Stamm (Ed.), *Secondary traumatic stress: Self-care issues for clinicians, researchers, and educators* (pp. ix–xii). Lutherville, MD: Sidran Press.

Stanley, T. J., & Danko, W. D. (1996). *The millionaire next door.* New York: Pocket Books.

Stevanovic, P., & Rupert, P. A. (2004). Career-sustaining behaviors, satisfactions, and stresses of professional psychologists. *Psychotherapy: Theory, Research, Practice, Training, 41*(3), 301–309.

Stevens, W. (1923). *Harmonium.* New York: Alfred A. Knopf.

Stiles, W. (1997). Multiple voices in psychotherapy clients. *Journal of Psychotherapy Integration, 7,* 177–180.

Stone, G. L. (1988). The heroic syndrome. *Journal of Counseling and Development, 67,* 108.

Strauss, J. L., Hayes, A. M., Johnson, S. L., Newman, C. F., Brown, G. K., Barber, J. P., et al. (2006). Early alliance, alliance ruptures, and symptom change in a nonrandomized trial of cognitive therapy for avoidant and obsessive-compulsive personality disorders. *Journal of Consulting and Clinical Psychology, 74*(2), 337–345.

Strupp, H. H., & Hadley, S. W. (1978). Specific vs. non-specific factors in psychotherapy: A controlled study of outcomes. *Archives of General Psychiatry, 36,* 1125–1136.

Sussman, M. B. (Ed.). (1995). *A perilous calling: The hazards of psychotherapy practice.* New York: John Wiley & Sons.

Swanson, K. W. (2010). Constructing a learning partnership in transformative teacher development. *Reflective Practice, 11,* 259–269.

Tarasoff v. Regents of the University of California. 118 Cal. Rptr. 129, 529 P 2d 533 (1974).

Thorson, T. (1994). *Reflections on practice.* Unpublished manuscript, Minneapolis, MN.

Tippett, K. (2007). *Speaking of faith.* New York: Viking.

Torrence, P. (1996). The culture and mentoring series. In A. M. Soliman, *Mentoring relationships in the Arab culture.* Athens, GA: Georgia Studies of Creative Behavior.

Trotter, M. J. (2009). *Effects of participation in a mindfulness-based stress reduction program on college students' psychological well-being.* Unpublished doctoral dissertation, University of Minnesota, Minneapolis.

Trotter-Mathison, M., Koch, J., Sanger, S., & Skovholt, T. M. (2010). *Voices from the field: Defining moments in counselor and therapist development.* New York: Routledge.

U.S. Census Bureau. (2009). *US and World Population Clocks.* Retrieved April 28, 2010, from www.census.gov/main/www/popclock.html

Vitaliano, P. P., Zhang, J., & Scanlan, J. M. (2003). Is caregiving hazardous to one's physical health? A metaanalysis. *Psychological Bulletin, 129*(6), 946–972.

Vygotsky, L. S. (1962). *Thought and language.* Cambridge: MIT Press.

Wampold, B. E., Mondin, G. W., Moody, M., & Stich, F. (1997). A meta-analysis of outcome studies comparing bona fide psychotherapies: Empirically "all must have prizes." *Psychological Bulletin, 122,* 203–215.

Ward, C. C., & House, R. M. (1998). Counseling supervision: A reflective model. *Counselor Education and Supervision, 38,* 23–33.

Warner, C. (1992). Chinese proverb. *Dictionary of women's quotations.* Englewood Cliffs, NJ: Prentice Hall.

Weis, A. C. (2010). Growing my perspective beyond the "secret knowledge" mindset. In M. Trotter-Mathison, J. M. Koch, S. Sanger, & T. M. Skovholt (Eds.), *Voices from the field: Defining moments in counselor and therapist development* (pp.52–54), New York: Routledge.

Wessells, D. T., Kutscher, A. H., Seeland, I. B., Selder, F. E., Cherico, D. J., & Clark, E. J. (Eds.). (1989). *Professional burnout in medicine and the helping professions.* New York: Haworth Press.

Williamson, C. (1975). Waterfall. On *The changer and the changed* [Record]. Oakland, CA: Olivia Records, Inc.

Winnicott, D. W. (1965). *The maturational processes and the facilitating environment.* New York: International Universities Press.

Wood, D. J., Bruner, J. S., & Ross, G. (1976). The role of tutoring in problems solving. *Journal of Child Psychology and Psychiatry, 17,* 89–100.

Woolf, V. (1990). *A moment's liberty: The short diary* (A. O. Bell, Ed.). San Diego, CA: Harcourt Brace Jovanovich.

Yalom, I. D. (1985). *The theory and practice of group psychotherapy* (3rd ed.). New York: Basic Books.

Yalom, I. D. (2002). *The gift of therapy: An open letter to a new generation of therapists and their patients.* New York: HarperCollins.

Yalom, I. D., & Leszcz, M. (2005). *The theory and practice of group psychotherapy* (5th ed.). New York: Basic Books.

Young, M. E. (1997). How to avoid becoming a zombie. In J. Kottler (Ed.), *Finding your way as a counselor* (pp. 45–48). Alexandria, VA: American Counseling Association.

Zeh, J. B. (1988). Counseling behind closed doors: How safe? *Journal of Counseling and Development, 67,* 89.

Zeigler, J. N., Kanas, N., Strull, W. M., & Bennet, N. E. (1984). A stress discussion group for medical interns. *Journal of Medical Education, 59,* 205–207.

Index